TEACHING WITH
THE ST☉RY BOX®
READING PROGRAM

RESOURCE GUIDE

TEACHING WITH
THE ST✸RY BOX®
READING PROGRAM

RESOURCE GUIDE

The Wright Group®

19201 120th Avenue NE • Bothell, WA 98011

Teaching with The Story Box® Reading Program: Resource Guide
©1999 Wright Group Publishing, Inc.

We gratefully acknowledge the following people for their contributions
to this resource guide:
Pat Large, Fourth-Grade Teacher, Orting, Washington
Sam Nofziger, Bilingual Teacher, Fresno, California
Susan O'Leary, Ph.D., First-Grade ESL and Reading Recovery Teacher,
    Madison, Wisconsin
Constance H. Wood, Multiage Kindergarten Teacher, Papaikou, Hawaii

We also acknowledge Wendy Cheyney and Judith Cohen for their permission
to adapt and reprint their vowel pattern chart on page 47. This chart appears
in *Focus on Phonics,* forthcoming from The Wright Group.

Photographed by David Perry

The Wright Group
19201 120th Avenue NE
Bothell, WA 98011

Printed in Canada

10 9 8 7 6 5 4 3 2 1

ISBN: 0-322-00638-4

CONTENTS

Chapter 4: Guided Reading

Chapter 5: The Story Box in Your Classroom

Welcome to The Story Box Reading Program

The Story Box is a balanced reading program centered around carefully sequenced and engagingly written and illustrated stories for early emergent and upper emergent readers. The stories and corresponding lessons introduce children to reading through **shared reading, guided reading,** and **independent reading**.

Because The Story Box is a *balanced* reading program, it provides, in addition to rich literary experiences, numerous and varied writing, listening, and speaking experiences and explicit skills instruction and practice. All of these experiences are tailored to different learning styles and include whole-group, small-group, and independent instruction.

In its skills instruction, The Story Box employs a teaching strategy in which students first learn how a skill or strategy is used in shared reading or guided reading story books. Then the teacher removes the skill or strategy from this context for in-depth instruction. Finally, students return to the text or engage in additional reading and/or writing activities to apply the skill. See the chart below for more information on in-context skills instruction.

WHAT'S THE EVIDENCE?

Weaver, 1994, writes that a "balanced reading program focuses on using skills like phonemic awareness and phonics knowledge in the service of strategies for constructing meaning from text." Support for the teaching of skills within the context of meaningful print comes from Adams, 1998, 1990; Strickland, 1998a; Weaver, 1996, 1994; Moustafa, 1997; Honig, 1996; and Routman, 1996.

References cited in the "What's the Evidence?" boxes are listed in a bibliography at the end of this guide.

Connecting Skills to Meaningful Print

In Context
Begin with authentic reading or writing. Use

- Read-alouds
- Read-Togethers
- Guided reading books
- Books for independent reading
- Model writing
- Process writing
- Guided writing
- Structure writing
- Independent writing

Explicit Instruction
Teach skills, such as

- Phonological awareness
- Concepts of print
- Phonics
- Word structure
- Vocabulary
- Mechanics
- Comprehension

In Context
Return to the text to apply what was learned, and then extend learning through

- Rereading familiar books
- Responding to reading through activities, journals, writing, and projects
- Reading new materials
- Creating reproductions, innovations, and retellings

Components of The Story Box Reading Program

The Story Box Reading Program is designed to be convenient and easy to use. It contains the following components:

◀ 32 Read-Togethers for shared reading, available in Big Book and pupil book sizes

▼ Guided reading books at instructionally appropriate levels
- 64 books in Sets A–D for early emergent readers
- 56 books in Sets E–H for upper emergent readers

▼ Audiocassettes to accompany each Read-Together book

▼ The Story Box Reading Program teacher guides include
- An overview and skills trace
- Shared reading and guided reading lesson plans
- A resource guide

▲ Take-Me-Homes™ Stories and Activities, available at both early and upper emergent levels. Engaging blackline masters promote reading at home and include
- Activities for each Read-Together book
- Small, reproducible versions of selected guided reading books

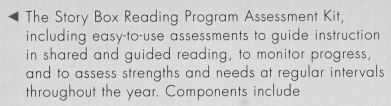

◄ The Story Box Reading Program Assessment Kit, including easy-to-use assessments to guide instruction in shared and guided reading, to monitor progress, and to assess strengths and needs at regular intervals throughout the year. Components include

- A comprehensive assessment guide
- A benchmark book and an Assessment of Reading Behavior for each guided reading set

Here Goes a Turtle

Here goes a turtle up the hill—
Creepy, creepy, creepy, creepy.
Here goes a rabbit up the hill—
Boing, boing, boing, boing.
Here goes an elephant up the hill—
Thud, thud, thud, thud.
Here goes a snake up the hill—
Slither, slither, slither, slither.
Here comes a rock down the hill—
Boom, boom, boom, boom, CRASH!

Covers

Glass covers windows
to keep the cold away
Clouds cover the sky
to make a rainy day

Nighttime covers
all the things that creep
Blankets cover me
when I'm asleep

► Poems for Sharing™, beautifully illustrated poetry posters that support each Read-Together book

- 16 posters for early emergent
- 16 posters for upper emergent

◄ *Poems for Sharing™ Teacher Notes,* available at both early and upper emergent levels. Components include

- Complete five-day lesson plans for each poem
- Blackline masters of sequencing images and activities
- Blackline masters of the poems

Additional Support Materials for The Story Box Reading Program

- **The Wright Skills™,** a comprehensive skills package that provides direct, explicit, and systematic instruction in phonological awareness, the letters of the alphabet, phonics, and word study skills
- **Enrichment Readers:** 30 early fluency and fluency titles
- **Audiocassettes to accompany the Enrichment Readers**

- *To Market, to Market* rhyme book
- Joy Cowley Author Study Book: *When I Was Young*
- Joy Cowley videos: *A Day Full of Joy* and *Get Writing! A Kid's Guide to Writing and Publishing*
- La Caja de Cuentos® (The Story Box Spanish Collection)
- *Paint, Write & Play!™* CD-ROM

The Story Box Lesson Plans

The Story Box teacher guides provide well-organized instructional plans that take you through the step-by-step processes for shared reading and guided reading. Lesson instruction offers a balanced reading approach that focuses on literature, language, and comprehension, while guiding emergent readers to draw meaning from text, acquire phonological awareness, learn sound-symbol relationships, and improve word-recognition skills. Individual lessons include detailed teaching strategies, suggestions for additional support for students needing it, and activity ideas that integrate reading, writing, speaking, and listening and that allow students to apply and practice what they have learned.

Above all, the research-based methodology offered in the teacher guides are meant to provide you with effective, flexible teaching strategies. These strategies will enable you to meet the learning needs of all your students as they acquire important skills and develop a love of reading.

WHAT'S THE EVIDENCE?

Research strongly indicates that a balanced reading program that focuses on literature, language, and comprehension along with the explicit systematic study of phonics produces the best readers. Recent findings by a panel of national experts suggest that children should learn to use letter sounds to decode words, in addition to predict story events, make inferences from clues in the text, and use developmental spelling in their writing. Honig, 1996, suggests that a language-rich, literature-based reading program should be used in conjunction with a comprehensive skills program. Research on balance in a reading program is referenced by Adams, 1998, 1990; Strickland, 1998a; Weaver, 1998; Braunger & Lewis, 1997; Moustafa, 1997; and Routman, 1996.

Shared Reading Lesson Plans

Detailed, five-day lesson plans are provided in individual booklets for each shared reading title. The booklets, which can be removed easily from the teacher guide binder, include the following items:

- An overview chart of the weekly plans for easy reference and planning
- Explicit skills instruction
- Highlighting of appropriate activities for ESL students, students requiring extra help, and students who need more challenge
- Activities for integrating the language arts
- Cross-curricular activities
- A bibliography of related literature
- Assessment opportunities

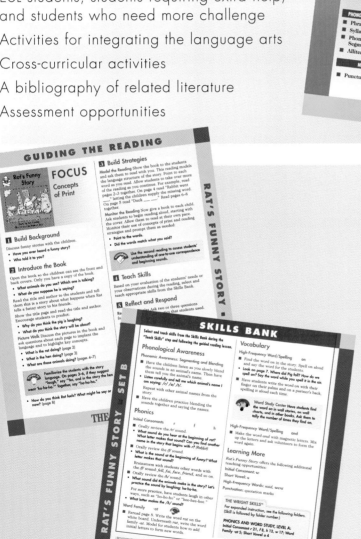

Guided Reading Lesson Plans

These detailed, two-sided lesson plan cards for each guided reading title can be removed easily from the teacher guide binder. They include the following items:

- A step-by-step process for each guided reading format
- Explicit skills instruction
- Highlighting of teaching opportunities for ESL students, students requiring extra help, and students who need more challenge
- Assessment opportunities

The Story Box Books and Reading Levels

The Story Box books have been designed specifically for early emergent and upper emergent readers. This program is most successful when instruction matches the level of the books, providing developmentally appropriate skills instruction and teacher support.

Early Emergent Reader Profile

What are the characteristics of an early emergent reader?

- Learning that text and illustrations tell a story
- Using oral language in reading
- Recognizing cover, title, and title page in books
- Noticing details in illustrations
- Hearing rhyming words, syllables, and onsets/rimes
- Knowing some letters, letter sounds, and words
- Predicting story line

What skills does an early emergent reader need?

- Book and text concepts of print
- Left-to-right progression
- Return sweep
- One-to-one correspondence
- Word-space, word-letter awareness
- Phonological awareness skills that include blending and segmenting
- Recognition of sound-symbol correspondence of consonants and short vowels
- Identify some high-frequency words
- Beginning reading strategies of reading for meaning, self-correcting, and monitoring
- Comprehension skills

Early Emergent Book Characteristics

What are the characteristics of early emergent books?

Language

- Rhyme, rhythm, repetition
- Simple language patterns
- Repetition of 1–2 sentence patterns with few changes
- Familiar vocabulary
- Repetition of simple high-frequency words

Illustrations

- Illustrations that match the text
- Illustrations that help tell the story
- Clearly identified objects
- Left-to-right flow of illustrations to reinforce left-to-right orientation of reading

Story structure

- Simple stories with beginnings, middles, and endings
- Strong use of picture clues, text clues, and meaning clues
- Surprise endings or twists on the story

Text layout

- A cover and title page that are integral to the entire book
- Consistent appearance of print on pages
- One to five lines of text per page
- One to two word changes per page

Theme

- A familiar experience
- Familiar objects or actions
- A single topic

The cow was hungry.

4

The donkey was hungry.

5

from *Green Grass*, Set B

Upper Emergent Reader Profile

What are the characteristics of an upper emergent reader?

- Knowing many of the basic concepts of print
- Ability to blend, segment, and manipulate sounds and words
- Hearing rhyming words, syllables, and onset/rimes in words
- Some integration of strategies
- Ability to gain meaning from print
- Knowing letters and sounds of letters
- Identifying many high-frequency words
- Using known words and other strategies to decode unknown words

What skills does an upper emergent reader need?

- Phonological awareness skills that include blending, segmenting, and manipulating
- The ability to identify high-frequency words
- The ability to identify letters and sounds
- Recognition and use of consonants, short vowels, and long vowels
- The use of consonant blends and digraphs
- Recognition of word families
- The ability to locate known chunks in words
- The ability to build on prior knowledge
- The ability to identify and use punctuation and capitalization
- Integration of the four cueing system
- The ability to self-monitor and self-correct
- The use of inference to gain meaning from text
- Comprehension skills

Upper Emergent Book Characteristics

What are the characteristics of upper emergent books?

Language

- More-challenging vocabulary
- Dialogue mixed with prose
- Increased vocabulary and text that may pose questions
- Less repetition
- Some descriptive language
- More-varied language patterns

Illustrations

- Illustrations that provide less support to text
- Illustrations that serve as sources of confirmation rather than of predictions
- Illustrations of main ideas

Story structure

- More-complex writing structure
- Stories with strong beginnings, middles, and endings
- More-varied repetitive patterns
- Messages contained in the print as opposed to in illustrations
- Clear story lines

Text layout

- Text that allows students to predict
- Longer sentences
- Two or more words introduced in writing structure
- Introduction of more punctuation
- Two to several lines of text on a page
- Text that no longer corresponds as directly to the illustrations

Theme

- Familiar topics
- Fantasy stories
- Books in other genres
- Less-familiar concepts

The baker said,
"I will make
a fantastic cake."

She got butter

and eggs

and sugar

and flour   and mixed them in a bowl.

2   3

from *The Fantastic Cake*, Set G

A Balanced Reading Program

The Story Box is a balanced reading program, which means that it provides a balance of literary experiences and skills. The chart at right lists these skills and literary experiences and describes ways in which a balanced reading program develops each one.

Components

Skills

Phonological awareness

- Promotes understanding that sentences are made up of words and words are made up of syllables or separate sounds
- Develops within-word awareness of rhyme, alliteration, and onset/rime and the phonemic awareness of blending, segmenting, and manipulating

Awareness of print

- Focuses on basic concepts of print (book, text, word concepts)
- Offers a print-rich environment
- Encourages awareness of environmental print
- Teaches alphabet recognition and letter formation

Sound-symbol relationships

- Teaches letter-sound correspondences
- Teaches vowel patterns and spelling patterns
- Teaches onset/rime and word families
- Teaches blending, segmenting, and manipulating sounds to decode words
- Provides reading materials that help students practice skills

Word identification and vocabulary

- Stresses high-frequency word recognition
- Uses spelling patterns and structural cues to teach word recognition
- Develops content vocabulary
- Increases students' knowledge of word meanings

Writing and spelling

- Identifies spelling patterns
- Encourages proofreading skills
- Helps students make the transition to conventional spelling

of a Balanced Reading Program

Literary Experiences

Rich literary experiences with Read-Togethers

- Enriches and expands children's literary experiences

- Builds students' background knowledge

- Introduces new vocabulary, concepts, and text structures

Oral language development

- Provides opportunities for discussion and activities that allow students to respond appropriately

- Includes rhymes, poems, songs, and chants that encourage participation

- Provides whole-group and small-group activities that involve talking and listening

Fluency

- Provides reading materials at instructional and independent levels

- Provides for self-selected reading time

- Promotes reading of a wide variety of books and genres

Comprehension

- Makes connections between students' prior knowledge and text

- Helps students monitor comprehension and use reading strategies to make sense of text

- Encourages higher-order thinking skills

- Introduces literary elements

Writing

- Promotes purposeful writing

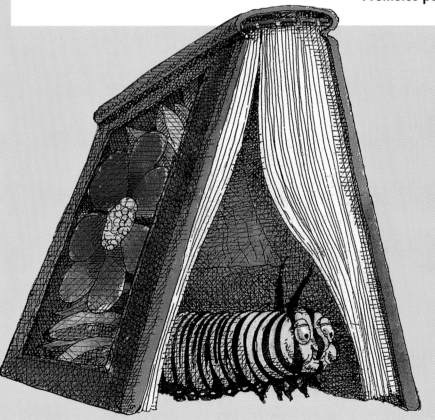

Instructional Processes in The Story Box

The elements of a comprehensive balanced reading program are **reading aloud, shared reading, guided reading, independent reading, paired reading, model writing, process writing, journal writing, guided writing, structure writing, content writing, independent writing** and **spelling**. These elements provide for a balance of reading, writing, listening, and speaking. Appropriate skills are taught in the context of each of these elements.

Reading Aloud

Reading aloud to children can be a mutually rewarding experience that reinforces your relationship with them and enriches their vocabulary, encourages their love of reading, and extends their imaginations.

It also offers young readers insights and the opportunity to develop skills they may not readily gain on their own.

When you enjoy reading a good story aloud, your enthusiasm for the story is contagious. When children observe you reading with expression, dramatic flair, and an obvious love of a good story, they become hooked and will want to read the story again on their own.

In addition to "hooking" young readers, there are several other benefits of reading aloud to them. First, when you read aloud to your students, they hear language that, while possibly above their independent or instructional reading levels, is still suitable for their listening level. Hearing stories read aloud thus allows them to reach cognitively beyond their independent reading levels. Second, hearing stories read aloud helps children develop important skills and abilities, including oral language skills,

comprehension skills, increased attention spans, reading skills, and the ability to visualize story events. Third, during read-alouds, children develop important knowledge, such as phonological awareness, improved vocabularies, and familiarity with the basic elements of a story.

Reading aloud also provides a crucial link to writing and speaking. As children become familiar with language through hearing it read to them, they soon adopt the same, more complex language structures and vocabulary in their own writing and speech.

Discussing read-alouds models for the children how to analyze the literary elements in stories, engages them in higher-level thinking and questioning strategies, and allows them to respond to a book on a personal level and make connections to other books they have read.

To strengthen the many positive effects of reading aloud to students, it is recommended that you read to them daily.

WHAT'S THE EVIDENCE?

Support for the benefits of reading aloud to children comes from Snow, Burns, & Griffin, 1998; Strickland, 1998a; Weaver, 1998; Morrow, 1997, 1992; Moustafa, 1997; Fountas & Pinnell, 1996; Routman, 1996; Adams, 1990; and Chall, 1990.

Choosing Stories to Read Aloud

It is important to select stories, poems, or nonfiction books that you yourself enjoy and want to read. Share with children your reasons for selecting books; by doing so, you will help them learn to think critically about books and make good choices of books on their own.

To keep students interested and optimize their learning, vary the type of materials that you read to them, balancing genres, styles, subject matter, and point of view. When selecting fiction books to read aloud, choose those with strong, identifiable characters, clearly described settings and events, and strong literary images that allow children to develop a rich sense of language. Choose poetry that expresses a range of tones and moods and a lively engagement with the musicality of language. Nonfiction books should stimulate listeners' curiosity and lead them to inquiry. Books with high-quality illustrations or photographs that are tied closely to the text will help emergent readers understand the concepts presented.

Two good resources for lists of appropriate fiction and nonfiction stories to read aloud are *Books Kids Will Sit Still For* and *More Books Kids Will Sit Still For*, both by Judy Freeman. For additional fiction and nonfiction books, poems, and songs that relate to each Read-Together book in The Story Box, consult the related literature Bookshelf at the end of each shared reading lesson plan.

Shared Reading

Shared reading is an interactive reading experience that involves the whole class. Shared reading begins with you reading a large-sized story (Big Book), poem, or song to your students and discussing it with them. On subsequent readings, invite your students to join in on words and phrases that they know. Share a reading with your students several times, and soon they will be able to read it independently.

Shared reading is enjoyable and purposeful. It demonstrates the reading process, scaffolds instruction, and provides support for beginning readers while giving them opportunities to behave as independent readers. During shared reading, students have numerous opportunities to develop and reinforce phonological awareness, oral language skills, and phonics skills; learn concepts of print; expand their vocabulary; and increase comprehension. You'll find that with shared reading you are able to guide questioning that involves children more actively in a story and increases understanding of story elements. Supporting writing, listening, and speaking activities helps students further relate to the shared reading experience. (For more information about shared reading, see chapter 3.)

WHAT'S THE EVIDENCE?

Shared reading is an important process for emergent readers. The benefits of providing shared reading are supported by Strickland, 1998a; Weaver, 1998; Moustafa, 1997; Eldredge, Reutzel, & Hollingsworth, 1996; Fountas & Pinnell, 1996; Routman, 1996; P. Cunningham, 1995; and Holdaway, 1979.

Guided Reading

Guided reading is central to the instructional reading program—it is the reading process that helps children move from shared reading to independent reading. In this process, you set up guided reading groups in which students read together, learn skills and reading strategies, discuss readings, and answer questions, all with your guidance.

Because guided reading groups are small and flexible, they encourage student participation and engagement. Guided reading achieves several other important effects. First, it provides opportunities for students to use developing reading strategies and skills as they attend to words in text. Second, it provides opportunities for students to problem-solve while they are engaged in reading for meaning. Third, it helps students at the same instructional level learn how to talk, think, and question their way through books while you challenge them to read and provide supports to assist them in reading. Fourth, through your ongoing assessments and careful monitoring of small groups and individual students, you can tailor instruction of skills and strategies to the specific developmental needs of your students. Fifth, guided reading teaches specific skills and understandings: phonological awareness, concepts of print, phonics skills, understanding of story elements, and effective reading strategies.

The Story Box guided reading books are carefully sequenced to gradually introduce appropriate skills and reading strategies. This sequencing enables you to scaffold instruction to ensure that all your students are making progress. (For an in-depth look at the guided reading process, see chapter 4.)

WHAT'S THE EVIDENCE?

The effectiveness of the small-group instructional model of guided reading is supported by Strickland, 1998a, 1989; Fountas & Pinnell, 1996; Honig, 1996; Routman, 1996; and Clay, 1991.

Independent Reading

Children need many opportunities to read on their own—reading achievement is positively influenced by the amount of time spent reading books. It is important that children read large amounts of text at their independent reading level with 95 percent to 100 percent accuracy. Independent reading is the single most valuable activity for developing comprehension, vocabulary knowledge, understanding of spelling structures, word analysis skills, and fluency. It also improves the quality and quantity of children's writing.

When you give children some control over and ownership of the reading process, they make great contributions to their own learning. You can develop this important sense of ownership by providing daily scheduled independent reading sessions. During these sessions, children will practice the reading strategies that they learned during shared and guided reading. They will work through print and word problems and the challenges presented by the books at their instructional and independent reading levels.

Selecting Books for Independent Reading

Emergent readers need to be able to make personal reading selections from a variety of books and genres. Books that you have read and taught during shared reading or guided reading make excellent choices for children.

To help students select appropriate books, you may wish to set up book boxes in your classroom. Organize instructionally appropriate books and other classroom reading material into the boxes according to reading levels. Make sure there is a box for each reading level in your classroom. Then direct students to look for their reading materials in the box that is appropriate for meeting their independent reading needs.

WHAT'S THE EVIDENCE?

Research shows that reading achievement is positively influenced by the amount of time children spend reading books. See Morrow, 1997, and Cunningham & Stanovich, 1991. Research also indicates that when children read independently, their writing quality improves and the quantity of their writing increases. See Adams, Treiman, & Pressley, 1996; Adams, 1990; Stanovich, 1986; and Anderson et al., 1984. The importance of independent reading in a balanced reading program is supported by Strickland, 1998a; Fountas & Pinnell, 1996; Honig, 1996; and Adams, 1990.

Paired Reading

During independent reading time, students may choose to read with partners. Paired reading gives children opportunities to practice solving print problems with the support of other readers and to receive reinforcement for their reading development. It also allows children to share their favorite stories or parts of stories with one another, which builds critical thinking skills and motivation for reading.

You may choose to pair students with similar reading ability levels or with different ability levels. You might even decide to pair students of different ages or from different grade levels.

Same-Ability Pairs

In same-ability pairs, children can collaborate to solve print problems and read stories that pose some reading challenges. A good time to use this type of paired reading is following a guided reading lesson; children can then work together to reread the text and practice the skills you just taught.

Mixed-Ability Pairs

Pairing children that need extra support with students who are more competent readers does not just benefit the student needing support. The more experienced reader develops feelings of self-worth, and his or her motivation increases from helping another student. To make these pairings most effective, instruct the more competent reader to listen to the other child work his or her way through the text. The listener should offer support only if the reader becomes stuck and is unable to use known reading strategies to continue.

Cross-Age Pairs

Most often in cross-age paired reading, older children support younger children as they read through texts. On occasion, it may be helpful for younger children to listen as older children read to them. Both children benefit from this type of reading, developing more positive attitudes toward reading.

WHAT'S THE EVIDENCE?

The benefits of independent and paired reading are supported by Strickland, 1998a; Morrow, 1997; Adams, Treiman, & Pressley, 1996; Fountas & Pinnell, 1996; Honig, 1996; Cunningham & Stanovich, 1991; Adams, 1990; Stanovich, 1986; and Anderson et al., 1984.

Writing

In The Story Box Reading Program, writing reinforces reading just as reading reinforces writing. A great deal of research supports the reciprocal relationship between reading and writing. Reading and writing are both interactive processes: good readers are usually good writers, and good writers tend to read well. Both skills require that students think about print and the relationships between sounds and letters. Both skills require that students have an understanding of letters, words, and sentences. By studying a child's writing, you can answer most of the following questions about his or her reading ability:

- Is the child able to hear phonemes in words?

- Can she relate the sound to the symbol? Does she exhibit an understanding of concepts of print in her writing, such as directionality, return sweep, and spaces between words?

- Does she form letters correctly, recognize and use spelling patterns, and correctly spell some words?

Writing, like reading, should occur throughout each day in a well-balanced curriculum involving a variety of activities. Children need to see different purposes for writing and explore different genres of writing, such as letters, journals, instructions, stories, poetry, fiction, and nonfiction. Children learn best when writing experiences are real and meaningful, when they are writing to learn, and when writing activities are enjoyable.

A balanced program includes seven types of writing experiences: **model writing, process writing, journal writing, guided writing, structure writing, content writing,** and **independent writing.** Each of these writing processes can be used in conjunction with shared reading and/or guided reading lessons. For example, following a shared reading or guided reading lesson, you might model writing about the story or one of the story's characters, guide students as they write about a favorite part of the story, provide a structured writing activity based on the language patterns in a story, or have students write independently about the story.

WHAT'S THE EVIDENCE?

Writing and reading have a strong relationship, according to Pikulski, 1995; Shefelbine, 1995; and Strickland, 1991. Strickland, 1998a; Weaver, 1998; P. Cunningham, 1995; and Tierney & Shannahan, 1991, support the importance of real, meaningful, and enjoyable writing experiences and the use of whole texts.

Characteristics of Emergent Writers

Beginning writers may exhibit many or even all of the following traits as they begin expressing themselves in writing.

Writers at the early emergent level

- Are developing an understanding of directionality (beginning writing in the upper-left corner of a page and writing from left to right)

- Can write some letters of the alphabet

- Use random letters to represent words

- Use a mix of uppercase and lowercase letters

- Are beginning to hear initial phonemes in words and can attach the correct symbol to those sounds

- Use drawings to tell a story

- Use artwork as an integral part of a story

- Understand that writing is for communication (they can "read" the random marks of their own stories)

Writers at the upper emergent level

- Leave spaces between words

- Use uppercase and lowercase letters

- Use some punctuation

- Spell some high-frequency words correctly

- Recognize and use some spelling patterns

- Are able to hear and write beginning, ending, and often medial sounds in words

- Are able to segment many words into their correct spellings

- Use artwork as an integral part of their stories

(Me and Lita were flying the kite)
Example of early emergent writing

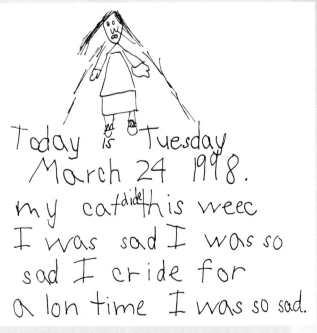

Example of upper emergent writing

Model Writing

Model writing is a whole-group shared writing activity that includes **Daily News** and **language experience**. It provides opportunities for you to model for children the thought processes and strategies of writing.

As students dictate sentences or stories, you write them on large chart paper or on an overhead transparency. Students participate in deciding what letters represent the sounds they hear in words, which helps them make sound-symbol connections in their minds and then transfer these understandings to print. The writing generated in this way then becomes an excellent source of reading material in your classroom, since children experience greater reading success when they read print that has come from their own experiences and oral language.

Daily News

An important form of model writing is the Daily News. Each day, select a child to share "news" orally with the rest of the class. This news item may be a piece of information, a personal story, a show-and-tell object, or an observation on local or world events. After the student shares, involve the class in composing a written message consisting of the date, a daily weather report, and a short statement summarizing the student's news item. Record the daily news on large paper or on an overhead transparency. As you write, invite students to help identify sounds, letters, punctuation, and some spelling.

You might then have students illustrate these news items, thereby connecting a visual representation with the written words. Display the finished news in the room or bind it into a Weekly News Big Book for the children to read.

Today is Monday.
It is raining.
Alicia said, "I went
to the store with my
Dad yesterday."

Print developed from oral language is some of the most effective reading material you can create in your classroom, serving as an important resource for teaching the skills that emergent readers and writers need. You might use the Daily News to teach or reinforce any of the following skills. Children can use markers to highlight their responses to the questions, or you can place a piece of laminate over the news and then write responses on it.

Concepts of Print
- Where did we start writing?
- Which way did we go?
- What did we put at the beginning and end of the sentence?
- What did we leave between each word?
- Find a letter in your name.
- Find your favorite letter. What is it?

Phonological Awareness
- What sound did you hear at the beginning of _____?
- Name another word that begins with the same sound as _____.
- Name a word that rhymes with _____.
- When I say _____, tell me the sounds you hear.
- How many syllables did you hear in _____?

Phonics
- What sound and letter does _____ begin with?
- What sound and letter does _____ end with?
- Find a word with the sound of _____.
- Find a word that rhymes with _____.
- Find a word in the _____ word family.
- Let's make a list of other words that begin with, end with, or rhyme with _____.
- What other words have the same vowel sound as _____?
- Can you find a small word in _____ that you already know?

High-Frequency Words
- Find the word _____.
- How did we spell _____?
- What will help you remember this word?

Language Experience

Language experience includes talking, writing, and reading about an experience shared by the class, such as a field trip, a visit from a community leader or expert in a particular field, a science observation, or a special school event. After such an event, discuss the experience with your students, encouraging them to explore their ideas, impressions, and feelings about it through spoken and written language.

You will want to write about their reactions and then later have them use this writing as a model for their own writing. Whenever possible, include illustrations and/or photographs in your discussions, and encourage students to illustrate their spoken and written ideas. By talking and writing about an experience, children come to a greater understanding of written expression and develop related vocabulary and background knowledge.

Following a classroom butter-making activity, students will write about their experience

Examples of Language Experience

Language experience can involve many different types of activities such as the following suggestions:

- Retelling a story

- Summarizing an experience

- Verbalizing thoughts and feelings about an experience

- Revising an experience

- Asking questions

- Predicting outcomes

- Discussing or explaining a concept

- Comparing and contrasting events

Process Writing

Children learn to write by writing, just as they learn to read by reading. Process writing provides a format in which students can write about their own experiences and for their own purposes. The goal of process writing is for students to find and develop their personal views and become comfortable with the writing process.

During daily process writing, encourage children to see themselves as authors and to think about the decisions they make as they write. Gradually, they will learn to view their experiences with a writer's eye, looking for meaning and considering how they can best express themselves.

During process writing, model your own writing for the students, demonstrating how your thought processes became print and what skills and strategies are needed to create a clear and readable piece of writing. You can use process writing to model revision and correct spelling, grammar, and punctuation. Gauge the depth and length of time you devote to modeling by the developmental needs of your students.

In their first writing attempts, allow students to focus on the meaning and expression of their ideas. At the early emergent level, children's writing is typically limited to pictures, random letters and/or a few words. You may choose not to have your beginning writers engage in the revision process. You may simply discuss the strengths their writing demonstrates and goals for future writing.

Once the children begin to gain some control over sounds and symbols and can spell several words, you can have them begin revising their work. Together, look at a first draft of their writing. You can provide guidance in spelling, punctuation, grammar, and story construction. Note that when it comes to spelling, it is important to permit beginning writers to make approximations. When learning through approximate, or phonetic, spelling, children use symbols of their own devising to represent the sounds they hear in a word. Very often, approximate spelling reveals remarkable solutions to the challenge of re-creating sound through symbol. A good way to assess children's level of understanding of the alphabetic principle and phonics is to study their use of approximate spelling.

WHAT'S THE EVIDENCE?

Wilde, 1992, found that the use of approximate spelling by children is a good indicator of their level of understanding of the alphabetic principle and phonics.

You will want to meet with a few students individually each day during the process writing time to discuss each student's writing strengths and an area on which they need to focus; for example, verbalizing a story idea; hearing and writing initial, medial, and final sounds in words; using correct punctuation and capitalization; or spelling known, high-frequency words correctly.

Occasionally, you will want students to publish finished stories. Publishing involves revising and polishing a piece of writing into a final form that can be shared with the class. The children may type their stories on the computer or handwrite the text themselves, or you or a classroom volunteer might help them write the text. If possible, make the publishing event special by providing high-quality paper, book covers, and art supplies that will give the writing the appearance of a real book.

Journal Writing

In journal writing, beginning writers experiment with language and discover writing as a medium of self-expression. Students' journal writing also provides a focus for instruction and a means of assessing writing development over time. As you observe and listen to students' journal entries, you can see what writing skills they are using and how their understanding of phonetic elements is growing.

Initially, you will want to model journal writing for the students by developing your own sample journal entry based on a personal story or experience. Involve the children in your thought process as you describe, for example, how you go about choosing the right words for your story, how you decide to begin each sentence, and how you remember the spellings of words you know.

Writing Responses to Reading

When students write about what they have read, they learn to think about ideas, emotions, different viewpoints, and various literary concepts. At the early emergent level, children's responses to literature may be only simple drawings. As children become more comfortable with the writing process, they begin to use words to convey their ideas.

After a shared reading or guided reading experience, help students make connections between the story and their own experiences and talk about the elements of the story, including character, setting, and events. Model a written response to the story. For example, write about how the character in the story is like you or about who your favorite character is and why. Children can use your model as a springboard for writing their own responses to the stories.

Guided Writing

Guided writing is a powerful approach to developing writing, especially phonics skills. In guided writing, you work with one child at a time, focusing on that child's knowledge of sound-symbol relationships. With this approach, you are able to observe what the child knows, assess exactly where the child is in the writing process, determine which phonics skills the child is using, and then tailor your instruction to suit the child's needs. Thus, you can model appropriate behaviors or strategies for learning that will guide and reinforce the child's approximations.

A guided writing session generally takes only two or three minutes. You may be able to meet with three to five students in individual sessions while the other children are writing in their journals. During a meeting, a student will write while you watch and offer guidance. You can use the following prompts during a guided writing session:

- What sound do you think _____ begins with?

- Let's use a sound-segment box to see if you hear all of the sounds.

- Let's try writing that word together. You write the sounds you know and I'll write the rest.

- Does your sentence make sense?

- Did you begin and end your sentence correctly?

Have your most inexperienced writers write only one sentence during your guided writing time with them. After they have developed as writers, you might write two or three sentences together.

A teacher prompts a student during a guided writing session

Structure Writing

Structure writing is an effective method of modeling, reinforcing, and providing practice in the use of the conventions of print. Through structure writing, children can practice basic grammatical and spelling conventions as they internalize the most common structures of our language.

Begin by modeling a simple writing task that you will later ask your students to do on their own. For example, after reading *Go, Go, Go* (The Story Box, Set A), you might model completing the structure pattern "I ____."

Beginning writers might add only a single letter to a structure pattern. Later, students can complete a structure on their own. For example, after reading *A Monster Sandwich* (The Story Box, Set B), you might have students complete the structure "Put some ___ on it," such as in the following example:

When students change the word or words that complete a structure, they are practicing the spelling of the *unchanged* words in the structure. For example, when completing the structure "I can ____," students practice the spelling of *I* and *can*.

Writing based on the structure of *In a Dark, Dark, Wood*

Content Writing

In content writing, students write about specific topics in any of the content areas, such as science, social studies, health, and math. Through this writing experience, students learn to use writing as a thinking tool to synthesize, summarize, and analyze information. Because content writing involves analysis, it can yield valuable insight into a child's cognitive development. In addition, content writing enhances students' long-term learning retention, increases students' metacognitive skills, builds students' decoding and comprehension skills, and helps students recognize and use language and text structures often found in nonfiction and content-area materials.

Encourage content writing in a variety of forms, such as journal entries, instructions, lists, recipes, charts, graphs, and maps. Content writing offers children opportunities to write in new and meaningful ways. They can summarize information, pose questions in their writing, solve problems, create directions, and make visual representations of information. In this way, students begin to experience some of the many applications of writing to learning and to all of the content areas.

Student content-writing sample from *Paint, Write & Play!™* CD-ROM

WHAT'S THE EVIDENCE?

The work of Armbruster, 1992, supports the positive effects of content writing on students' recognition of language and text structures.

Independent Writing

The goal of model, guided, structure, and content writing is independence in writing. As children learn the tools of self-expression and gain confidence in their mastery of writing conventions, they begin to develop as independent writers.

To encourage independent writing, capitalize on any and all writing opportunities. Have students write their own stories, take notes as reminders to you or to themselves, make lists of things, create directions, write recipes, write notes to others, make class charts, and record classroom rules. The key to helping students become independent writers is creating an abundance of opportunities for children to write, write, write.

WHAT'S THE EVIDENCE?

Support for the writing process and all of the formats of writing can be attributed in part to Strickland, 1998a, 1991; Weaver, 1998; Braunger & Lewis, 1997; Fountas & Pinnell, 1996; P. Cunningham, 1995; Shefelbine, 1995; Richardson & Morgan, 1996; Armbruster, 1992; and Wilde, 1992.

(Happy Birthday, Natalie)

Spelling

Spelling is an integral part of reading and writing instruction. It enhances children's ability to read unknown words and helps them hear and pronounce words correctly. When children are exposed daily to reading and writing, they internalize not only the spellings of words, but spelling patterns as well. Shared reading, guided reading, model writing, guided writing, and independent writing all provide avenues for teaching spelling strategies.

As you and your students read, have them look for and name letters, sounds, and high-frequency words in the Read-Togethers or guided reading books. As they progress in their reading ability, have them look for spelling patterns and word endings as well.

Build and display word lists around the classroom to assist children in correctly spelling frequently used words. These lists might, for example, consist of color words, number words, words having to do with a particular theme or topic, words in the same word family, words with the same beginning or ending sounds, or words with similar vowel patterns. Students will make cognitive links with the words in these lists that will aid them in developing their visual memory of the words.

WHAT'S THE EVIDENCE?

Moustafa, 1997, writes about the link between reading and writing practice and improved spelling . The importance of teaching spelling in conjunction with reading and writing is supported by Moustafa, 1998; Strickland, 1998a; Weaver, 1998; Moats, 1997; Honig, 1996; Routman, 1996; P. Cunningham, 1995; Shefelbine, 1995; Woloshyn & Pressley, 1995; Juel, 1994; and Adams, 1990.

Stages of Spelling

Developing writers and readers go through several stages of learning about letters and sounds. The development of spelling strategies at the emergent level is usually sequential, beginning with the use of pre-phonetic and early phonetic strategies and gradually moving toward advanced phonetic strategies. As children develop as spellers, they move toward transitional and then standard spelling.

At the early emergent level, when children generally use pre-phonetic or early phonetic spelling, they are just beginning to learn that the marks that they put on paper represent letters and words and tell stories. These marks often consist of consonant sounds to represent words or shapes that may or may not resemble letter forms.

Early emergent spellers need practice in becoming phonemically aware of sounds and syllables. Phonological understandings in early spellers can predict later reading ability. Phonetic spelling correlates with word reading and word attack skills.

Upper emergent spellers interact with more print. They have a fairly good grasp of letter-sound relationships and recognize several words and word chunks. At the advanced phonetic stage of spelling, children use auditory strategies to match sounds with symbols, and they use increasingly sophisticated spelling strategies. Children at this level pay more attention to the visual features of words and so are able to recognize word chunks and word families and see patterns in spelling.

A child's writing and spelling ability correlates highly with word recognition and reading comprehension and increases as the students' writing ability increases.

WHAT'S THE EVIDENCE?

Routman, 1996, and P. Cunningham, 1995, discuss research on the spelling development of writers and readers. Links between students' level of spelling development and later success in reading are supported by Adams, 1990. The research of Juel, 1994, supports the high correlation between writing and spelling ability and word recognition and reading comprehension.

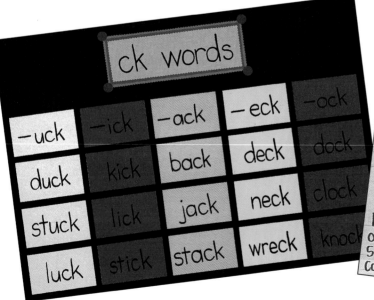

Example of a spelling-pattern wall chart

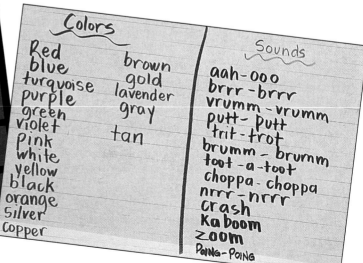

Example of a word-wall chart

Characteristics of Early Emergent Spellers

Pre-phonetic/primitive spelling: random letters

An early emergent speller may

- Reproduce scribbling or shapes that resemble letter forms

- Use random letters and numbers to represent words

- String writing together with no concept of a word

- Show no relationship between spelling and words

- Copy some words and phrases

Early phonetic spelling: consonants

An early emergent speller may

- Attempt to represent with letters the sounds heard in words

- Use initial consonants or a few consonants to represent a whole word

- Understand that longer words have longer spellings

- Match some consonants with their sounds

- Find reading what he or she writes difficult but possible if there is a clear illustration

Mixes uppercase and lowercase letters

Uses initial and final consonants to represent a word

Spells some high-frequency words correctly

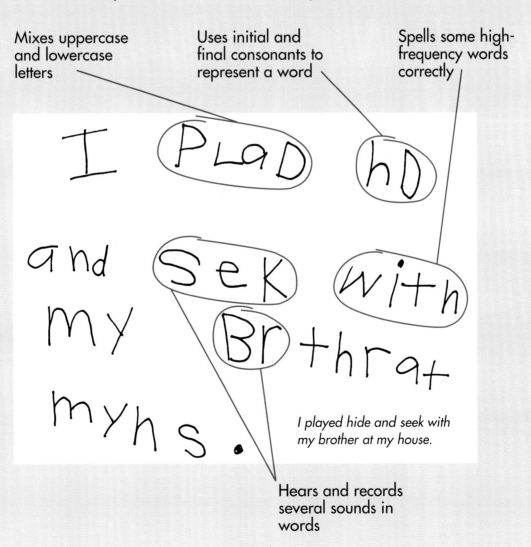

I played hide and seek with my brother at my house.

Hears and records several sounds in words

Characteristics of Upper Emergent Spellers

Advanced phonetic spelling: initial, medial, and final consonants

An upper emergent speller may

- Write letters based on how words look as well as on how they sound

- Analyze and record most consonant sounds

- Use some long vowels as markers but often not correctly

- Spell words the way they sound

- Spell some high-frequency words correctly

- Easily read passages of his or her writing

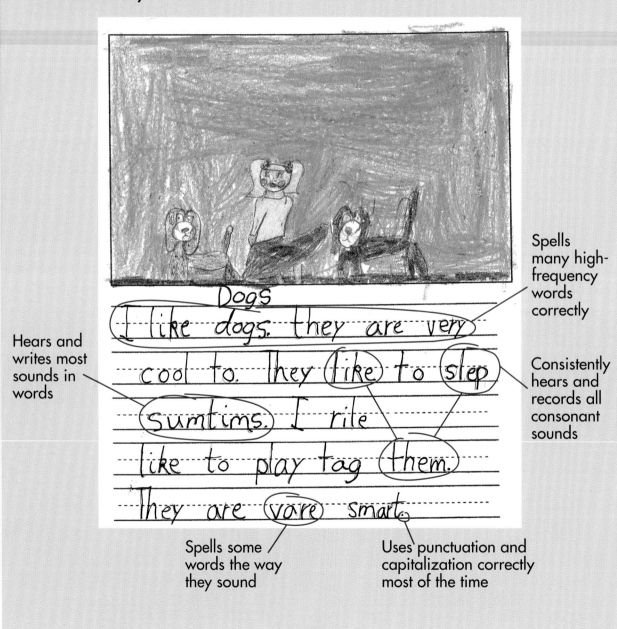

Hears and writes most sounds in words

Spells many high-frequency words correctly

Consistently hears and records all consonant sounds

Spells some words the way they sound

Uses punctuation and capitalization correctly most of the time

Strategies for Teaching Spelling

There are numerous strategies for developing students' spelling ability. Three are discussed here: (1) teaching spelling patterns, (2) encouraging phonetic spelling, and (3) implementing a formal spelling program.

Spelling Patterns

The skills and writing activities in the Story Box shared reading and guided reading lessons focus attention on spelling patterns, how words are put together, and correct spellings of high-frequency words.

There are three major spelling patterns—sound, function, and meaning.

Sound patterns can be found in words with rhyming sounds, such as *hen, men,* and *pen.* In these words, the initial consonant sounds, known as **onsets,** may change, but the endings, known as **rimes,** remain the same. Early emergent readers tend to focus on sound representations, so sound patterns are usually the easiest spelling cues for them to learn.

Function patterns describe the forms of words and the ways in which words are used in sentences. Sentence structure requires that particular words have specific endings; for example, plural words often end with -*s* or -*es*, past tense verbs often end with -*ed,* some nouns become adverbs when they take an -*ly* ending, and some verbs become nouns when they take a -*ment* ending.

Meaning patterns are found in words with the same roots, bases, or origins. These words have similar spellings and related meanings, even though they may have very different pronunciations. For example, *two, twice,* and *twins* are all related to the concept of "two" and begin with the same letters. Another example is the pattern found in *medicine, medical,* and *medication.*

Phonetic Spelling

Children who are just beginning to write and spell words are often called inventive or developmental spellers. Phenix (1998) states, "We might understand it better if we called it phonetic spelling. It is not a children's invention; it is real spelling done with minimal information. Nor is it temporary; we use sound-patterns all our lives. Nor is it developmental; improved spelling is largely the result of more information and practice."

> ## WHAT'S THE EVIDENCE?
>
> Strickland, 1998a, indicates that student spelling becomes more conventional with practice in reading and writing. P. Cunningham, 1995, suggests that students should be encouraged to make the transition from approximate to conventional spelling as soon as they are developmentally ready to do so. See Phenix, 1998, for a discussion on phonetic spelling.

For many emergent level children, writing and spelling is an activity they do aloud. As young children write, they sound out each word and attempt to match the sounds they hear to the appropriate letters. Because of this sounding-out strategy, writing and spelling are perhaps the best way for children to learn and practice phonics. The more children manipulate and construct words as they practice writing and spelling, the more phonics practice they get.

Students feel freer to write in learning environments that encourage the use of phonetic spelling. In turn, writing gives students a context for learning to spell and helps them internalize spelling strategies. As students concentrate on conveying written messages, they naturally begin to self-correct and apply their phonics skills. With students' continued exposure to reading and writing, their spelling becomes more conventional. As you see students making this transition to correct spelling, assist the process by offering positive feedback and encouragement.

Formal Spelling Instruction

Children need to learn as soon as possible how to spell high-frequency words that they use in their writing. The sooner children memorize the correct spelling of high-frequency words, the less chance there is of them practicing and internalizing incorrect spellings.

With students who are in the middle of first grade and who are ready, you may want to implement a more formal spelling program. When children combine their phonetic spellings with a formal spelling program, they experience rapid growth in both correct spelling and word recognition. A formal spelling program at the upper emergent level should help students identify sounds in words, patterns in words, and consistent spellings for consonants, vowels, syllables, and word families. A formal spelling program should be purposeful, supporting both the reading and writing processes.

WHAT'S THE EVIDENCE?

The works of Moats, 1997, and Shefelbine, 1995, support well-conceived and purposeful formal spelling programs.

Instructional Cycle in The Story Box

As you begin working with The Story Box, you may wish to follow a complete instructional cycle. A complete instructional cycle begins with assessment and ends with assessment, so that instruction is based on what your students know and on the skills and strategies they have yet to learn. As you continue the cycle, you plan what needs to be focused on, devise a way to model necessary skills and strategies, guide children in their learning, and then give them time to practice and apply what they have learned. Finally, you reassess the students to evaluate their understanding of what was taught.

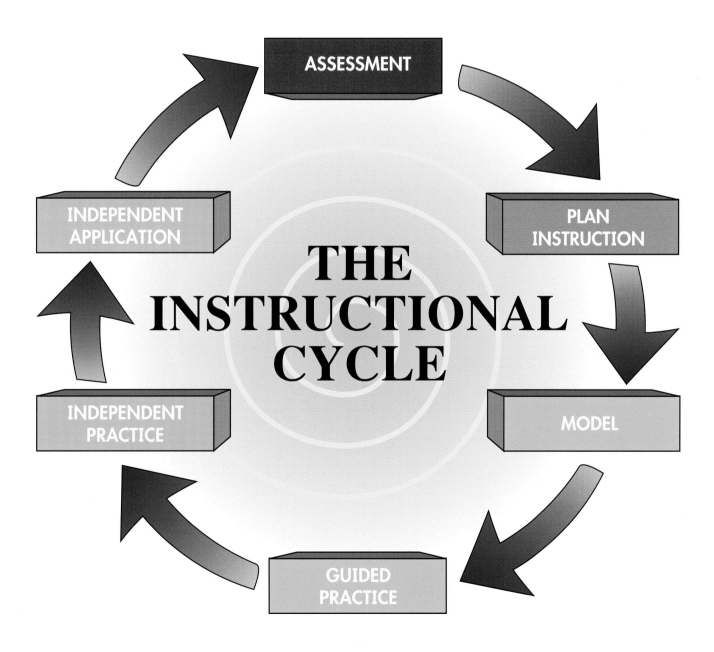

Plan Instruction

You will want to select the books and strategies that your assessments indicate will most effectively teach a skill. Plan how you will introduce a skill or strategy and how you will guide students toward independent application of the skill. You may choose to teach the skill within the context of a reading and then move on to more explicit instruction. This direct, explicit teaching provides students with multiple strategies for learning the skill. Once students have an understanding of the skill, you can move them back into the context of the book.

In its skills instruction, The Story Box employs a teaching strategy in which students first learn how a skill or strategy is used in shared reading or guided reading story books. Then the teacher removes the skill or strategy from this context for in-depth instruction. Finally, students return to the text or engage in additional reading and/or writing activities to apply the skill.

Pre-Instruction Assessment

The assessment that you do prior to instruction can come from a variety of sources. Assessments involve observing students' performances or their demonstration of knowledge of a skill or concept. Instruction is based on daily observations; anecdotal notes from previous lessons; checklists that you maintain daily, weekly, or monthly; and informal assessments, such as an Assessment of Reading Behavior, a Concepts of Print Checklist, a Phonological Awareness Assessment, and a Phonics Assessment. (See The Story Box Assessment Kit for a complete exploration of assessment.)

Once you have determined what skill or concept your students need to learn, you can begin to plan your instruction.

Model

After introducing students to a new skill or strategy by using a shared reading or guided reading book, you may choose to model use of the skill in writing activities and think-alouds; and webs, charts, or other graphic organizers. Demonstrations help bring to a conscious level the application of the skill or strategy being taught.

Once students have an understanding of a new skill, they need opportunities to practice it with your support.

Guided Practice

In guided practice, you work with an individual student, a small group, or the entire class on developing specific skills or strategies. Encourage students to find examples of applications of a skill in the Read-Togethers, guided reading books, or in their own writing samples. Use webs and charts that build on the skill; for example, you might have students help you create a web of words that begin with a particular sound or letter.

Independent Practice

Provide many opportunities for students to independently practice a skill. These opportunities may include independent reading of a book, searching for examples of a skill in reading books, making word charts, practicing saying or spelling new words, and working with a partner or small group to practice a skill. Children should have a variety of contexts in which they can practice what was taught.

Independent Application

Once students have learned a concept or skill, they need to be able to apply this new knowledge in new situations. For example, after students have learned the spelling of a particular sound, they should be able, on their own, to find that same sound in words they come across in their reading. It is helpful to have students keep in their journals lists of words they find that relate to a concept or skill they've learned.

Post-Instruction Assessment

Once your students have learned and practiced a skill or strategy, you can assess their understanding of it. If your assessment suggests that student understanding is high, you can use the information from your assessments to begin a new teaching cycle. The instructional cycle can be long. For example, in shared reading, you might focus on the same skill for two or more days. The cycle can also be short, lasting for a single class period, as in a guided reading or writing lesson.

As you continue using the instructional cycle to plan new lessons and skills, keep in mind that you will need to periodically reassess and reinforce skills you have already taught.

The Four Cueing System

Reading is a complex undertaking that requires readers to use several strategies for full comprehension. When reading, children use several sources of information, such as words, sentences, and organizational structures, to help them understand text. To become good readers, children need to develop strategies that will enable them to make simultaneous use of different reading cues that help them know if and how what they read makes sense, sounds right, and looks right.

The four cueing system model explains how a reader's schema and semantic cues, syntactic cues, and graphophonic cues all contribute to a reader's comprehension.

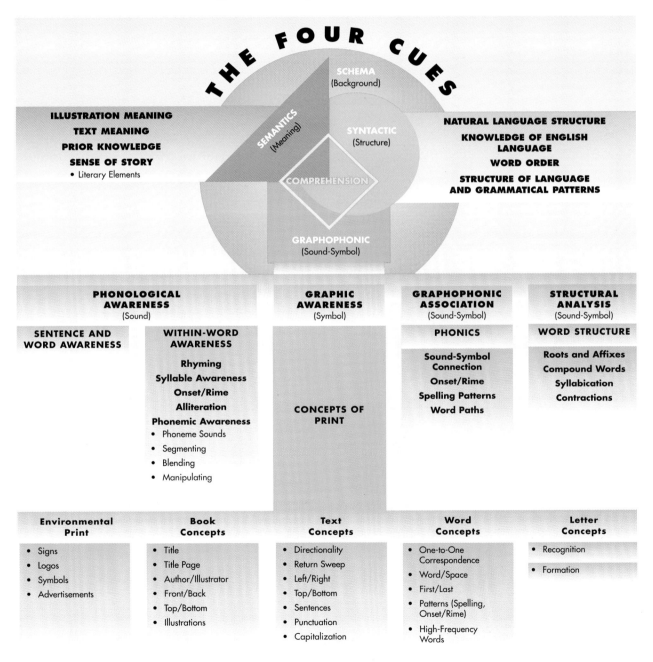

THE FOUR CUES

SCHEMA (Background)

SEMANTICS (Meaning)

SYNTACTIC (Structure)

COMPREHENSION

GRAPHOPHONIC (Sound-Symbol)

ILLUSTRATION MEANING
TEXT MEANING
PRIOR KNOWLEDGE
SENSE OF STORY
• Literary Elements

NATURAL LANGUAGE STRUCTURE
KNOWLEDGE OF ENGLISH LANGUAGE
WORD ORDER
STRUCTURE OF LANGUAGE AND GRAMMATICAL PATTERNS

PHONOLOGICAL AWARENESS (Sound)

SENTENCE AND WORD AWARENESS

WITHIN-WORD AWARENESS
Rhyming
Syllable Awareness
Onset/Rime
Alliteration
Phonemic Awareness
• Phoneme Sounds
• Segmenting
• Blending
• Manipulating

GRAPHIC AWARENESS (Symbol)

CONCEPTS OF PRINT

GRAPHOPHONIC ASSOCIATION (Sound-Symbol)

PHONICS
Sound-Symbol Connection
Onset/Rime
Spelling Patterns
Word Paths

STRUCTURAL ANALYSIS (Sound-Symbol)

WORD STRUCTURE
Roots and Affixes
Compound Words
Syllabication
Contractions

Environmental Print
• Signs
• Logos
• Symbols
• Advertisements

Book Concepts
• Title
• Title Page
• Author/Illustrator
• Front/Back
• Top/Bottom
• Illustrations

Text Concepts
• Directionality
• Return Sweep
• Left/Right
• Top/Bottom
• Sentences
• Punctuation
• Capitalization

Word Concepts
• One-to-One Correspondence
• Word/Space
• First/Last
• Patterns (Spelling, Onset/Rime)
• High-Frequency Words

Letter Concepts
• Recognition
• Formation

Schema Cues

A reader's schema are all the prior knowledge and experiences that he or she brings to reading. Schema cues are crucial to a reader's comprehension of a text and ability to make use of the other reading cues. When reading skills are linked to a child's schema, that child has a much greater chance of learning the skills.

Semantic Cues

Semantic cues tell readers if what they read makes sense. Semantic cues provide readers with meaning, helping them understand words as well as the broader messages, including literary elements, of a story. Illustrations and text clues also help students gain meaning from books.

Syntactic Cues

Syntactic cues tell readers if what they read sounds right. Syntactic cues reside in the structure of language, grammatical patterns, and word order. Syntactic cues help readers predict what types of words, such as nouns, verbs, or adjectives, will appear in the text. The ordinary language children hear and use daily and their understanding of the English language are key factors in this cueing system.

Graphophonic Cues

Graphophonic cues tell readers if what they read looks right. Graphophonic cues focus on the relationship between sounds and symbols and visual and spatial concepts. Graphophonic cues include phonological awareness, graphic awareness (concepts of print), graphophonics association (phonics), and structural analysis (word structure).

WHAT'S THE EVIDENCE?

Efficient readers use the four cueing system while reading. See Strickland, 1998a; Weaver, 1998; Braunger & Lewis, 1997; Fox, 1996; Morrison, 1994a, 1994b; Share & Stanovich, 1995; Adams, 1990; and Clay, 1985, 1979. Stanovich, 1986, found that less-skilled readers use semantic (meaning) and syntactic (structure) cues to identify words and tend to neglect graphophonic cues, while successful readers use graphophonic cues along with semantic and syntactic cues.

References cited in the "What's the Evidence?" boxes are listed in a bibliography at the end of this guide.

Skills Instruction in The Story Box

The Story Box Reading Program provides a wide variety of strategies for teachers to model and guide skills instruction, as well as appropriate experiences for children to practice and apply the skills. Through shared reading and guided reading lesson plans, students learn skills in the context of engaging stories and poems and related writing activities.

WHAT'S THE EVIDENCE?

Support for the effectiveness of embedding skills instruction in the context of real reading and writing experiences comes from Strickland, 1998a; Weaver, 1998, 1996, 1994; Moustafa, 1997; Honig, 1996; P. Cunningham, 1995; Routman, 1991; Adams, 1990; and A. Cunningham, 1990.

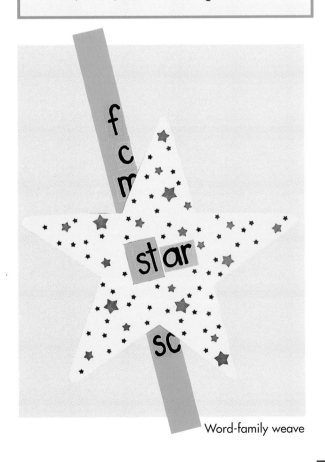

Word-family weave

Because skills instruction is an instrumental part of teaching reading, it is a key component in The Story Box. The Story Box teaches children to

- Recognize concepts of print and books
- Hear and identify sounds
- Decode words
- Identify high-frequency words
- Comprehend what they read
- Analyze word patterns
- Read with fluency and accuracy

The specific skill areas taught in the Story Box lessons are (1) phonological awareness, (2) concepts of print and mechanics, (3) phonics, (4) word structure, and (5) vocabulary. The Story Box lessons also include questions and activities to build students' comprehension skills.

Each shared reading and guided reading lesson provides references to The Wright Skills for additional skills practice. Informal assessments for skills are available in The Story Box Assessment Kit.

Phonological Awareness

Phonological awareness, a component of the graphophonic cueing system, is an overall understanding of the sound structure of spoken language, including rhyming and alliteration. It is an awareness that oral speech can be divided into sentences and words and that within words there are syllables, onsets and rimes, and phonemes. Phonological awareness includes

- **Sentence Awareness**—an awareness that a sentence is an expression of a complete thought. Sentence awareness is the ability to break speech into sentences and to recognize that oral and written language is organized into sentences.

  One way to teach sentence awareness is to have children listen as you read a page or several sentences from a story and clap their hands when they hear the end of a sentence.

- **Word Awareness**—an awareness of words in spoken and written language. It is the ability to hear individual words in sentences. This awareness will help students later understand that text is actually the spoken word written down.

  An activity to teach word awareness is to have students listen as you read a sentence from a story and tap their fingers each time they hear you say a word.

- **Rhyming**—an awareness that rhyming words end with the same sounds. Rhyming is one of the easiest phonological awareness tasks for children. Rhyming awareness is the first step toward being able to blend and manipulate sounds in words.

  One way to help children discriminate rhyming words is to say pairs of words, some that rhyme and some that don't. Have the children clap or raise their hands when they hear a pair of words that rhyme.

Phonological Awareness
Rhyming

- Read page 3 to the children and have them listen for the rhyming words *see, me,* and *jigaree.* Read other pages aloud and ask students to clap when they hear the rhyming words. Brainstorm other words that rhyme with *see, me,* and *jigaree.*

- Say several word pairs: *bee/hat; man/see; key/bag; tree/book.* Instruct the children to listen for the word in each pair that rhymes with *me* and then say the word.

Phonological awareness activities for *The Jigaree,* Read-Togethers 1

- **Alliteration**—the ability to hear and generate words that begin with the same initial sounds. The initial sound may be a consonant, a vowel, a blend, or a digraph.

  Saying tongue twisters and alliterative sentences or phrases helps children hear sounds that are alike.

- **Syllable Awareness**—the within-word awareness that allows students to hear the parts or syllables that make up a word. For many children, hearing syllables in words may be easier than hearing individual sounds or phonemes.

  Asking children to do an action such as clapping or tapping as they listen for word parts will help them hear syllables in words.

■ **Onset/Rime**—the within-word understanding that words are made of sound chunks or segments. The onset is the consonant or consonants that precede a vowel in a one-syllable word, and the rime is the vowel or vowels and any consonants that follow it. For example, in *big*, *b* is the onset and *-ig* is the rime. It is easier for children to hear and identify onsets and rimes than it is for them to hear individual phonemes.

Help students use analogy to hear onsets and rimes. Have them listen to a word as you drop the onset and just say the rime. Ask children to suggest other onsets that can be added to the rime to make new words.

■ **Phonemic Awareness**—the ability to hear and distinguish individual phonemes within words and to recognize that spoken words are made up of sequences of speech sounds. Phonemic awareness is also the ability to blend, segment, and manipulate the phonemes in words. (A phoneme is the smallest sound segment of a word.) Development of phonemic awareness is a key factor in becoming a successful reader and writer. Most phonemic awareness studies show that phonemic recognition facilitates learning to read, and in turn, learning to read helps develop phonemic recognition.

Develop students' phonemic awareness by engaging them in informal, game-like activities that help them hear like sounds and play with the sounds. These activities can include blending, segmenting, and manipulating.

■ **Blending**—a level of phonemic awareness that helps children hear and blend isolated phonemes in words to make a word. For example, if you say /r/ /u/ /n/, you would have the students say /r/ /u/ /n/, *run*.

■ **Segmenting**—the ability to break a word down into its separate phonemes. For example, you would say *bed* and then slowly say each phoneme /b/ /e/ /d/. The children would repeat the sounds /b/ /e/ /d/ and then blend the sounds together and say the word *bed*.

■ **Manipulating**—the most difficult concept of phonemic awareness, manipulating is the ability to substitute one phoneme for another in a word. For example, changing *bat* to *hat*, *bat* to *bar*, and *bat* to *bit*.

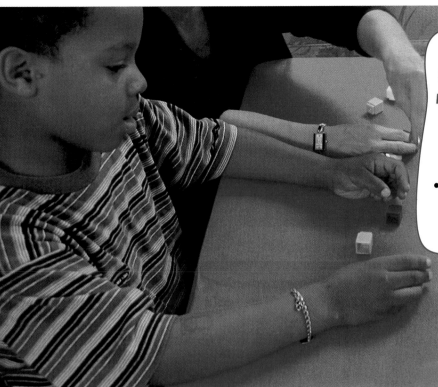

Phonological Awareness

Phonemic Awareness: Segmenting and Blending

■ Invite the children to build the words *want*, *don't*, and *get* with connecting cubes. Tell them to connect one cube for every sound they hear in a word; for example, *get* would have three cubes connected.

● Touch the cubes from left to right with your finger as you say each sound. Now sweep your hand from left to right and blend the sounds together to say the word.

Phonological awareness activities for *Lost*, Set E

Initially, it is easiest for children to hear words in sentences, especially ones including rhymes or alliterations. As they develop auditorially, children begin to hear syllables, onsets, and rimes in words. Then they develop phonemic awareness, hearing the individual phonemes in words and the blending and segmenting of these sounds. By the middle of first grade, most children are able to manipulate the sounds in words by omitting, adding, and substituting phonemes.

Instruction in developing phonological awareness skills is included throughout the shared reading and guided reading lesson plans. These plans provide appropriate activity suggestions for teaching each of the levels of phonological awareness. The activities provide children with engaging and enjoyable experiences as they develop their reading skills.

WHAT'S THE EVIDENCE?

Adams, 1990, says that difficulty with phonemics is the "single most significant predictor of reading and written language problems." The importance of hearing and recognizing the sounds of language is supported by Nation & Hulme, 1997; Adams & Bruck, 1995; Beck & Juel, 1995; Foorman, 1995; and Yopp, 1992. Additional support for teaching skills within meaningful contexts comes from Strickland, 1998a; Weaver, 1998, 1996, 1994; Braunger & Lewis, 1997; Moustafa, 1997, 1995; Nation & Hulme, 1997; Routman, 1996; P. Cunningham, 1995; Snider, 1995; and A. Cunningham, 1990.

Concepts of Print

Fundamental to learning to read is an awareness that print represents knowledge and ideas, carries a message, and has conventions. An understanding of print and mechanics generally includes an awareness of environmental print concepts, book concepts, text concepts, word concepts, letter concepts, and punctuation and capitalization concepts. To make sense of written language, children need to recognize that writing is composed of letters, that it moves left to right on a page, that spaces separate words, that written words represent what is spoken, and that sentences tell a story.

Components of Concepts of Print

Concepts of print, or graphic awareness, is part of the graphophonic cueing system. Concepts of print includes the following components:

- Environmental print—what children know about the print they see in their lives: their own names; books; written messages; company logos; and print on charts, signs, products, and posters.

  To help students use environmental print, you might want to encourage them to bring in environmental print and use this to create a "print wall."

- Book concepts—what children know about books, including the title and title page, the front and back cover, identification of the author and illustrator, the top and bottom of a book or page, and the role of illustrations in conveying a book's story or ideas.

  Ask students to point to parts of a book to determine their understanding of book concepts.

- Text concepts—what children know about the features of text, including that print has directionality and moves from left to right; return sweep, which involves reading to the end of a line and then going back to the beginning of the next line; and sentences, which begin with capital letters and end with punctuation.

  To determine students' understanding of directionality, encourage them to point to where they would begin reading on a page.

- Word concepts—what children know about words in text, such as that what is read and what is printed have a one-to-one correspondence, words are separated by spaces, words are made up of letters and have similar patterns or phonograms, and words may be instantly recognized by sight.

  You might want to evaluate students' understanding of word concepts by having them use a fun pointer to point to the words as a story is read.

- Letter concepts—what children know about the alphabet, such as the names of alphabet letters, letter order, and how to reproduce these letters.

  To teach letter concepts, you might want to have children match uppercase and lowercase letters.

Concepts of print is taught through direct and explicit skill instruction in the shared reading and guided reading lesson plans. A variety of activities incorporate both reading and writing opportunities.

WHAT'S THE EVIDENCE?

According to Juel, 1996, understanding concepts of print along with phoneme segmentation ability and knowledge of letter names are the best predictors of reading success. Research on metalinguistic awareness comes from Dechant,1993.

Adams, 1990, writes that the two best predictors of early reading success are alphabet recognition and phonemic awareness. The importance of using concepts of print instruction in reading is discussed by Strickland, 1998a; Braunger & Lewis, 1997; Chall, 1996; Juel, 1996; Beck & Juel, 1995; MacHado, 1995; Dechant, 1993; Adams, 1990; and Clay, 1985.

Concepts of Print

Directionality/Return Sweep

■ Open the book to pages 2–3. Have students show the class the answers to the following questions.

- Which page do we read first?
- Which way do we go when we are reading?
- Where do we go when we get to the end of the line?

Phonics

Phonics is a component of the graphophonic cueing system. Phonics instruction enables readers to connect sounds to letters, blend sounds to decode words, and use recognizable spelling patterns in decoding. In writing, students use their knowledge of phonics as they link letters to sounds, segment sounds to encode (write) words, and use spelling patterns to write words. According to current research, balanced, systematic phonics instruction that is connected to reading and writing results in better comprehension skills, word recognition skills, and spelling skills.

The phonics instruction in The Story Box involves meaningful print and follows an in-context, explicit, in-context approach. Students first learn about sounds and symbols by reading stories, then looking at words and word parts taken from the stories, and, finally, returning to the stories and related activities to apply what they've learned. Activities are designed to help you explicitly teach phonics skills and provide opportunities for children to extend their understanding by blending, segmenting, and manipulating print to form new words.

An important skill in beginning reading and writing is helping children make sound-symbol connections. Phonics instruction begins with sounds and letters and how they are blended together to form words; for example, /p/ /i/ /g/ makes *pig*. It also asks students to hear the individual phonemes in a word.

As children develop as readers they begin looking at whole words and separate their sounds and letters into familiar patterns. Once children recognize patterns within words, such as consonant blends, known word chunks, and known small words, they can manipulate the parts and letters in the words to form new words based on the same patterns.

Phonics

Short Vowel i

■ Have the students look at page 6. Ask a volunteer to find and frame the word *in*. Ask students what sound they hear at the beginning of *in*. Tell them that several words with the short *i* sound appear on this page. Have volunteers use waxed string to circle the short *i* words. Have students work with a partner to look through their own copy of the small book to find other examples of short *i* words. Together create a chart of short *i* words.

I will go to town
in my vintage c
big gree

Phonics activity for *To Town*, Read-Togethers 1

When children are familiar with rimes in words and can manipulate onsets, they are able to use analogies to decode unknown words. For example, if children know the word *jump* and see the new word *thump*, they will recognize the *-ump* rime and be able to substitute the onset *j* with the new onset *th* to make *thump*. The following word-family chart shows the rimes used in the Story Box lessons.

Word Families in The Story Box

-ack	-ash	-est	-it	-ow
-ad	-at	-et	-ive	-own
-ade	-ate	-ick	-ock	-oy
-ain	-ave	-ide	-og	-ub
-air	-aw	-ig	-oke	-uck
-ake	-ay	-ight	-old	-ug
-all	-eam	-ike	-one	-um
-am	-eat	-ile	-oo	-ummy
-ame	-ed	-ill	-ook	-ump
-an	-ee	-im	-op	-unk
-and	-eep	-ime	-ot	-up
-ar	-eet	-ine	-ound	-ut
-ark	-ell	-ing	-ouse	
-arm	-ent	-ish	-out	

Vowel Patterns

Vowel patterns, or spelling patterns, are the conventional placements of vowels and their surrounding consonants in words.

The vowel pattern chart provides an effective structure for learning vowel patterns. Seventy-five percent to 90 percent of all words will fit into one of the six vowel patterns included in the vowel pattern chart on the next page. If a word doesn't fit, it becomes a memory word, such as *was, do, to,* and *night,* that students need to learn to recognize by sight.

When you initially teach students to use the vowel pattern chart at the upper emergent level, you will want to categorize words with only one syllable, such as *run, me,* and *name.* Once students are familiar with categorizing one-syllable words and comfortable with the vowel pattern chart, begin analyzing words with more syllables. Place these words under the correct heading on the chart and highlight the appropriate sound. For example, the word *over* could fit under two headings: Open and Closed. You may wish to highlight the long *o* in the first syllable of *over* under the Open heading, or the short *e* in the second syllable under the Closed heading. The vowel patterns in the vowel pattern chart are described in the following list:

- **Closed Vowel**—Syllables with a closed vowel pattern have one short vowel and end with one or more consonants, as in *step*. Most of the word families fit this vowel pattern.

- **Open Vowel**—Syllables with an open vowel pattern end with one long vowel, as in *go*. *Y* can sometimes be a vowel.

- **Vowel with Silent *e***—Syllables with the vowel/consonant/silent *e* pattern have one long vowel that is followed by a consonant and a silent *e*, as in *cake*.

- *r*-**Controlled Vowel**—Syllables with this pattern have a vowel followed by an *r* that alters the sound of the vowel, as in *car*.

- **Two Vowels**

  Vowel Digraph—Syllables with this pattern have two adjacent vowels, in which the first vowel is long *(boat)*. *W* and *y* can work as vowels.

  Vowel Diphthong—Syllables with this pattern have two adjacent vowels, in which the vowels make a sound that is neither short nor long *(shout)*.

- **Syllable Ending with Consonant Plus -*le***—Syllables with this pattern end with a consonant that is followed by -*le*. Two-syllable words that end with a consonant plus -*le* will always divide before the consonant plus -*le*, as in *bub/ble, ta/ble, mum/ble*.

VOWEL PATTERN CHART

Closed	Open		Silent *e*
pig at step print	go she I my		cake name slice

r-Controlled	Two Vowels		Consonant Plus -*le*
car corn her first fur	vowel digraph	vowel diphthong	apple table eagle
	rain see play slow	now out coin toy	

WHAT'S THE EVIDENCE?

Honig, 1996, explains that phonics should be taught in an "active, problem-solving manner that develops a conscious understanding of the sound/symbol system; tailored much more precisely to the specific needs of children; and taught by providing students with numerous opportunities to use and practice the skills in the context of reading." Adams, 1990, writes that if children recognize only thirty-seven of the most commonly used rimes, they will be able to decode over five hundred primary words. The connection between recognizing phonograms and decoding words is discussed by Honig, 1996; Eldredge, 1995; and Adams, 1990.

Whole-to-part-to-whole phonics instruction is discussed by Weaver, 1998; Braunger & Lewis, 1997; Moustafa, 1997; Honig, 1996; P. Cunningham, 1995; and Adams, 1990. Additional discussions on phonics have been presented by Strickland, 1998a; Weaver, 1998, 1994; Fountas & Pinnell, 1996; Routman, 1996; Dechant, 1993; and A. Cunningham, 1990. The connection between looking for vowel and spelling patterns in words and identifying known chunks in new words is supported by Cheyney & Cohen, forthcoming; Strickland, 1998a; and P. Cunningham, 1995.

Word Structure

Word structure, or structural analysis, is part of the graphophonic cueing system and involves developing strategies for decoding words. Structural analysis refers to understanding how words are constructed. As a skill, structural analysis includes recognizing the changes that occur when prefixes are added to words and when endings are added to words in the form of plurals, possessives, or suffixes. Structural analysis also includes understanding syllabication, contractions, possessives, and compound words.

Structural analysis skills are important tools as children encounter increasingly challenging text and vocabulary. These skills show students how to use strategies they already know to make sense of new words. For example, students learn how to use their ability to decode one-syllable words to read multisyllabic words, and they learn to use their ability to look at spelling and vowel patterns in words to identify known chunks of new words.

The Story Box shared reading and guided reading lesson plans support the development of structural analysis skills.

WHAT'S THE EVIDENCE?

The importance of developing structural analysis skills is supported by Strickland, 1998a, and P. Cunningham, 1995.

Word Structure

Word Ending   -ed

■ Read the sentences from the story that contain the words *roared* (page 4), *looked* (page 8), and *zoomed* (page 16). Write the words on sentence strips, cut off the -*ed* portions, and then display the words and -*ed* cards in a pocket chart. Have the class practice saying the words as you insert or remove the -*ed* card after each word.

Point out the sounds -*ed* makes at the end of different words: /-ed/ as in *painted*, /d/ as in *framed*, and /t/ as in *walked*. Brainstorm and write other words ending in -*ed* on sentence strips.

Pocket Chart Center Put the word cards and -*ed* cards in this center so that students can practice manipulating word endings.

Word-structure activity for *The Hungry Giant*, Read-Togethers 3

Vocabulary

Vocabulary instruction expands children's understanding of text and develops their background knowledge and linguistic abilities and draws on all four cueing systems. The Story Box's vocabulary instruction focuses on helping students recognize high-frequency words and understand the meaning and use of content words, synonyms, antonyms, homographs, homonyms, abbreviations, onomatopoeia, and similes. Lessons provide explicit instruction in word meaning and usage as well as extensive exposure to words in a variety of meaningful contexts.

Children who have well-developed vocabularies comprehend text better. Since words encountered in print are best understood if they have been heard first, reading aloud to children is an important part of vocabulary instruction. To reinforce what they hear and to provide meaningful contexts for learning new words, it is also important to give students many opportunities to read independently.

WHAT'S THE EVIDENCE?

The work of Mason, 1992, and Elley, 1989, supports the theory that children learn new words best when they encounter them in meaningful contexts.

Opposites

big — little
loud — quiet
will — won't
hard — soft
hot — cold

High-Frequency Words

Fundamental to reading is understanding what words mean and recognizing them in print. In speaking, listening, and reading, a great number of words need to be recognized instantly. High-frequency words, or sight words, are words that children encounter frequently in their reading, that they often cannot decode, and that they find difficult to attach meaning to; for example, *the*, *of*, *was*, and *to*. Having automatic recognition of these words gives children the freedom to focus their attention on more difficult words and overall text comprehension. Mastering high-frequency words also helps students speed up their reading, which enhances their confidence and keeps them from forgetting passages they have just read.

Since it takes the average child between four and fourteen exposures to automatize the recognition of a new word, the activities in the Story Box's shared reading and guided reading lessons provide many opportunities for children to build word recognition skills and expand their vocabularies.

WHAT'S THE EVIDENCE?

Children must have four to fourteen exposures to a word before they can automatically recognize it. The importance of vocabulary development in a reading program is discussed by Strickland, 1998a; Honig, 1996; P. Cunningham, 1995; Mason, 1992; Stahl, 1992; Adams, 1990; and Elley, 1989.

Vocabulary

High-Frequency Words/Spelling   in   goes

■ Use magnetic letters to demonstrate the spelling of the word *in*. Have students practice remaking the word.

Writing Center Have students write the word *in* on several word cards and then put the cards in something, such as a box or bowl.

■ Reread page 2. Model writing the word *goes*. Have students use a paintbrush and water to write the word *goes* on the chalkboard.

Vocabulary activities for *Salad*, Set B

Comprehension

Comprehension, a reader's ability to make sense of what he or she reads, is the ultimate goal of reading. To make sense of what they read, children must be able to automatically decode the words in a text and connect them to their schemas—their existing knowledge and background experiences.

There are a number of prereading, during-reading, and post-reading comprehension strategies that can help children decode text and link it to their schemas.

Prereading Strategies

Activities and discussions prior to reading enable students to use schemas to access their level of understanding of a topic. Activities to access background knowledge include questioning; brainstorming; creating story webs, word webs, semantic maps, mind maps, KWL charts, and pictures; using props; reading additional fiction or nonfiction books that relate to the topic; and real-life experiences.

Each of the shared reading and guided reading lesson plans in The Story Box has a component to guide children's thoughts and help them link what they know to the story or theme.

> **Build Background** Ask questions that will help the children tap prior knowledge.
> - **Have you ever seen flowers growing in a garden?**
> - **Have you ever seen a red rose?**
> - **How would you describe the rose you saw?**

Build Background questions for *The Red Rose*, Read-Togethers 2

During-Reading Strategies

Discussions during reading can help students stay focused on the meaning and purpose of reading. Questions asked during reading should be open-ended, help students confirm or amend their predictions and purposes for reading, assist in visualizing the story, and summarize events that have been read up to that point in the story.

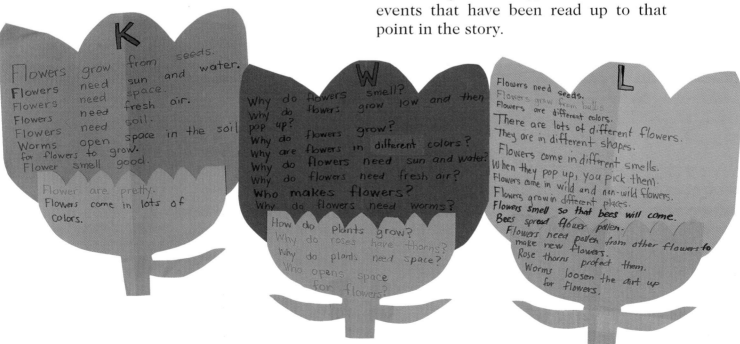

In The Story Box, sections of the shared reading and guided reading lesson plans engage students in purposeful during-reading discussions, in making predictions, and in making confirmations.

Read the Big Book

Build Comprehension Encourage the children to discuss the sequence of events in the story. Help them understand that the rhyming pattern will help them remember the sequence.

- **How do you know what Obadiah is going to do next?**

Read the story together. As you come to each pair of words that rhyme, pause and allow the children to supply the missing rhyme. For example: "The pool was wet, so he jumped in a ____."

Rhyming Observe which children are hearing the rhyming pairs. Record your observations.

Read the Big Book activities for *Obadiah*, Read-Togethers 3

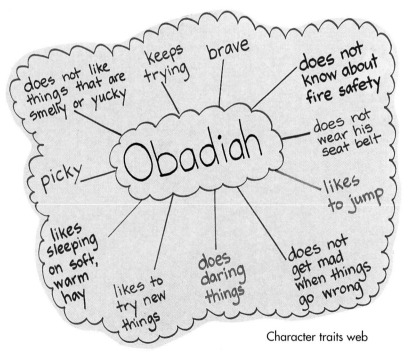

Character traits web

Post-Reading Strategies

Discussing a story after reading it can be a very effective way to bring further meaning to the text. Post-reading discussion in the shared reading and guided reading lesson plans helps students make personal connections to the story while encouraging them to articulate their understandings and interpretations of the story. Children are able to confirm predictions, discuss important details, summarize what was read, and make additional inferences about the story's meaning.

In addition to discussions, activities that support the post-reading questions include webs; charts; story maps; art projects; dramatic reenactments; writing activities that relate to the story; and innovations, reproductions, or retellings of stories.

Comprehension Levels

In postreading discussions, it is important to ask questions that access and foster students' reading comprehension at literal, inferential, and critical levels.

Literal-level comprehension questions are based on details or information that can be found in the actual text. These tend to be who, what, where, and when questions, such as

- Who were the characters in the story?
- What did the characters do?
- Where did the story take place?
- When did the story take place?

Inferential-level questions help readers understand a writer's ideas or purpose, make generalizations about the story, anticipate and predict outcomes, or infer what might happen next.

- How did you know that...?
- What is the difference between...?
- What, do you think, was meant by...?
- What was the main idea?

Critical-level questions help children evaluate and make judgments about what was read. This type of questioning involves the highest level of thinking and allows students to express opinions about a story, evaluate the validity of the text, or apply what was learned to a different situation.

- What if...?
- What is your opinion of...?
- Do you agree or disagree that...? Why?

The Story Box lessons provide suggested questions at all three levels of comprehension. The comprehension sections of the shared reading lesson plans and the guided reading lessons prompt students to discuss the books, share opinions, make predictions, and make personal connections to the story. Questions provided in these sections can also be used to enhance and assess comprehension.

> ## Talk About It
>
> **COMPREHENSION: Mood/Tone** Together, look carefully at the illustrations in the book noting the meanies' facial expressions, actions, and gestures. Ask questions that will help students understand how the meanies feel.
>
> - **What do you see in the illustrations that tells you more about the meanies?** (identifying details)
> - **What might the meanies be thinking in this story?** (drawing conclusions)
> - **How do you think they feel about what they are doing?** (drawing conclusions)
>
> Discuss the supporting role of the rats that appear throughout the story. Have the children look at the rats' expressions and how they react to the meanies.

Talk About It activities for *Meanies*, Read-Togethers 2

> ## WHAT'S THE EVIDENCE?
>
> Good readers comprehend what they have read. The importance of teaching comprehension skills and strategies is addressed in the works of Beck et al., 1997; Brady & Moats, 1997; Braunger & Lewis, 1997; Moustafa, 1997; Booth, 1996; Fountas & Pinnell, 1996; Honig, 1996; Gunderson, 1995; Dechant, 1993; and Adams, 1990.

I like the meany that is laughing because he is cute and he is funny.

What Is Shared Reading?

Children come to school with varying amounts of literacy knowledge and different cultural literacy practices. The task primary teachers face is to provide learning experiences that support and challenge children, regardless of their literacy level. Shared reading is an instructional strategy that allows all students to experience success and extend their understanding of reading, starting on the first day of school.

Shared reading is the whole-group instructional model of a balanced reading program. Teachers model the reading process while students participate in a cooperative reading experience that takes place in a supportive environment similar to the lap reading some children experience at home. During shared reading, the teacher uses a Read-Together Big Book, which contains large, vivid illustrations and enlarged text for students to see easily. After a brief introduction, the teacher reads the story aloud, using a pointer to track the printed text. The teacher asks open-ended questions and uses natural conversation to encourage students to participate in making predictions and discussing the story. This initial shared reading experience enables the teacher to scaffold instruction of the book's language structures and vocabulary to fit students' reading level.

Over the course of a week, or longer if student interest is high, the teacher rereads the featured story many times. During these repeated readings, the teacher gradually releases the responsibility for reading the text to the students, inviting them to "share" the reading. During rereadings, the featured Read-Together serves as a vehicle for explicit skills instruction based on assessed student needs. The Read-Together can also be linked to integrated language arts and cross-curricular learning experiences. These activities help solidify students' understanding of the story and provide resources for creating a print-rich environment.

A great deal of learning occurs during shared reading. This is a time when students are consolidating their fundamental understanding of reading and how it works. They are learning about print directionality, voice-print matching, sentence structure, story structure, letter names, sound-symbol correspondence, and new vocabulary. As they become

familiar with reading fundamentals, they acquire important skills, such as finding meaning in print, rereading a sentence to see if it sounds right and makes sense, predicting and confirming, and self-correcting.

An essential goal of shared reading is to help students become confident, enthusiastic readers who are ready to read new books without hesitation and generate their own learning projects. Shared reading will help make your classroom a cooperative learning community. The more students hear your good expression as you read and reread, the better they will understand how book language works. The more opportunities you give them to talk about books, the more they will use words from those books in their own vocabularies. The more they hear and see stories, the more they will use these story structures in their own writing.

Why Is Shared Reading Important?

- Students see that reading is enjoyable and purposeful.

- Students experience confidence and success as they begin to read.

- Students develop an understanding that reading should make sense.

- Students gain an understanding of how books are organized and how reading works.

- Students understand how readers solve print problems.

- Students develop their vocabulary and oral language.

- Students gain a sense of book language and an understanding of story structures and literary elements.

- Students are given the opportunity to manipulate language as they extend and personalize stories.

Shared reading is appropriate for students at both the early and upper emergent levels. The following chart provides an overview of how shared reading changes from the early emergent level to the upper emergent level.

Shared Reading at the Early Emergent Level	Shared Reading at the Upper Emergent Level
• Focuses on oral language development	• Helps students use story language in their own speaking and writing
• Develops listening vocabulary	• Provides opportunities for students to manipulate language • Develops sight vocabulary
• Helps students discover how print works	• Helps students solve print problems • Uses books that have more print on the page
• Emphasizes concepts of print	• Has less emphasis on concepts of print
• Suggests that the teacher points to each word as it is read	• Suggests that the teacher may only need to point to the beginning of each line and not every word
• Suggests that the teacher provides more support during the initial readings	• Suggests that the teacher may provide less support during initial readings
• Uses books with predictable story structures	• Encourages students to be more responsible for predicting and then confirming the predictions
• Develops sense of story	• Has more focus on main ideas and story elements
• Develops sense of language structure	• Encourages the use of story language structures in own writing
• Develops comprehension skills	• Strengthens comprehension skills
• Develops recall or retelling strategies for story elements	• Teaches literary elements
• Introduces reading strategies	• Supports and strengthens reading-strategy development
• Introduces beginning skills of phonological awareness, letter recognition, sound-symbol correspondences, and a few high-frequency words	• Provides for more focus on phonetic elements such as vowel patterns, consonant blends and digraphs, known word parts, word families, word structures, and more high-frequency words • Teaches decoding strategies

WHAT'S THE EVIDENCE?

Shared reading is an important process for emergent readers. The benefits of providing shared reading are supported by Iversen & Reader, 1998; Strickland, 1998a; Weaver, 1998; Au, Carroll, & Scheu, 1997; Christie, Enz, & Vukelich, 1997; Moustafa, 1997; Eldredge & Reutzel, 1996; Fountas & Pinnell, 1996; McIntyre & Pressley, 1996; Routman, 1996; Cunningham, 1995; and Holdaway, 1979.

A study by Combs, 1987, in which shared reading in one kindergarten class was compared to the reading of traditional books in another kindergarten class, has shown that shared reading with Big Books (1) significantly improves children's recall of story elements, as well as their descriptions and the level of detail they recall; (2) increases children's interest in the stories read to them; (3) greatly improves children's attentiveness and interaction with the teacher and classmates; and (4) increases children's interest in print and its relationships to a story's language and meaning.

A study by Elley, 1985, found that teachers who produced the largest gains in reading achievement over a school year spent more time on shared reading. The same study indicated that students who showed the strongest positive interest in reading spent more time on shared reading, listening to stories at the listening center, listening to teachers read aloud, and reading silently.

Elley, 1991, found that students who had daily shared reading and language experience had higher gains in reading, writing, and language use than did students in a control group. These gains have been reflected in the recent International Association of the Evaluation of Educational Acheivement survey of international literacy achievement.

References cited in the "What's the Evidence?" boxes are listed in a bibliography at the end of this guide.

Elements of Read-Togethers

Milwaukee cow number one
likes to tap dance in the sun.

2

Milwaukee cow number two
likes to moo and moo
and moo.

3

The Story Box Read-Togethers are specifically designed to ensure a successful shared reading experience. The following key features of the Read-Togethers provide a rich, supportive context designed to help all children succeed at reading:

Predictable structure: Stories provide text with repeated pattern, refrain, rhyme, or rhythm. A predictable structure makes it easy for your students to read along with you during repeated readings. This participation gives your students confidence and helps them understand how reading works.

Enlarged text, extra spacing between words, and limited print on each page: These features allow all your students to easily see the print and pictures during shared reading and skills lessons.

Illustrations that support the text: The story illustrations are carefully designed to provide students with all the information they need to understand the meaning of the story and to connect that meaning to the printed text.

Many high-frequency words imbedded in the text: This helps students learn to read the high-frequency words in the context of meaningful stories. Reading these sight words over and over helps students develop automaticity.

A predictable story line: This allows students to predict what is coming next as they read and makes the story easy to interpret so you can incorporate movement and dramatization as you read.

A story that is engaging, fun, and easily remembered: Appealing stories help students learn to love reading and value books as sources of meaning and pleasure.

Assessment and Shared Reading

In order to effectively plan your shared reading lessons to meet the needs of all the students in your class, you will want to pre-assess your students to determine their strengths and needs. The knowledge you gain from the assessments will help you identify the skills and strategies you should model and teach during the shared reading lessons. (For more information on the instructional cycle, see pages 33–35.)

The Story Box Assessment Kit provides a variety of literacy assessments for you to use throughout the year, as well as forms to help you compile this information into class profiles for whole-group planning. Assessments helpful for planning shared reading lessons cover the following skill areas:

- **Phonological awareness:** to determine if students can hear rhymes, syllables, sentences, words, onsets and rimes; and can orally blend, segment, and manipulate sounds

- **Concepts of print:** to determine if children have an awareness of books, text, words, and letters

- **Letter recognition:** to determine which letters students can identify and reproduce

- **Phonics:** to determine what sound-symbol correspondences students have and if they can blend, segment, and manipulate them; and to determine if students are able to transfer their knowledge to dictated sentences and use their knowledge of the alphabetic principle to decode text

- **Reading behaviors:** to determine the strategies and cues students are using at their instructional reading level

- **Comprehension:** to determine if students understand what they read; can make inferences, predictions, and judgments about the reading; and are learning to identify literary elements

- **Writing:** to determine if students are using their knowledge of sounds and can transfer that knowledge to their writing

- **Self-reflections:** to determine how students feel about themselves as readers and about the reading process

Literacy Centers and Shared Reading

Literacy centers are places where students can revisit and reread print by engaging in purposeful and authentic reading, writing, listening, and speaking activities independently or collectively. Enhancing the physical setting of literacy centers increases children's use of these centers, which, in turn, results in children doing more reading and writing and thus enhancing literacy achievement.

Items that work well in literacy centers include Read-Togethers and guided reading titles; additional books you provide; other forms of print such as magazines and posters; and displays of student artifacts, such as wall stories, charts, murals, and student-authored books. Surrounding children with books and functional print in the classroom stimulates their interest in literacy and gives them models of conventional print to emulate. It also provides the children who have limited literacy experiences with opportunities to learn about the functions and structures of written language, and helps children who already have rich literacy experiences at home make the leap to written language use at school. For more on literacy centers, see pages 127–132.

WHAT'S THE EVIDENCE?

The importance of using literacy centers with emergent level children is supported by Morrow, 1997, 1992; Fountas & Pinnell, 1996; Christie, 1987; and Loughlin & Martin, 1987.

Shared Reading Lesson Plans

Cover

On the cover of every shared reading lesson plan, you will find two regular features: **About the Story,** which is a summary of the featured story, and **Focus Skills,** which identifies the skills activities suggested in the lesson.

Weekly Overview

The next two pages of the shared reading lesson plan provide thematic links ideas, topic studies ideas, the cross-curricular activities from pages 14–15 of the lesson, and the literacy centers involved in the week's activities.

The weekly overview chart is also found on these pages and presents an overview of all five days of lessons. The grid is divided into three areas that correspond with the three-part structure of each daily lesson plan: (1) Sharing the Reading, (2) Skills Bank, and (3) Integrating Language Arts.

Thematic Links identifies themes such as relationships, exploration, celebrations, creativity, community, environment, cycles, change, and perspectives for each Read-Together. These themes help students make connections between the stories and their own lives.

Topic Studies identifies topics for each Read-Together to help connect the book to content areas. You can build courses of study around the topics to extend students' knowledge and understanding.

Cross-Curricular Activities lists the content area activities that accompany the Read-Together. These activities are described in the Cross-Curricular Activities section on pages 14–15 of the lesson.

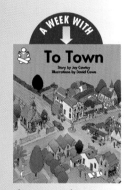

A WEEK WITH

To Town
Story by Joy Cowley
Illustrations by David Cowe

Thematic Links
Creativity, Community

Topic Studies
Transportation, Sound, Safety

Cross-Curricular Activities
- Art
- Building
- Math
- Social Studies

 Literacy Centers

Materials created or used during the week are added to the following centers:
- Big Book Center
- Poetry Center
- Pocket Chart Center
- Listening Center
- Drama Center
- Alphabet Center
- Word Study Center

SHARING THE READING

	Warming Up	Read the Big Book	Read It Again	Talk About It
DAY 1	• Reread familiar poem • "The Bus Song" Poetry Poster: Listen and respond • Reread familiar Big Book	• Build Background: Discuss towns • Introduce the Book • First Reading: Elicit predictions and responses	• Read with Participation: Join in on sounds and vehicle names	• Comprehension: Elicit personal response *(personal response; recalling)*
DAY 2	• Reread familiar poem • "The Bus Song" Poetry Poster: Listen and respond • Reread familiar Big Book	• Recall the Story: Discuss story details and characters • Read with Participation: Read using cloze technique	• Read Parts: Groups read characters' lines or vehicle sounds	• Comprehension: Discuss setting *(observing; establishing prior knowledge; comparing and contrasting)* • Discuss Small Towns: Create chart about small towns
DAY 3	• Reread familiar poem • "The Bus Song" Poetry Poster: Sing and make up hand motions • Reread familiar Big Book	• Build Comprehension: Recall beginning, middle, and end • Read with Audiocassette	• Read and Mime: Create mimes for each form of transportation	• Comprehension: Discuss characters *(comparing and contrasting; making generalizations; personal response)*
DAY 4	• Reread familiar poem • "The Bus Song" Poetry Poster: Sing and play instruments • Reread familiar Big Book	• One-to-One Correspondence: Focus on matching text and voice	• Take Roles: Read characters' parts with vehicle sounds and hand motions	• Comprehension: Discuss characters *(inferring; drawing conclusions)* • Discuss Safety Rules: Discuss vehicle safety rules
DAY 5	• Reread familiar poem • "The Bus Song" Poetry Poster: Sing while walking in a circle; illustrate and take home reproducible • Reread familiar Big Book	• Dramatize the Story: Read with hats, steering wheels, and other props	• Reading Strategy: Read story, pausing to find known word parts in words	• Comprehension: Discuss theme *(identifying details; synthesizing; observing; drawing conclusions)*

2

Literacy Centers identifies the centers used or added to throughout the lesson. The materials in these centers consist of previously read Read-Togethers, skill activities you have introduced, manipulatives that the children need to use to develop skills, and poetry and books that have been read aloud. Literacy centers allow children to practice and reinforce what they have learned.

Shared Reading Icons

Here is a guide to icons found in the shared reading lesson plans:

 Assessment opportunities occur throughout the lesson plans.

 ESL icons indicate activities that include movement, vocabulary development, or other strategies that work well for students acquiring English.

 Extra Help icons alert you to suggestions for additional support for students who need it.

 Challenging lessons are available for advanced students.

 Think Aloud icons show how you can demonstrate reading strategies to your students.

 See the **Literacy Center** icon for suggestions on how to use centers during the lesson.

 Find helpful tips and interesting background information where you see the **Teacher Tip** icon.

 See the **Technology** icon for suggestions on how to integrate *Paint, Write & Play!*™ into your instruction.

 Fun activities involve students and their families at the **School to Home and Back** icon.

 Students can reinforce important skills they have learned during the lesson with activities to take home.

SKILLS BANK   INTEGRATING LANGUAGE ARTS

Phonological Awareness	Concepts of Print	Phonics	Vocabulary	
Word Awareness: Listen for words that describe vehicles	• **Return Sweep:** Demonstrate and practice return sweep • **Letter Recognition and Formation: Tt** Locate upper- and lowercase *t*s and practice forming them	• **Initial Consonant:** *t* Brainstorm words that begin with *t*	• **Content Words:** *bulldozer, vintage, helicopter, pogo stick* Discuss and demonstrate meaning of words	• **Describing Transportation:** Children brainstorm types of transportation and color and sound words to describe them • **Writing:** Children write about their favorite type of transportation • **Independent Reading** • **Reading More:** Read aloud a book about transportation
Syllable Awareness: Listen for syllables in transportation names **Phonemic Awareness: Initial Sound: /b/** Listen for words that begin with /b/	• **One-to-One Correspondence:** Use pointer to practice matching voice and text	• **Initial Consonant:** *b* Find words that begin with *b*; make a word wall	• **High-Frequency Words:** *I, go, to* Match words on self-stick notes to words in book	• **Making a Mural:** Children discuss features of a small town and create a mural • **Writing:** Children write about where they could go in one of the vehicles in *To Town* • **Independent Reading** • **Reading More:** Read aloud a book about a trip to town
Rhyming: Change onsets to make words that rhyme with *way*	• **Concepts of Word and Letter:** Find first and last words and letters	• **Initial Consonant:** *v* Make a chart of vintage items and circle the *v*s	• **High-Frequency Words/Spelling:** *in, on* Use manipulatives to make the words	• **Making a Graph:** Children discuss and graph the types of transportation they use to get to school • **Writing:** Children complete a sentence structure • **Independent Reading** • **Reading More:** Read aloud a poem about transportation or about a town
	• **Concept of Word:** Count words on page	• **Short Vowel:** *i* Find short *i* words in book and make a chart	• **Content Words:** Write descriptive phrases and circle color words in matching color	• **Making a Class Big Book:** Pairs describe how they go to town and create pages for a Big Book innovation • **Writing:** Children write about a time they rode in a vehicle • **Independent Reading** • **Reading More:** Read aloud a book that has good sound words
Alliteration: Listen for words that begin with the same sound and brainstorm alliterative phrases		• **Initial Consonants:** *b, v* Listen for words that begin with *b* or *v*; sort *b* and *v* word cards	• **Spelling:** *in, go* Find *in* and *go* in bigger words	• **Making an Innovation:** Children create an innovation on the story using descriptive phrases for new vehicles and sounds • **Writing:** Children write about a family adventure to someplace special • **Independent Reading** • **Reading More:** Read aloud a book about traveling or an outing

Children complete and take home a story-wheel activity for *To Town.*

3

Weekly Lesson Plans

The weekly shared reading lesson plans will help you organize your shared reading time and maximize learning for your students. Each weekly plan features a Read-Together, with explicit skills instruction and a variety of language arts and cross-curricular activities.

Begin shared reading with Warming Up activities

Read aloud text that appears in boldface type

- On Day 1, build background knowledge and introduce the Read-Together
- On Days 2–5, recall and/or retell the story before the first reading

Invite children to become more involved in the story through participation

Help your students make predictions and respond to the story

DAY 1

SHARING THE READING

Warming Up

Coming Together Begin with a familiar poem a child has chosen from your poetry center. Invite the children to recite, sing, or move as you point to the text.

Share the Poetry Poster Read the poetry poster "The Bus Song" from Poems for Sharing™. Invite the children to respond to the poem.

- **Have you ever taken a ride on a bus like this before?**
- **Who do you see riding the bus in this illustration?**

The Bus Song
The wheels on the bus go 'round and 'round,
'Round and 'round, 'round and 'round.
The wheels on the bus go 'round and 'round
All through the town.

Favorite Books Ask a child to select a familiar Big Book from the Big Book center. Invite the children to read with you as you point to the text.

Read the Big Book

Build Background Ask questions that will help students tap prior knowledge.

- **Do you live in a big or small town?**
- **What is your town like? What kind of vehicles do you see in your town?**

Introduce the Book Show the children the front and back covers of the book.

- **What do you see in the picture?**
- **Is this a small town or a large town?**

Read the title, author, and illustrator of the book.

- **What do you think this story might be about?**
- **Where do you think the people are in the story?**

Show the students the title page and read the title, author, and illustrator again. Invite the children to make predictions about the story.

- **Have you seen a sign like this one before?**
- **What does the sign tell you?**
- **What do you think is going to happen in this story?**

First Reading Read the story to the students, modeling fluent reading. Pause on page 11 to discuss different ways of going to town. Ask children to make predictions.

- **How do you think the next person will get to town?**

Continue reading, stopping on page 15 to elicit more predictions.

- **What will the little boy do once he gets to town?**

Read It Again

Read with Participation Invite the children to read the sound of each vehicle and join in reading the vehicle name or any other parts of the story they know.

Talk About It

COMPREHENSION: Personal Response Ask two or three questions to support comprehension.

- **What did you like best about this story?** (personal response)
- **What different ways did people go to town?** (recalling)
- **What would be your favorite way to go to town?** (personal response)

Colors		Sounds
Red	brown	aah-ooo
blue	gold	brrr-brrr
turquoise	lavender	vrumm-vrumm
purple	gray	putt-putt
green		trit-trot
violet	tan	brumm-brumm
pink		toot-a-toot
white		choppa-choppa
yellow		nrrr-nrrr
black		crash
orange		Kaboom
silver		zoom
copper		Poing-Poing

Describing Transportation
listening, speaking

Develop oral language by having students brainstorm types of transportation. Write their ideas on a transportation web. Tell students that they will be drawing and writing about one type of transportation. Work with them to make a list of the colors they might use and the sounds that vehicles make. Display the lists for students to use as reference for their writing throughout the week.

4

Develop critical thinking and evaluate the students' comprehension of the story

Use story-related activities from this section to integrate reading, writing, listening, and speaking

Choose lessons from the Skills
Bank that teach your students the
skills they need to focus on

SKILLS BANK

Phonological Awareness

Word Awareness

■ Read phrases from the story that describe a
vehicle, and ask the students to listen for and
count the words. For example, on page 2 read
"big, yellow bulldozer." Students should count
three words.

Concepts of Print

Return Sweep

■ Think aloud about reading from the end of one
line to the beginning of the next (return
sweep).

 **Return Sweep "When I'm reading a
long story and come to the end of a line,
I need to remember to go on to the
beginning of the next line."**

■ As you read *To Town*, have a student point to
the words and show what to do at the end of
the lines.

Letter Recognition and Formation   T t

■ Show the students the cover of *To Town* and
point out that both words in the title start with
uppercase *T*. Look at the title page together,
and ask students to compare the *T*ts with those
on the cover. Have students locate other upper-
and lowercase *t*s in the story.

■ Model the formation of both *T* and *t*, using
either a white board or chart paper. Have the
students practice writing *T* and *t* in the air, on
the palm of their hands, and/or on white boards.

Letter Recognition Randomly place
several magnetic letters, letter cards, or
letter tiles on a table, and ask students to
find the *t*s.

 Alphabet Center Children can make *T*s
and *t*s with modeling clay.

Phonics

Initial Consonant   t

■ With the children, brainstorm a list of words
that begin with *t*. Write the words on a wall
chart and display.

Vocabulary

Content Words

bulldozer   vintage   helicopter   pogo stick

■ Discuss the meanings of the more difficult
words in the story; for example, *bulldozer,
vintage, helicopter,* and *pogo stick*. Bring in
something old and have children use the word
vintage to describe it. If possible, bring in a
pogo stick for the children to try.

INTEGRATING LANGUAGE ARTS

Writing

Invite children to draw and write
about their favorite form of transportation. Encourage them to use
color and sound words in their
writing.

Save the illustrations to include in
a mural later in the week. (See
"Make a Mural," Day 2.)

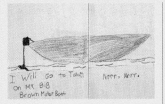

A child writes about a favorite form of
transportation: "I will go to town on my big,
brown motorboat. Nrrr, Nrrr."

Independent Reading

Invite students to read familiar
books of their choice alone or
with a buddy.

Reading More

Read aloud a book about transportation. Compare and contrast the
types of transportation with those
found in *To Town*.

Invite children to
read independently
or with a partner

5

Have children respond
to the story through
writing

Read aloud a book that
relates to a theme of the
Read-Together

Sharing the Reading

This first component of the shared reading lesson plan has four main parts: (1) Warming Up, (2) Read the Big Book, (3) Read It Again, and (4) Talk About It.

Warming Up

Just as athletes and musicians need to warm up before they perform, your students need to prepare themselves for reading. Each day, the shared reading time begins with several Warming Up activities designed to do the following:

- Welcome students to the shared reading experience
- Develop community
- Provide models of fluent reading
- Develop oral language
- Demonstrate print conventions
- Provide rich language experiences for the development of phonological and phonemic awareness, and phonics skills

Warming Up includes three steps: Coming Together, Share the Poetry Poster, and Favorite Books. Students read a familiar poem, then the featured poetry poster from Poems for Sharing, and finally a familiar Big Book.

Coming Together

Use the Coming Together step to familiarize students with poems and nursery rhymes that they will remember and enjoy for many years. During this initial step of Warming Up, you will first want to ask a student volunteer to select a familiar poem from the poetry box. Then you will lead students in an interactive rereading of the poem. They can recite, sing, chant, or do creative movements as you read. Use a pointer to track print as you read.

Share the Poetry Poster

Use the poetry poster from Poems for Sharing that accompanies the Read-Together for the week. For example, "The Bus Song" is thematically linked with *To Town*. You will want to lead students in a participatory reading of the poem as you point to the words. Then invite students to discuss the poem.

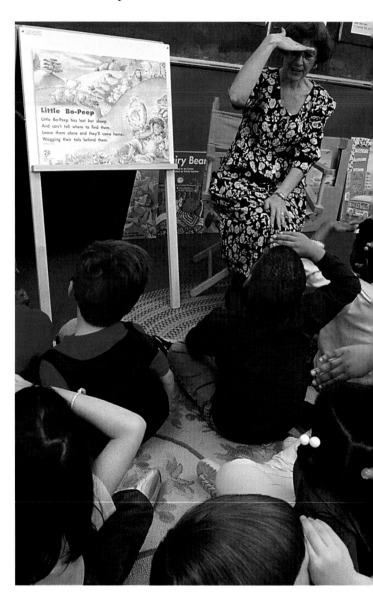

Favorite Books

After the poetry reading, read a favorite story. Ask a student volunteer to select a book that the class is already familiar with from the Big Book center. Use a pointer to track the print as the class participates in rereading the story. Rereading familiar Big Books allows students to practice previously taught skills and strategies and develop fluency.

Children's favorite books are often ones they create themselves

Read the Big Book

On Day 1, this second part of Sharing the Reading features three steps: Build Background, Introduce the Book, and First Reading.

Build Background

Before the first reading, help students build background knowledge and connect students' experiences to the themes and topics of the book. To expand the students' knowledge, you might want to do activities related to the themes and topics, such as reading other books, showing a movie or video, providing manipulatives or models, going on a field trip, creating webs or charts, or researching the topic on the Internet.

Introduce the Book

Introduce the Read-Together to students by focusing their attention on the cover and telling them the title and author's name. Discuss the function and purpose of the title and explain the roles of the author and illustrator. Share what you notice about the cover and invite students to talk about what they notice. Encourage them to make predictions about the story before you begin reading.

WHAT'S THE EVIDENCE?

Snow, Burns, & Griffin, 1998, found that how well children understand text and word meanings depends on their background knowledge and understanding of the concepts being presented.

According to Anderson & Pearson, 1984, and Rumelhart, 1980, readers understand what they read only as it relates to what they already know. Because text is not fully explicit, readers must draw from their existing knowledge to understand the text. Research from Anderson & Pearson, 1984, suggests that readers build meaning by combining text information with what they already know.

The joint position paper of the International Reading Association (IRA) and the National Association for the Education of Young Children (NAEYC), 1998, discusses the improvement of students' comprehension and vocabulary when they are engaged in predicting and analyzing text before and after reading.

First Reading

The purpose of the first reading is to help your students understand and appreciate the story. You are presenting the book language of the story, demonstrating the pleasure that comes from reading, and modeling how good readers think and react to books. As you read together, be sure to do the following:

- Read the story with enthusiasm and expression.

- Vary your voice to depict different characters and emphasize the repetitions, rhymes, and colorful language in the story.

- Read the story slow enough for your students to use the pictures for making meaning and forming mental images of the story.

- Model delight, surprise, curiosity, excitement, and interest in the language and illustrations in the book as you read.

During the first reading, give students time to look carefully at each page. Select a couple of places in the story to stop and allow your students to spontaneously react to the story events. This will allow them to confirm or amend any earlier predictions and make further ones. Invite your students to explain why they are making the predictions they suggest. After the reading, invite students to respond to and discuss the story.

Before reading the book on Days 2–5, always have students try to recall, review, and/or retell the story in their own words. Encourage them to describe story elements, characters, setting, problems, and resolutions. You may also wish to have them sequence the story, explaining what happened in the beginning, middle, and end.

Read It Again

This third part of Sharing the Reading invites children to become more involved in the story through participation in drama, movement, and other activities. This feature is meant to

- Help students internalize the vocabulary and story structures;

- Enhance students' reading comprehension;

- Enhance students' reading fluency;

- Provide students with more listening experience; and

- Allow students to participate in the reading using the cloze technique. This helps students develop self-confidence.

The Cloze Technique

Pause before a predictable word or phrase and allow students to orally complete the sentence. This allows your students to use reading strategies and make decisions about what would make sense in the text. Some students will fill in the word from memory. Others will focus on the print, looking closely at the beginning letter or letter clusters and familiar letter patterns to figure out the word.

What follows are suggested activities for the Read It Again section of the lesson plan.

Reading Chorally: Break the story into parts. Assign different groups of students different parts of the story to read. For example, have one group read the dialogue and another group read the transitional phrases and sentences.

Using Movement: Have your students brainstorm a movement, action, mime, or sound effect to accompany the reading of selected words, such as verbs, nouns, or repeated phrases.

Using Rhythm: Have students chant, clap, snap, or use a rap beat as they read repetitive parts of the story. Provide rhythm instruments for selected students to play to correspond with repeated phrases or words.

Dramatizing the Story: Provide simple props, puppets, or name tags with characters' names for your students to use to dramatize the story. Selected students might use movement to portray the story while the story is being read by the remainder of the class. Students can also recite the lines associated with or spoken by a story character.

WHAT'S THE EVIDENCE?

Soundry, 1993, and Martinez, Cheyney, & Teale, 1988, suggest that engaging in dramatic play and reenacting a story can build a sense of story structures and enhance comprehension. Christie, 1987, suggests that drama reenactments can facilitate comprehension by building children's knowledge of story structures.

Think-Alouds

In think-alouds, the teacher verbalizes what he or she is thinking about while reading, modeling the process for children to use later on their own. Think-alouds allow you to explain how to use print conventions, familiar words, and the reading strategies of rereading and self-checking to solve print problems. Think-alouds also help students learn how to use prediction and questioning to comprehend text.

WHAT'S THE EVIDENCE?

The works of Spiegel, 1995 and 1992, support the use of modeling during reading instruction. McNeill, 1992, shows that an effective way to teach reading comprehension is to model the thinking process that accompanies reading.

A centipede came by. ... a good house for a centipede," it said, ...d it went in.

Talk About It

Talk About It is the fourth and final part of the Sharing the Reading component. After reading the story again, you will want to evaluate the students' comprehension of the story by allowing time for a lengthier discussion of the book. Begin the week with open-ended personal responses to, and discussions about, story events. As the week progresses, extend students' thinking by posing questions that encourage them to draw on their background knowledge and evaluate, problem solve, and connect the story to other stories they have read.

Throughout the five days of the lesson, your questions should focus on developing students' comprehension at the literal, inferential, and critical levels. Students should also develop their comprehension of the basic literary elements of character, setting, problems and solutions, mood, theme, and genre. All of the comprehension questions in Talk About It have critical-thinking labels.

How to Create a Good Discussion

At the beginning of the week, encourage your students to share their ideas and reactions to the book. Avoid asking questions that lead to only one- or two-word responses. Instead, invite your students to use descriptive language to tell about characters, setting, or plot. You might use questions like the following:

■ What did you think of this book? Why?

■ What was your favorite part of the story? Why?

■ What character did you like best? Why?

■ Was there anything that confused you? What?

WHAT'S THE EVIDENCE?

The works of Rascon-Briones & Searfoss, 1995, and Peterson & Eeds, 1990, suggest that comprehension is enhanced when several readers discuss their responses and construct shared understanding. Guthrie, 1996, argues that children who are engaged in discussion about what they have read tend to be more interested in the reading process and score better on achievement tests. Having students explain or support their understanding of what they read can help them become more thoughtful readers. According to Snow, Burns, & Griffin, 1998, the ability to recall a story and recall sentences from a story are strong predictors of reading success.

Skills Bank

The Skills Bank section of each daily shared reading lesson plan provides activities and techniques for teaching the focus skills for the featured book. The Skills Bank may include the following sections:

- Phonological Awareness
- Concepts of Print
- Phonics (including Spelling and Word Families)
- Word Structure
- Vocabulary (including Spelling)
- Mechanics

To teach skills effectively, follow these steps:

1. **Assess students' needs:** Use The Story Box Assessment Kit and daily observations to evaluate students' ability levels. Determining students' strengths and needs is the foundation of the instructional process.

2. **Create an instructional plan:** Once you have determined your students' ability levels, decide on an instructional plan. Use the Skills Bank to plan and carry out explicit instruction. Review the weekly overview grid to see when the different skills are introduced.

3. **Model the skill using the Read-Together:** The familiar text in the featured Big Book will enable your students to connect what they know from the story with the new skill they are learning. This will help them retain what they are learning and transfer the skill to new contexts.

4. **Provide guided and independent practice opportunities:** After introducing the skill with the Read-Together, choose other contexts in which students can practice and extend their understanding of the skill.

5. **Provide time to apply the skill:** Give students opportunities to apply the skill to new reading and writing activities.

6. **Assess students' needs:** Continue the instructional cycle.

For more on teaching skills, see Chapter 2.

WHAT'S THE EVIDENCE?

Teaching skills is vital to helping students become successful readers. Teaching skills within the context of a shared reading is supported by Snow, Burns, & Griffin, 1998; Morrow, 1997; Moustafa, 1997; Honig, 1996; and Adams, 1990.

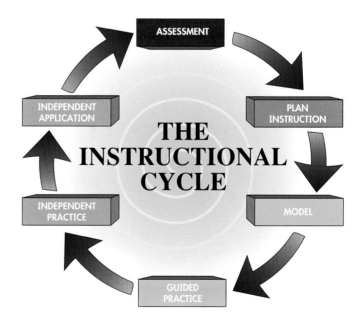

THE INSTRUCTIONAL CYCLE

ASSESSMENT — PLAN INSTRUCTION — MODEL — GUIDED PRACTICE — INDEPENDENT PRACTICE — INDEPENDENT APPLICATION

Integrating Language Arts

Integrating Language Arts activities provide opportunities for students to respond to the text, solidify their understanding of what they have read, and practice skills. Each shared reading lesson plan presents story-related activities, suggestions for writing, independent or partner reading, and stories to read aloud.

Story-Related Activities

Students may participate in a variety of literacy-building activities that integrate reading, writing, listening, and speaking:

- Reproductions
- Innovations
- Structure writing
- Retellings
- Graphic organizers
- Written responses

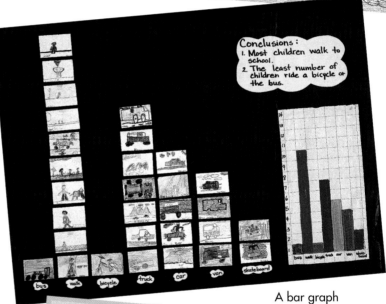

An example of structure writing

A bar graph

A puppet for a retelling

A written response

Centipeda

And the best thing I like about centipedes is if you put it in a box it won't bother you.

The End

By Megan

Types of Reproductions

A reproduction is the re-creation of a story in a new format. Students illustrate the text, the characters, or other meaningful elements of the story. This helps them bring further meaning to the print and internalize the story structure. The following reproductions are appropriate for the emergent level:

Big Book Reproductions

Before doing a reproduction, make sure you have shared the Read-Together with your students many times so they are comfortable with its content and language. Discuss characteristics of the book's illustrations. Encourage students to use these as guidelines when making their own reproductions.

- The illustrations should fill the entire page.
- The pictures match the text.
- The setting is shown in the picture.

Next, provide each student or student pair with a sentence or phrase written on a strip of paper. Have students match the sentence or phrase to the text in the book and read it to you. Then give them art materials so they can illustrate the words. Have them work together to sequence their sentences or phrases and drawings. Then invite the students to recreate the book by placing the sentences and drawings in a blank Big Book you provide. Reread the reproduction and then put the book in the Big Book center.

Accordion Book Reproductions

Give the children sentences or phrases from a story and invite the children to illustrate them. Then tape the sentences and drawings together in order and in one long strip to create a book that folds like an accordion. Once you create the accordion story, you may wish to unfold it and put it under a clear plastic runner on the floor. Allow the children to walk on it and read the print. Finally, display the accordion book as a wall story or fold it into a Big Book and place it in the Big Book center for students to enjoy.

Roller Story Reproductions

Invite the children to illustrate sentences or phrases from a story. Tape the sentences and drawings together in order and in one long strip. Then find an empty box and cut out a large square hole on the front of the box. Push two dowels horizontally through both sides of the box and attach each end of the story strip to a dowel to create a roller story. Have the children "roll" the story onto the dowels like a filmstrip and reread the new reproduction during shared reading. Place the roller story in the Big Book center.

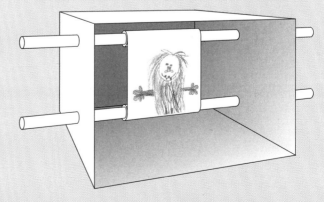

Types of Reproductions (cont.)

Transparency Story Reproductions

Put sentences or repeated phrases on transparencies. Have students use transparency markers to illustrate their sentences on the transparencies. Place each finished page in a clear plastic folder. Use the transparency story during shared reading in place of the Big Book. Put the transparency folder in the overhead projector center for students to access during center time.

Transparency Shadow Puppet Reproductions

Have students illustrate the story settings on transparencies. Then invite the students to create shadow puppets by cutting out the shapes of the characters in the story and attaching them to tongue depressors. They can retell the story using their shadow puppets and transparencies on the overhead.

Wall Story Reproductions

Have students paint the story setting(s) on large pieces of butcher paper. Then invite them to look at each page of the story and draw on separate pieces of paper the characters and what they are doing. Have the children cut the characters out

and attach them in the correct order to the painted story setting(s). Write each sentence from the story on a sentence strip, or a speech bubble if there is story dialogue. Then ask the children to place the sentences or speech bubbles in the correct order next to the characters on the wall. Read the wall story during shared reading time. Provide pointers for students to use to read the wall during literacy center time.

Character Cutout Reproductions

Have students make large cutouts of the main characters. Then invite the children to add large speech bubbles next to the characters with dialogue from the story or statements describing what each character does, thinks, or likes.

Innovations

In an innovation, the basic sentence structure or language pattern of a story is retained, but the character(s), setting, or theme changes. To make a new story, students substitute nouns, verbs, or adjectives with new words. In creating a new story, students combine what they each know about oral language, stories, and print. Making innovations enriches vocabulary, reinforces knowledge of high-frequency words, and develops an understanding of language structures. The Story Box Read-Togethers provide excellent story structures for creating innovations.

Begin by selecting a story students know well. Decide on which aspect of the story to change. (With early emergent students, it may be appropriate to change only one sentence. Don't try to change too much when you begin to do this activity.) Write the story on sentence strips or a chart, leaving blanks in the sentences for the students to fill in with new words. Another option is to place self-stick notes over the text you want to replace in the Big Book and write students' new words on the notes. For an example of an innovation, see below.

Writing

Writing ideas are provided in the Integrating Language Arts section for each day of the shared reading lesson plan. Students may use a structure writing format, write entries in their journals, write their own stories, make lists, and engage in a wide range of other writing activities as they make additional connections to a story.

At the early emergent level, writing activities require teacher support because students are just beginning to learn to record their thoughts and ideas. Some students may "write" by drawing a picture or a few marks on a page. Others will be able to write a few letters or words.

Writing activities at the upper emergent level do not need to be as structured. This allows students to be more independent and creative in their writing. After reading a story, you might have children write about and illustrate favorite characters or parts of the story. They can write a new ending or complete a sentence structure from the story. They can also create their own innovation, turn the story into a play, or write personal reactions. Finally, always allow time for children to share their writing with others.

For more on writing, see pages 18–27.

Independent Reading

The goal of The Story Box Reading Program is to help students become capable, independent readers. To help accomplish this goal, allow time at the end of shared reading for students to select and read from the print materials you have accumulated in your classroom. This independent reading time gives your students control and ownership over the reading process and provides them with the opportunity to practice reading strategies and skills modeled during shared reading.

WHAT'S THE EVIDENCE?

Taylor, Frye, & Maruyama, 1990, found that the amount of independent reading children do both in and out of school is related to gains in reading achievement. The work of Adams, Treiman, & Pressley, 1996; Adams, 1990; Stanovich, 1986; and Anderson et al., 1984, suggests that independent reading is the single most valuable activity for developing comprehension and vocabulary knowledge, general knowledge, and more and better writing. Morrow, 1991, found that when children are given ample opportunities to engage in book-related activities, they are more likely to engage in voluntary reading. The research of Stotsky, 1983, reveals that reading and writing are closely related and that teaching the two processes together has a positive effect on literacy learning.

Reading More

At the end of the shared reading time, you may choose to read aloud to the whole class. Use the Bookshelf feature at the end of the lesson as a resource for related theme and topic books to read aloud. For more information on read-alouds, see pages 12–13.

Begin by gathering your students close to you. Introduce the story and tell why you chose it. As you read, allow time for students to respond to the pictures, the meaning of the story, and language. Stop periodically and model your own thinking as you read. Demonstrate your enjoyment of reading, showing your reaction to the story as you read it. After the reading, invite students to share their insights and impressions in open-ended conversation.

Take-Me-Homes

Included in the fifth day of the lesson plan is a Take-Me-Home activity from *Take-Me-Homes Stories and Activities*. Take-Me-Home activities are designed to extend and enrich the Read-Together; are varied; and include retellings, story wheels, sequencing, and story innovations. Once students have completed the Take-Me-Home activities, they can share them at home with family members.

WHAT'S THE EVIDENCE?

A large part of the educational research and practices of the last twenty years confirms that the best way to raise a reader is to read to the child in the home and in the classroom. Reading aloud should also be used to expose children to informational text. See Snow, Burns, & Griffin, 1998; Au, Carroll, & Scheu, 1997; Christie, Enz, & Vukelich, 1997; Allington & Walmsley, 1995; Hiebert & Taylor, 1994; and Adams, 1990.

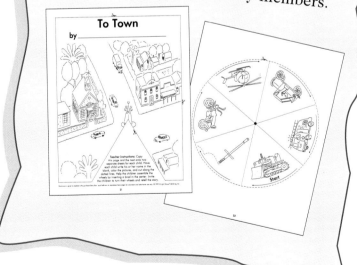

Give each child the take-home activity for *To Town*. Have the children write their names on the front, color the pictures, and assemble the story wheel. Invite the children to use their story wheels to retell *To Town*. Encourage the children to take home their story wheels to share with family members.

On Day 5, invite the children to complete a Take-Me-Home activity

Cross-Curricular Activities and Other Resources

Following Day 5, you will find the final two pages of the shared reading lesson plan. Three sections are featured: (1) Cross-Curricular Activities, (2) Skills Bank, and (3) Bookshelf.

Cross-Curricular Activities: These suggested activities are organized by subject area.

Skills Bank: This Skills Bank suggests additional teaching opportunities. The skills listed in this section may be used for review, additional instruction, and prac-

CROSS-CURRICULAR ACTIVITIES

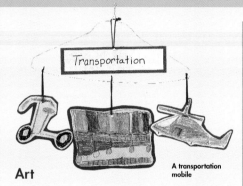

A transportation mobile

Art

- Invite children to make transportation mobiles. They can draw pictures of different types of transportation, cut them out, and mount them on construction paper. Students can then use yarn to tie the illustrations and a label that reads "Transportation" to a coat hanger. If possible, hang the transportation mobiles in your classroom.
- Use a large refrigerator box to make a class school bus. Cut windows out of the box and invite the children to paint it like a bus. The children can "ride" in the finished bus and sing "The Bus Song."
- Discuss safety rules for riding a bike, riding in a car or school bus, or taking any other form of transportation. Then invite the children to illustrate posters that promote safety rules. Children can write the safety rule on the poster or dictate it to you.

Building

- Invite the children to build different types of transportation using blocks.

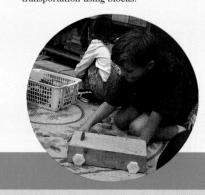

Math

- Encourage the children to discuss all of the different ways that they have traveled. Write the types of transportation across the bottom of a chart and write the names of the students who have used the form of transportation above each label. Discuss the results of the class transportation graph. Which form of transportation is the most commonly used? Which one is used least? Write the children's conclusions on the graph.

Social Studies

- Develop oral language by discussing safety features of cars. Draw a picture of a car on a large sheet of butcher paper. As the children name safety features, discuss where they are located on the car and label them.

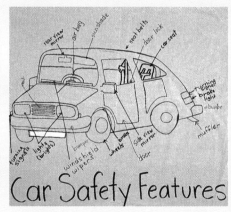

- Discuss with students how small towns and big towns are alike and different. Create a class chart or Venn diagram that compares and contrasts small towns and big towns.
- On a world map, mark the city and state or country where each child in the class was born. Graph the number of children who were born in your school's state, those born outside of the state, and those born in other countries.

14

tice or as challenge activities for some students.

A cross-reference to The Wright Skills is also provided for many of the skills taught in the lesson. You can use the Wright Skills lessons to provide explicit instruction, practice, application, and assessment.

Bookshelf: This list provides suggestions for fiction, nonfiction, poems, rhymes, and songs that can be read aloud to students and then added to the library center. The titles suggested relate to the themes or topics of the Read-Together. These titles provide several options for extending topic or theme studies, enriching students' background knowledge, and making connections to content-area studies.

SKILLS BANK

To Town offers the following additional teaching opportunities:

Phonemic Awareness: **blending**

Initial Consonant: **w**

Word Family: **-ig**

THE WRIGHT SKILLS™

For expanded instruction, see the following folders. (Skill is followed by folder number.)

FOCUS ON PREPHONICS:
Word Awareness 1; Syllable Awareness 4; Initial Sound /b/ 18; Rhyming 2; Alliteration 5; Letter Recognition and Formation Tt 16; Blending 7

PHONICS AND WORD STUDY, LEVEL A:
Initial Consonants t 3, b 16, v 26, w 17; Short Vowel i 18; Word Family -ig 19

BOOKSHELF

Fiction

Mr. Gumpy's Motor Car by John Burningham
Not So Fast Songololo by Niki Daly
Silly Sally by Audrey Wood
Tap-Tap by Karen Lynn Williams

Nonfiction

100 Words About Transportation by Richard Brown
Cars by Anne Rockwell
City Storm by Rebel Williams (TWiG® Books Read-Togethers, Set 1, The Wright Group)
Trucks by Rebel Williams (TWiG® Books, Set B, The Wright Group)

Poems, Rhymes, and Songs

And the Sidewalk Went All Around, lyrics by Cricket Rohman (The Song Box®, Set C, The Wright Group)
"City" by Langston Hughes in *The Random House Book of Poetry for Children*
"Taxis" by Rachel Field in *Favorite Poems Old and New*
This Is the Way We Go to School: A Book About Children Around the World by Edith Baer
"To Market, to Market" (traditional) in *Heritage Readers*, Book AA (The Wright Group)
Wheels on the Bus, The, by Maryann Kovalski
"Yankee Doodle" (traditional)

- Make a mural showing your community and its relationship to the state, country, continent, and planet. In the center of a large sheet of butcher paper, you might write, for example, "We live in a house in a neighborhood." In another section, you could write, "The neighborhood is a part of the city." Divide students into groups and have each group illustrate one section of the mural. Display the mural, and have students describe it to classroom visitors.

15

The Four Cueing System and Shared Reading

Good readers use the following four types of cues simultaneously to gain information from text: (1) schema, (2) semantic, (3) syntactic, and (4) graphophonic. (For more information on the four cueing system, see Chapter 2, pages 37–38.) The shared reading lesson plans are designed to help students use all four cues as they read.

Each major component of the shared reading lesson plans helps students develop and use the four cueing system. The following chart shows how the lessons support the four cueing system.

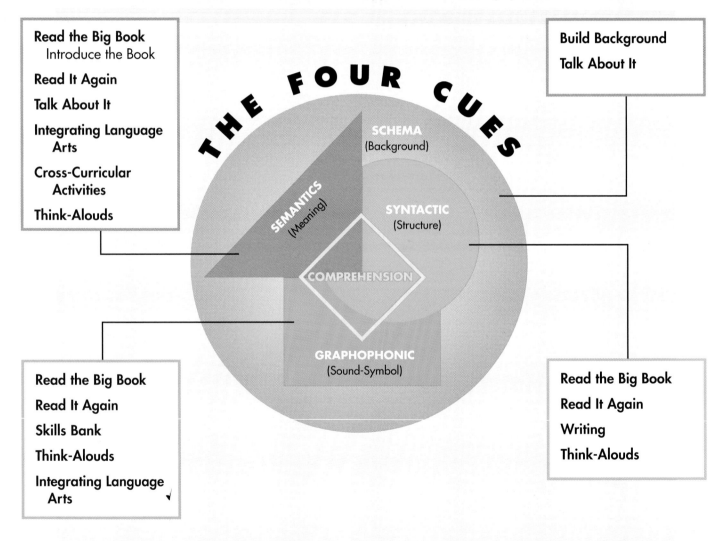

Read the Big Book
Introduce the Book

Read It Again

Talk About It

Integrating Language Arts

Cross-Curricular Activities

Think-Alouds

Build Background

Talk About It

THE FOUR CUES

SCHEMA
(Background)

SEMANTICS
(Meaning)

SYNTACTIC
(Structure)

COMPREHENSION

GRAPHOPHONIC
(Sound-Symbol)

Read the Big Book

Read It Again

Skills Bank

Think-Alouds

Integrating Language Arts ✓

Read the Big Book

Read It Again

Writing

Think-Alouds

Schema Cues and Shared Reading

Discussions during the Build Background step of the shared reading lesson establish a link between students' backgrounds, or schemas, and the story being read. This facilitates story comprehension and broadens students' schemas. If these activities indicate that students do not have adequate schemas to understand the text, then providing concrete experiences to build schemas is vital to story comprehension. Discussions after reading the Big Book during Talk About It ask students to connect the story to personal experience, which also supports and develops students' schemas.

Semantic Cues and Shared Reading

Many components of shared reading model the use of semantic cues during reading. Students develop an understanding of the story during the Introduce the Book step and through readings of the Big Book. Discussing the story after reading during the Talk About It step helps students gain meaning as they recall information and respond to the story's events. Teacher think-alouds, the cloze technique, student participation during reading, and the Integrating Language Arts and Cross-Curricular activities following the reading also help students connect to meaning in stories.

Syntactic Cues and Shared Reading

The repetitive language structures and natural language text of the shared reading books facilitate students' use of syntactic cues while reading during the Read the Big Book and Read It Again steps. Teacher demonstrations, think-alouds, and modeling help students understand how to use oral language structures while reading. Syntactic cues are also developed during structure, journal, and content writing, and text innovations found in the Writing section of the lesson.

Graphophonic Cues and Shared Reading

Developing students' use of graphophonic cues is an integral part of the shared reading process. During shared reading, teachers can explicitly teach the graphophonic skills of phonological awareness, concepts of print, mechanics, phonics, word structure, and vocabulary, found in the Skills Bank. Integrating Language Arts activities in which children are encouraged to use phonetic spelling to respond to the story also helps them use graphophonic cues. Teachers can help students develop their use of graphophonic cues during the Read the Big Book and Read It Again steps by using a pointer during shared reading and think-alouds to highlight letters and word chunks of unfamiliar words.

WHAT'S THE EVIDENCE?

To be successful in the reading process, children need to use all four types of cues: see P. Cunningham, 1995; Robb, 1994; Adams, 1990; Stanovich, 1986; and Clay, 1979.

Shared Reading Planning Form

The Story Box shared reading lesson plans provide a variety of suggestions for teaching each Read-Together book, as well as skills to introduce or review. What you teach during shared reading time will be determined by the strengths and needs of the students in your classroom and from your daily observations and assessments. You will need to identify any concepts and vocabulary that are challenging for the students, determine which reading strategies your students need to work on, and identify specific skills that you plan to introduce or review. You may wish to fol-low the shared reading lesson plan for each Read-Together title or make copies of the blank planning form on page 173 to organize, plan, and record your own shared reading lessons. This form, which will allow you to monitor your students' progress and record an entire week of completed lessons for future review, may also be used with any shared reading book.

An example of a completed shared reading lesson form has been provided to show how the lesson plan for *One Cold, Wet Night* can be adapted to meet different teaching needs.

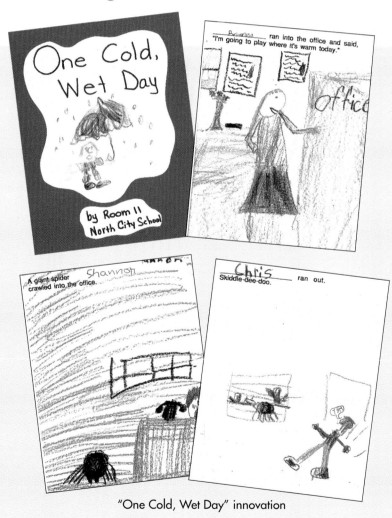

An example of an *-ight* word-family chart

"One Cold, Wet Day" innovation

84

A Week with *One Cold, Wet Night*   Date Nov 17

Day	Sharing the Reading	Skills Bank	Integrating Language Arts	Comments/ Observations/ Assessments
Day 1	• Introduce the book • Discuss the animals and the weta • Read using sounds for each animal • Comprehension: personal response	• Phonological awareness: /ed/ rime • Phonics: initial consonant *j* (review)	• Illustrate characters and props • Write about a toy they like to sleep with	• JB and AN need 1–1 practice and directionality • CR knew sound of *j* today
Day 2	• Recall events • Read with expression • Focus on directionality • Comprehension: discuss setting	• Phonological awareness: rhyming words with *wet* • Phonics: short vowel *e* • High-frequency words: *jumped, into, out*	• Make a retelling of story • Write about a rainy night	• Had JB and AN help point to words, continue monitoring • Short *e* pretty solid with most students
Day 3	• Role play while reading • Read with audiocassette • Comprehension: discuss character traits, make web of farmer's traits	• Phonological awareness: segment and blend *ee* words from story • Phonics: vowel digraph *ee* • High-frequency words: review words and practice spelling	• Combine retelling and illustrations into a wall story • Write about bedtime routines	• Most caught on fast to *ee* digraph—AS, PK, TT, & RM need more support • Checked DH, GW, NM for blending and segmenting—need additional practice
Day 4	• Read character parts • Read wall story from Day 3 • Comprehension: discuss problem and solution	• Phonics: word family *-ight* • Word structure: compound word *outside* • High-frequency words: *said, be, to*	• Create an innovation for "One Cold, Wet Day"; change characters and setting • Write about an unusual day or night	• Reviewed *ee* digraph with AS, PK, TT, and RM; continue reinforcing • Checked individual word-family lists. Most students have caught on to manipulating initial consonants in word families.
Day 5	• Read using sound effects for rain, animals, farmer • Read innovation from Day 4 • Comprehension: create story-structure chart	• Phonological awareness: listen for hard and soft *g* sound • Phonics: hard and soft *g* • Phonics: vowel diphthong *ou (out)* • Word structure: *-ed* ending	• Create a three-part retelling of story with partner • Write about favorite character in story	• Challenged BD, GT, and BS to chart additional hard and soft *g* words; they had fun with this activity and found several words • Continue reviewing *ou* diphthong and *-ed* ending

A blank blackline master of this form can be found on page 173.

What Is Guided Reading?

Guided reading is the formal instructional component in a balanced reading program. This small-group instructional process uses gradually leveled books to build a bridge between whole-group shared reading and independent reading. Guided reading begins by grouping two to five students together who are reading at the same instructional level, and giving each student a copy of the same book. Grouping students according to their skill levels allows teachers to tailor skill and strategy instruction to the students' specific needs. Guided reading also provides an effective structure in which to extend previous instruction, introduce and model new skills and strategies, and assess individual progress.

Guided reading groups should be flexible. As students' skills and needs change, the reading groups should change to accommodate them. Flexible grouping means that students are always reading text at the appropriate level of difficulty—challenging but not frustrating or discouraging.

In the Story Box guided reading formats, teachers scaffold instruction, providing a strong instructional foundation and then gradually decreasing support as students master skills. Students take increasing responsibility for their learning as teachers guide them to work together to develop reading strategies, problem solve, and discuss what they have read. Scaffolding instruction helps students successfully engage in the reading process and ensures that their learning occurs within the zone of proximal development. Vygotsky (1987) defines this as the "difference between the child's actual level of development and the level of performance that he achieves in collaboration with the adult." Scaffolding allows students to complete a task that would have been impossible without teacher support. Teaching children at their appropriate instructional level in guided reading is an ideal way to ensure their reading success. The work of Pearson (1985) found that when instruction is scaffolded, students take increasing responsibility for their learning.

The guided reading lessons in The Story Box provide a means of scaffolding instruction by adjusting the support given to students as they develop as readers. At the early emergent level, students are carefully guided through the reading process step by step. At the upper emergent level, students begin to take on more responsibilities in their reading.

To further ensure that your students are learning at their instructional level or within their zone of proximal development, you will need to determine which aspects of each lesson will require additional scaffolding or support. Here are some questions to consider as you teach the guided reading lessons:

- Which skills need to be taught or re-taught and at what depth of instruction?

- What skills and strategies require support?

- Which text will best support the teaching of these skills?

- How much support will each student group need?

- How much schema needs to be developed?

- How should I phrase questions to elicit prior knowledge and allow students to predict?

- Which words or concepts might need additional explanation?

- Which strategies might need prompting?

- What questions can I ask that will best support comprehension of the story?

- What and how much teacher-student interaction is needed?

In this chapter, we will explore the ways in which you can successfully use the guided reading books and guided reading lessons of The Story Box to scaffold instruction, helping your students successfully make the transition from shared reading to independent reading.

WHAT'S THE EVIDENCE?

The guided reading process has been discussed by Tompkins, 1997; Fountas & Pinnell, 1996; Routman, 1996, 1991; Tancock, 1994; Adams, 1990; and Pearson, 1985. Flexible groups in reading best meets the needs of students in those groups. See Au, Carroll, & Scheu, 1997; and Allington & Walmsley, 1995. Research on scaffolding and the zone of proximal development supports teaching children to read at their instructional levels and comes from Johnson & Graves, 1996/97; Graves, Van Den Broek, & Taylor, 1996; and Vygotsky, 1987, 1978.

References cited in the "What's the Evidence?" boxes are listed in a bibliography at the end of this guide.

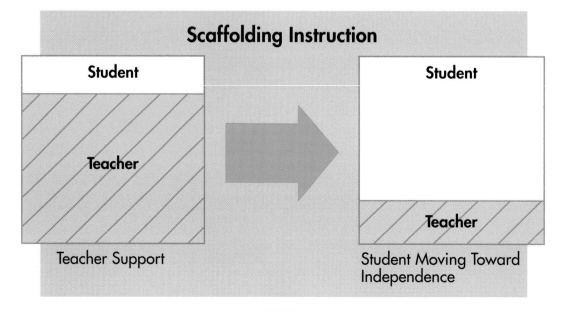

Scaffolding Instruction

Student / Teacher — Teacher Support

Student / Teacher — Student Moving Toward Independence

Assessment and Guided Reading

Before you organize guided reading groups, you will need to assess each student's reading level and determine what strategies and skills to focus on. (For more on the instructional cycle, see pages 33–35.) The Story Box Assesment Kit provides a variety of assessments to assist you in evaluating students and placing them in appropriate reading groups. These assessments cover the following skill areas:

- **Phonological awareness:** to determine if children can hear rhymes, syllables, sentences, words, alliteration, onsets and rimes; and if they can blend, segment, and manipulate sounds

- **Concepts of print:** to determine if children have an awareness of books, text, words, and letters

- **Letter recognition:** to determine which letters students can identify and reproduce

- **Phonics:** to determine what sound-symbol correspondences students have and if they can blend, segment, and manipulate them; and to determine if students are able to transfer this knowledge to dictated sentences

- **Reading behaviors:** to determine students' instructional reading level and how they use strategies and cues in their reading

- **Comprehension:** to determine if students are understanding what they read, can make inferences and judgments about the reading, and are learning to identify literary elements

- **Writing:** to determine if students are using their knowledge of sounds and can transfer that knowledge to their writing

- **Self-reflections:** to determine how students feel about themselves as readers and about the reading process

Opportunities for informal assessment present themselves throughout the guided reading process. You may wish to keep a clipboard with assessment forms, tracking charts, and self-stick notes handy during the guided reading lesson to jot down your observations. Here are some areas you might wish to informally assess during the different steps of the guided reading lessons:

- **Build Background:** schema development, prior knowledge, ability to relate to a topic

- **Introduce the Book:** prior knowledge, concepts of print (cover, author, illustrator), ability to predict events
- **Build Strategies:** ability to supply missing words/phrases in cloze sentences, ability to use concepts of print strategies and reading strategies, level of independence during the first independent reading, skills and strategies used or that need introduction or additional support
- **Teach Skills:** ability to understand and apply new skills
- **Reflect and Respond:** ability to verbalize strategies used while reading, level of comprehension of a story, ability to relate a story to personal experiences, critical thinking skills
- **Read Independently:** ability to cooperate with others while reading, success with reading strategies and the four cueing system (Note: This is an ideal time to take an Assessment of Reading Behavior on one child each day.)
- **Writing:** ability to express in writing an understanding of elements such as the structure of the story, character relationships, and how the story relates to personal experiences

For more on assessment, see The Story Box Assessment Kit.

Instructional Reading Levels

The four levels of reading development are early emergent, upper emergent, early fluency, and fluency. The Story Box covers the early emergent and upper emergent reading levels and offers enrichment books at the early fluency and fluency levels. The early emergent and upper emergent levels each have two guided reading lesson formats that gradually help students become more independent in the reading process.

Below is a chart that shows the four guided reading formats and lists the corresponding Story Box sets.

The Story Box's four guided reading formats are scaffolded to guide and support early emergent and upper emergent readers at the levels at which they learn best. The leveled books within each format become more challenging to meet students' increasingly sophisticated reading demands. Reader characteristics, focus skills, and book characteristics for the early emergent and upper emergent levels are presented in the table on the next two pages.

Focus of Formats

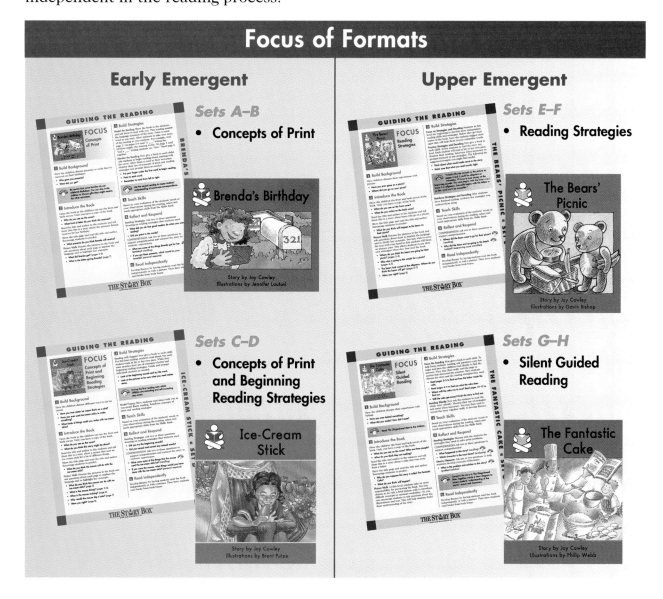

Early Emergent

Sets A–B
- Concepts of Print

Brenda's Birthday
Story by Joy Cowley
Illustrations by Jennifer Lautusi

Sets C–D
- Concepts of Print and Beginning Reading Strategies

Ice-Cream Stick
Story by Joy Cowley
Illustrations by Brent Putze

Upper Emergent

Sets E–F
- Reading Strategies

The Bears' Picnic
Story by Joy Cowley
Illustrations by Gavin Bishop

Sets G–H
- Silent Guided Reading

The Fantastic Cake
Story by Joy Cowley
Illustrations by Philip Webb

Early Emergent Level Overview

Reader characteristics

- Shows interest in books
- Recognizes that illustrations and books tell a story
- Acquires beginning skills of concepts of print and reading strategies
- Predicts story events
- Responds to print
- Knows some letters and sounds
- Recognizes a few high-frequency words

Focus skills

- Book concepts of cover, title page, author, illustrator
- Text concepts of pictures, sentences, punctuation, capitalization
- Word concepts of directionality, word-space, one-to-one correspondence, word families
- Concept that print contains meaning
- Letter concepts of recognition, formation
- Word recognition
- Four cueing system

Book characteristics

- Consistent placement of print
- Left-to-right orientation of text and illustrations
- Short, repetitive sentences with one- or two-word changes
- Natural language structures
- Illustrations that match the text
- Surprise endings or twists
- Familiar vocabulary

Upper Emergent Level Overview

Reader characteristics

- Recognizes and uses concepts of print
- Has begun to integrate reading strategies
- Gains meaning from print
- Recognizes most letters and sounds
- Identifies several high-frequency words

Focus skills

- Solidifying concepts of print
- Letter-sound correspondences
- Word recognition
- Four cueing system
- Reading strategies
- Word families
- Locating known words or word chunks
- Gaining meaning from text by making inferences

Book characteristics

- Sentences replacing captions or longer sentences replacing shorter ones
- Dialogue mixed with prose and introduced in a variety of formats
- Text that no longer corresponds as directly to the illustrations
- Illustrations that increasingly serve as sources for confirmation rather than prediction
- Two or more words, rather than one, introduced in a writing structure
- Text that allows children to predict
- Familiar objects and actions

Determining Instructional Reading Levels

Based on your observations and assessments, you can determine each student's appropriate instructional reading level to ensure he or she has a successful reading experience. A student who reads with 90 percent to 94 percent accuracy, using the Assessment of Reading Behavior from The Story Box Assessment Kit, is in the correct reading level. Students in the correct reading level should be able to read most of the text but should still find challenges and opportunities for practicing new strategies and skills. If students read with accuracy below 90 percent, they are having difficulty with the level you selected for them and should move to the next easier level. Similarly, if students read with 95 percent to 100 percent accuracy, they would be at the independent reading level on that selection and should move up to the next level of difficulty.

Each format for the Story Box guided reading levels provides the process that best meets the needs of children reading at that instructional level. For example, if a student reads a book from Set C in The Story Box with 92 percent accuracy on an Assessment of Reading Behavior, he or she would benefit most from the early emergent guided reading format Concepts of Print and Beginning Reading Strategies. If, however, the child reads the same story with 85 percent accuracy, the book is too difficult. You would want to place the child in a reading group that focuses on the early emergent guided reading format Concepts of Print and use books from Sets A or B. Finally, if the student reads the Set C book with 98 percent accuracy, you would want to move the child up to the next format at the upper emergent level.

WHAT'S THE EVIDENCE?

The importance of placing students at their appropriate instructional levels in guided reading is supported by the research of Johnson & Graves, 1996/97; Graves, Van Den Broek, & Taylor, 1996; and Vygotsky, 1987, 1978.

Teacher and Student Responsibilities

Both teachers and students have responsibilities to make the guided reading process successful.

Teacher Responsibilities

- Use a variety of assessment tools to evaluate the students' skill levels and strategy development.
- Determine appropriate instructional levels for students.
- Plan the guided reading lessons by selecting the appropriate guided reading format and the correct level of text, and determining the concepts and vocabulary skills to teach.
- Scaffold the instruction based on students' needs.
- Model correct reading behaviors and strategies.
- Observe students' reading behaviors.
- Provide constructive feedback.
- Prompt correct strategy use.
- Guide discussions.
- Maintain ongoing assessment and monitoring of students' progress.
- Reevaluate and regroup as needed.
- Provide a variety of reading and writing experiences.
- Encourage independence and responsibility in students.

Student Responsibilities

- Interact with the teacher, other students, and the text.
- Engage in the entire reading process.
- Predict events.
- Use appropriate reading strategies and behaviors.
- Use problem-solving strategies to read difficult text.
- Use decoding skills to construct meaning.
- Locate specific text features.
- Discuss and react to the text.
- Make personal connections to the text.
- Read independently and/or with a partner.
- Extend learning through writing and center activities.

Guided Reading Formats

At the early emergent level, the focus of the first guided reading format is concepts of print, which includes reading from left to right, understanding one-to-one correspondence, knowing that text tells the story, and having an awareness of books and print. The focus of the second early emergent format is on concepts of print and beginning reading strategies. At this level, students already understand many of the concepts of print and are starting to look at letters and words in text. They recognize more words and try to decode words using what they know about sounds and letters.

At the upper emergent level, the focus of the first format is reading strategies. These lessons help students utilize the four cues and develop reading strategies that can be used to decode unknown words. Children at this level are encouraged to verbalize the cues and strategies that can be used when reading text and approaching unknown words. The second upper emergent format focuses on silent guided reading. This format is a brief transition to the early fluency level. Children should not be moved into this format until they can confidently use reading strategies. Once they have mastered the use of reading strategies, they can begin reading silently and move into more advanced books and discussion of literary elements.

Each of the four formats involves a six-step process. These steps are modified from format to format, based on students' developing reading behaviors. This scaffolding provides the appropriate amount of teacher support during guided reading. The chart at right shows the six steps of each format.

Concepts of Print Format

Concepts of Print and Beginning
Reading Strategies Format

Reading Strategies
Format

Silent Guided Reading Format

Guided Reading Formats

	Early Emergent		Upper Emergent	
	Concepts of Print	Concepts of Print and Beginning Reading Strategies	Reading Strategies	Silent Guided Reading
Step 1	*Build Background*	*Build Background*	*Build Background*	*Build Background*
Step 2	*Introduce the Book* • Picture Walk	*Introduce the Book* • Picture Walk	*Introduce the Book* • Picture Walk	*Introduce the Book* • Picture Walk
Step 3	*Build Strategies* • Model the Reading • Monitor the Reading	*Build Strategies* • Reading with Support • Model Fluency	*Build Strategies* • Focus on Strategies and Decoding • Practice Strategies and Decoding • Reinforce Strategies and Decoding	*Build Strategies* • Focus the Reading • Reading Silently
Step 4	*Teach Skills*	*Teach Skills*	*Teach Skills*	*Teach Skills*
Step 5	*Reflect and Respond* • Reading Strategies • Comprehension	*Reflect and Respond* • Reading Strategies • Comprehension	*Reflect and Respond* • Comprehension	*Reflect and Respond* • Reading Strategies • Comprehension • Literary Elements
Step 6	*Read Independently*	*Read Independently*	*Read Independently*	*Read Independently*

Step 1: Build Background

For students to have a successful reading experience, they need to be able to connect with the story by activating their own prior knowledge, or schema. To determine what students know and what they still need to know about the topic of a book, you need to ask questions about experiences they have had that might be related to the topic. Prereading questions set purposes for reading and help students organize information. They also help develop critical-thinking and confirming skills that students can use both during and after reading to evaluate their understanding of the text.

Books that tend to have more difficult concepts or vocabulary often require more background building. For ESL students or others requiring extra support, you may wish to enhance the Build Background step of the lesson with activities such as field trips, film strips, related literature, and cognitive webs. Cognitive webs help facilitate students' abilities to make connections to a story and build scaffolds for learning. Such webs may be developed through discussion or various activities, including reading familiar books, poems, or songs; creating KWL charts; mapping; and using manipulatives.

1 Build Background

Have the children discuss kangaroos.

- **Have you ever seen a kangaroo?**
- **How do kangaroos move from place to place?**

from *Jump, Jump, Kangaroo*, Set C

WHAT'S THE EVIDENCE?

The following works support developing schema by building background prior to introducing a story: Tancock, 1994; Richards & Gipe, 1992; White & Lawrence, 1992; Dole et al., 1991; and Nolan, 1991.

Step 2: Introduce the Book

For each of the four guided reading formats, an effective way to introduce the book to students is to have them focus on the cover, title, author and illustrator, and title page. Then they should make predictions about the story based on what they notice. During the introduction, you will want to scaffold what students know about book concepts and focus on the main idea of the story. As students take over more of the reading, usually toward the end of the upper emergent level, you may have them begin reading the title of the story themselves. The introduction is a good place to give extra support to ESL students or others needing assistance.

Picture Walk

As you look at each page of the story during the Picture Walk, ask open-ended questions that require students to focus on the book's illustrations and story events. This is an opportunity to highlight concepts that are important to the meaning of the story, provide the general plot or main idea, call attention to the sequence of the story, and analyze any unusual or difficult language structures.

At the early emergent level, the Picture Walk section is quite supportive. You will probably want to focus on nearly every page and ask students to predict story events and the story ending. Once students have developed some reading strategies and are using the upper emergent guided reading format Reading Strategies, you may wish to cover the text of the story with your hand during the Picture Walk. This focuses the children's attention on interpreting the illustrations and allows them to use their own reading strategies when they read the book on their own for the first time.

---

2 Introduce the Book

Open the book so the children can see the front and back covers. Only you have a copy of the book.

- **Where do you think the kangaroo might be?**
- **How does the illustrator show that the kangaroo is jumping?**

Read the title and author to the students and tell them this is a story about a kangaroo that jumps over different things.

Show the title page and read the title and author. Encourage students to predict:

- **Where is the kangaroo now?**
- **What might the kangaroo be thinking?**

Picture Walk Discuss the pictures in the book and ask questions about each page to implant the language and to highlight key concepts.

- **What does the kangaroo jump over here?** (pages 2–6)
- **What do you think will happen next?** (page 7)
- **Were you right?** (page 8)

from *Jump, Jump, Kangaroo*, Set C

Picture Walk Discuss the pictures in the book and ask questions about each page to implant the language and to highlight key concepts.

- **What color is this box?** (pages 2–6)
- **What kind of box is this? Maybe this is a "gotcha" box.** (page 7)
- **What happened? Who is in this box? What could he be saying?** (page 8)

from *The "Gotcha" Box*, Set B

Picture Walk At this level, students take on more responsibility for previewing the book. You may choose to do only a brief picture walk to introduce difficult concepts or unusual vocabulary. Or, you can encourage students to ask questions about the illustrations and text. This will help students build their understanding of the story.

from *Roy G. Biv*, Set G

Picture Walk Discuss the pictures in the book and ask questions about them to implant the language and to clarify key concepts. You may wish to cover the text with your hand so that students will focus on picture cues. This allows students to use their own strategies when they first read the book.

- Which way is the little spider going? (page 2)
- What does the little spider see? Do you think he'll try to catch it? (page 3)
- Do you think he'll try to catch the bee or the butterfly? (pages 4–5)
- What do you think the little spider thought when he saw the big bird? (pages 6–8)

from *Too Big for Me,* Set F

During the upper emergent guided reading format Silent Guided Reading, the Picture Walk section shortens and is typically only used to introduce difficult vocabulary or concepts. Eventually, students take over more of the responsibility for previewing the book and can be encouraged to ask their own questions.

WHAT'S THE EVIDENCE?

Providing a good introduction to a book before reading helps set the stage for reading success by determining how much students observe or know about the book being introduced. See Fountas & Pinnell, 1996; Tancock, 1994; and Clay, 1991.

Step 3: Build Strategies

Teaching reading strategies is a key component in the guided reading process and is essential to helping students become independent readers. At both the early emergent and upper emergent levels, the Build Strategies step of the lesson focuses on showing students how to use fundamental reading strategies to get meaning from the text and decode unknown words using all four cues. The components of the Build Strategies step vary among the four lesson formats as shown below.

Guided Reading Formats			
Early Emergent		**Upper Emergent**	
Concepts of Print	Concepts of Print and Beginning Reading Strategies	Reading Strategies	Silent Guided Reading
Build Strategies • Model the Reading • Monitor the Reading	*Build Strategies* • Reading with Support • Model Fluency	*Build Strategies* • Focus on Strategies and Decoding • Practice Strategies and Decoding • Reinforce Strategies and Decoding	*Build Strategies* • Focus the Reading • Reading Silently

(Step 3 is indicated in the leftmost "Step 3" column spanning the Build Strategies rows.)

Concepts of Print (Early Emergent Guided Reading Format)

3 Build Strategies

Model the Reading Show the book to the students and ask them to read with you. This reading models the language structure of the story. Point to each word as you read. Allow students to take over more of the reading as you continue. For example, read page 2. Students may read pages 3–6. On page 7 chime in with "gotcha." Read page 8 together.

Monitor the Reading Now give a book to each child. Ask students to begin reading aloud, starting with the cover. Allow them to read at their own pace. Monitor their use of concepts of print and reading strategies and prompt them as needed:

• Look at the pictures to check the story's meaning.

• Think about the color of each box.

from *The "Gotcha" Box*, Set B

Model the Reading

The early emergent guided reading format Concepts of Print provides a great deal of support in the Model the Reading section. In this section, you demonstrate one-to-one correspondence between printed and spoken words by pointing to words as you read them. Use a cloze technique as you model the reading, allowing students to take over more of the reading on each page. The cloze technique helps you focus on strategies that you want students to use when reading the text. During the Model the Reading section, you may want to support students by providing or implanting difficult vocabulary or language patterns. You may also wish to have students predict what a word might begin with and/or have them frame a particular word in the text.

WHAT'S THE EVIDENCE?

The research of McIntyre & Pressley, 1996, suggests that the cloze technique helps teachers focus on strategies that the students need to use when reading the text.

Monitor the Reading

Monitor the Reading is the other Build Strategies section in the format Concepts of Print. This section assists you in monitoring whether students are using concepts of print and reading strategies, including pointing to words, returning to the next line, reading in the right direction, looking at illustrations to gain meaning, trying to make sense of the story by rereading or self-correcting errors, decoding words, making predictions about the print, and learning how to confirm.

During Monitor the Reading, students receive their own copy of the book and read aloud at their own pace. This may sound similar to choral reading, but each child is actually reading independently out loud. Emergent readers gain meaning by recoding, which is reading aloud and hearing the words inside their heads.

Concepts of Print and Beginning Reading Strategies (Early Emergent Guided Reading Format)

3 Build Strategies

Reading with Support Now give a book to each child. For this first reading, students read aloud, but each student reads at his or her own pace. While they read, monitor their use of concepts of print and beginning reading strategies. Guide and prompt individual students as needed:

- Think about what is happening in the story.
- Look at the beginning sounds of words.
- Use words you know to help you read.

Model Fluency Have students read aloud with you as you model fluent reading. Reinforce concepts of print and reading strategies.

from *Jump, Jump, Kangaroo*, Set C

Reading with Support

The early emergent guided reading format Concepts of Print and Beginning Reading Strategies gives more reading responsibility to students. You will not need to model the reading of the story at this level. Once you reach the Reading with Support section of the Build Strategies step, the students will have just experienced a thorough Picture Walk and will be ready to independently read their own copies of the book out loud at their own pace. They should be using beginning reading strategies, including looking at the words, trying beginning sounds, pointing to each word,

and beginning to self-correct and reread to make sense of the story. In this section, you will need to closely monitor students' reading to see what strategies they are using and/or to prompt them to try particular strategies.

Model Fluency

The other section of Build Strategies in this format is Model Fluency, in which you do a second reading of the story to model fluent reading. Invite the students to read along with you as you model good expression and fluent phrasing. In this section you have an opportunity to remind students about what strategies they can use to get through challenging parts of the text. Suggested strategy prompts are shown in the table at right.

Strategy Prompts for Early Emergent Readers

Focus on schema

- What do you know about _____?
- Have you ever _____?

Focus on concepts of print

- Where do you start reading?
- Put your finger on the first word.
- Which way do you read?
- Now where do you go to read the next part?
- Can you find the title page?
- Point to the title.

Focus on one-to-one correspondence

- Point to each word as you read.
- Read it with your finger.
- Did that match?
- Were there enough words?

Focus on meaning

- Did that make sense?
- What happened in the story when _____?
- Use the pictures to make sure what you read made sense.

Focus on structure cues

- Did that sound right?
- What might be another way to say that?
- Can you think of another word that would fit here?

Focus on graphophonics: Locating known words

- Can you point to _____?
- Show me _____.
- How did you know that word was _____?

Focus on graphophonics: Locating unknown words

- What did you see in the word _____?
- Can you find _____?
- How did you know that word was _____?
- What do you think that word might be?

Focus on cross-checking

- How did you know that word was _____?
- Is there another way to tell?
- It could be _____, but look at _____.

Focus on self-correcting

- Try that again.
- What did you see?
- Were you right?
- How did you know?
- Why did you stop?

Reading Strategies (Upper Emergent Guided Reading Format)

3 Build Strategies

Focus on Strategies and Decoding Students at this level are beginning to develop more independent reading skills and strategies. Before they get their copies of the book, have the students suggest strategies that will help them decode unfamiliar words.

Practice Strategies and Decoding Now give a book to each child. Invite students to read the story out loud. Each student will read at his or her own pace. Monitor their reading. Intervene when necessary to prompt students to use strategies. The following are suggested prompts you might find useful:

- Look for familiar parts in the word.
- Look at the whole word and try it.

 THINK ALOUD "When I see a word I don't know, I try to find a part of the word that I do know. Like in this word. (*butterfly*, page 5) I know the little word *fly*. Then I look at the whole word and try to figure it out."

Reinforce Strategies and Decoding After students have finished reading, reinforce the strategies you noticed them using.

from *Too Big for Me*, Set F

Focus on Strategies and Decoding

The upper emergent guided reading format Reading Strategies focuses on using the four cueing system and reading strategies to successfully decode text. During Focus on Strategies and Decoding section of the Build Strategies step, you will want to elicit from the students the reading strategies that they might use. Verbalizing the strategies before reading helps students think about what they can do to figure out difficult vocabulary and better understand what they are about to read.

Practice Strategies and Decoding

During the Practice Strategies and Decoding section of the Build Strategies step, students will have their own copy of the book, read the book out loud at their own pace, and use reading strategies when appropriate. If students come to a difficult part in the text, you will need to prompt them to try a strategy for decoding the words.

Reinforce Strategies and Decoding

During this part of the Build Strategies step, the students think about, discuss, and analyze the reading strategies they used or the tricky parts of the text. You will want to reinforce the strategies that you noticed students using and the successes they had with decoding. Students can describe a behavior or a strategy that helped them decode a difficult word, or others in the group might offer suggestions. This social interaction helps develop cognitive strategies and fosters self-monitoring by students.

Suggested questions to prompt students to think about reading strategies are listed below:

- What did you do to help you with a word?
- Did what you read make sense?
- How did you know what that word was?
- Can you find _____?
- Did you look at all the letters in a word?
- Did you try the beginning sound?
- Did you look for known parts in a word?
- Did you reread when you had trouble with a word?

Silent Guided Reading (Upper Emergent Guided Reading Format)

3 Build Strategies

Focus the Reading Now give a book to each child. To help focus students' reading, ask questions every few pages and have the children read silently to find the answers. They may then orally read the page or section that answered the question. Have students discuss the story and the reading strategies they used.

- Read pages 2–14 to find out where Roy G. Biv lives and what clothes he likes to wear.

- Look on page 11. What color are the shoes? Indigo is a shade of purple. How will you remember this word is indigo?

- Read pages 15–16 and find out what Roy G. Biv will help you know.

Reading Silently Now ask the students to read the whole story silently. Monitor their use of strategies and assist when necessary. You may then wish to reread the story together orally to develop fluency.

from *Roy G. Biv*, Set G

Focus the Reading

During the Focus the Reading section of the upper emergent guided reading format Silent Guided Reading, students will have their own copy of the book and you will ask questions for every two to four pages of the story. Then you will guide the students to read those pages silently to find the answers. To confirm their answers, they can locate and read aloud the supporting text.

If students have any problems with the text during this focused silent reading, encourage them to discuss the strategies they used to solve them.

Reading Silently

Next, students can silently read the whole story to themselves during the Reading Silently section of the Build Strategies step. If you notice a student having trouble with the text, assist him or her with strategy development or reinforcement. You may wish to reread the story or parts of the story with the students to provide a fluent model and an opportunity for them to practice fluent reading. Suggested strategy prompts for the upper emergent level are listed in the table on page 106.

WHAT'S THE EVIDENCE?

The importance of teaching reading strategies and the correct usage of strategies in the reading process comes from the works of Schwartz, 1997; Goodman, 1996; McIntyre & Pressley, 1996; Tancock, 1994; Garner, 1992; Marlow & Reese, 1992; Richards & Gipe, 1992; and Clay, 1985.

Strategy Prompts for Upper Emergent Readers

Focus on schema
- What do you know about _____?
- Have you ever _____?

Focus on meaning cues
- Did that make sense?
- What happened in the story when _____?
- What do you think it might be?
- Were you right?
- Use the pictures to make sure what you read made sense.

Focus on structure cues
- Did that sound right?
- Can you say that another way?
- What is another word that might fit here that looks right and makes sense?

Focus on graphophonic cues
- Did you use what you know about sounds and letters to decode the word?
- What letter/sound does it start/end with?
- What would you see at the beginning/in the middle/at the end?
- Do you know another word that might start/end this way?
- Is there any part of the word that you already know?
- Does that look right?

Focus on cross-checking
- How did you know that word was _____?
- Is there another way to tell?
- It could be _____, but look at _____.

Focus on self-correcting
- Take a closer look at _____.
- Were you right? Could it be _____?
- How did you know that this word was _____?
- Can you find the tricky part?

Focus on self-monitoring
- Try that again.
- What did you see?
- Were you right?
- How did you know?
- Why did you stop?

Step 4: Teach Skills

> ### 4 Teach Skills
>
> Based on your evaluation of the students' needs or your observations during the reading, select and teach appropriate skills from the Skills Bank.

from Roy G. Biv, Set G

In the guided reading process, skills instruction is essential to developing independent readers. The Teach Skills step in all four guided reading formats is a time to teach skills that apply to the story students have just read, including areas you observed students having difficulty with during the Build Strategies step.

Teaching skills within the context of the reading process helps students retain in long-term memory what they learn because it helps them attach what they learn to their schema, or previous knowledge. Once students have stored skills in long-term memory, they can transfer the skills, generalize the skills, and apply the skills in new contexts. See the Skills Bank discussion on pages 112–113 for more on ways to teach skills.

WHAT'S THE EVIDENCE?

Skills taught in isolation are stored only in short-term memory because they are not connected to anything the learner knows. Skills taught in isolation versus skills taught within the context of the reading process is discussed by Moustafa, 1997; Honig, 1996; Dechant, 1993; and Adams, 1990.

Step 5: Reflect and Respond

5 Reflect and Respond

Reading Strategies Ask two or three questions focusing on reading strategies that students used.

- **What did you do that helped you read the story?**
- **Did you look at the beginning sounds?**
- **Did you use words you know to help you with tricky words?**

COMPREHENSION Ask two or three questions to support comprehension and connect the story to students' experiences.

- **What did the kangaroo jump over?** (recalling)
- **Why was the kangaroo jumping over the other animals?** (inferring)
- **How do you think the kangaroo felt after he jumped out of the zoo?** (inferring)

from *Jump, Jump, Kangaroo*, Set C

Once students have finished reading a story, they need time to reflect on what they have read and discuss their understanding of it. The Reflect and Respond step in all four guided reading formats provides opportunities for students to discuss the strategies they used while reading and evaluate their understanding of the story. The components of the Reflect and Respond step vary among the four formats as shown below.

Guided Reading Formats			
Early Emergent		**Upper Emergent**	
Concepts of Print	Concepts of Print and Beginning Reading Strategies	Reading Strategies	Silent Guided Reading
Step 5 *Reflect and Respond* • Reading Strategies • Comprehension	*Reflect and Respond* • Reading Strategies • Comprehension	*Reflect and Respond* • Comprehension	*Reflect and Respond* • Reading Strategies • Comprehension • Literary Elements

Reading Strategies

A Reading Strategies section is featured in both the early emergent formats, as well as the upper emergent guided reading format Silent Guided Reading. (The upper emergent guided reading format Reading Strategies covers reading strategies thoroughly in the Build Strategies step.) The Reading Strategies section presents an opportunity for students to discuss tricky parts of the text and analyze the reading strategies they used. During this section, students can share with other members of their group the strategies they found helpful and the reasons they were helpful. This type of social interaction helps develop cognitive strategies and fosters self-monitoring. You may want to encourage students to participate by asking questions like the following:

- What did you do to help you with a word?
- Did you point to the words?
- Did what you read make sense?
- Did you read from left to right?
- How did you know what that word was?
- Did you look at all the letters in a word?
- Did you try the beginning sound?
- Did you see a little word inside a big word?
- Did you see a part of a word you know?
- Did you check the illustrations to be sure what you read made sense?

Comprehension

All four guided reading formats feature the Comprehension section in the Reflect and Respond step. This part of the lesson gives students an opportunity to demonstrate how well they understood what they read. Discuss the story with students to assess what they recall and how it might relate to their lives. Ask questions that prompt critical-thinking skills, such as inferring, making judgments, analyzing, comparing and contrasting, sequencing, and drawing conclusions.

WHAT'S THE EVIDENCE?

When children are engaged in discussion about what they've read, they tend to be more interested in the reading process. The importance of developing comprehension skills in reading is supported by Fountas & Pinnell, 1996; Guthrie, 1996; Honig, 1996; Guthrie et al.,1995; Tancock, 1994; Garner, 1992; Adams, 1990; and Pearson, 1985.

Literary Elements

Literary Elements Ask one or two questions to help students develop concepts of literature.

- **How does the setting in this story compare with where you live?** (setting)

from *Roy G. Biv*, Set G

Once students have mastered many of the reading strategies and become more fluent readers, they begin to focus on the literary elements of a story. In the upper emergent guided reading format Silent

Guided Reading, children are asked to think about literary elements. For example, they may consider the characters in a story and how they interact and develop; how the setting affects the events; the story's problem and solution; the author's intent; and point of view. Careful questioning can help students develop these literary skills as they begin to read longer and more complex books.

Step 6: Read Independently

6 Read Independently

Develop fluency by having students read the book independently or with a partner. Then have students read books from book boxes.

from *Roy G. Biv*, Set G

The primary goal of teaching reading is getting students to successfully read independently. At the end of each guided reading lesson, students practice rereading the story so they can apply the strategies and skills they've learned. This rereading assists them in developing fluency by building their word-recognition skills, and it improves their comprehension as they become more familiar with the story's events.

During this final part of the lesson, you may wish to have students read individually or take turns reading with partners. Partner reading provides extra support by allowing students to share strategies and help one another problem solve. One partner should read the story all the way through before the other partner reads. (See page 17 for more on paired reading.)

In addition to rereading the lesson story, students may practice reading familiar books from their book boxes. These boxes should contain books that they have read in previous lessons and that are at their instructional and independent reading levels. When allowed to select their own reading materials, students tend to be more motivated and engaged in reading. As students reread familiar books, they notice more details about the text, make generalizations about their knowledge of word patterns, gain confidence in their ability to read, and generally develop more independence as readers.

While children are reading independently, you may wish to meet with individual students to assess their reading behaviors, skills, and strategy use or to further reinforce skills and strategies. This is an ideal time to take an Assessment of Reading Behavior on individual students to assess how they are using strategies and the four cueing system. During your assessment, you may wish to have students read the book just used during the lesson, a familiar book at their instructional level, or an unfamiliar book at their instructional level to evaluate how they are dealing with text.

WHAT'S THE EVIDENCE?

Cunningham & Stanovich, 1991, found that independent reading and student achievement have a positive correlation. Independent reading provides time for students to practice their reading skills. The importance of this is supported by Taylor et al., 1997; Fountas & Pinnell, 1996; Honig, 1996; Allington & Walmsley, 1995; Hiebert & Taylor, 1994; Cunningham & Stanovich, 1991; Adams, 1990; Juel, 1990; Stanovich & West, 1989; Samuels, 1988; and Juel & Roper-Schneider, 1985.

Skills Bank

As a comprehensive reading program, The Story Box includes a component that addresses the skills that students need in order to become successful readers. The Skills Bank, included in each guided reading lesson of all four formats, delineates the skills that are most appropriate at each instructional level, as well as those that are most appropriate for each guided reading title.

With the Skills Bank, you select the skills you wish to cover with each guided reading group. You will base this on your ongoing observations and assessments of students. Each skill discussed in the Skills Bank can be taught either implicitly, within the context of the guided reading lesson, or explicitly, after the guided reading lesson. The Skills Bank features strategies and activities to help you teach each skill, as well as opportunities for students to practice what you've taught. The Skills Bank also provides opportunities to teach phonological awareness; concepts of print; phonics; vocabulary words, including high-frequency words, spelling words, and content words; word structure; and mechanics. See the section on skills on pages 39–53 for an in-depth discussion of skills instruction.

Learning More

The Learning More section in the Skills Bank suggests additional teaching opportunities that might be appropriate for some guided reading groups. The skills listed in this section may be used for review, additional instruction, practice, or as challenge activities for some students.

The Wright Skills

The Wright Skills provides explicit instruction, practice, application, and assessment for skills covered in The Story Box.

WHAT'S THE EVIDENCE?

Dechant, 1993, writes that "reading moves from whole to part to whole and that when we focus on the parts we are implicitly talking about skills teaching." Teaching reading skills is vital to developing successful readers. Teaching skills within the context of a lesson and/or explicitly after a lesson is supported by Strickland, 1998; Weaver, 1998b, 1996, 1994; Morrow, 1997, 1992; Moustafa, 1997; Honig, 1996; P. Cunningham, 1995; Dechant, 1993; and Adams, 1990.

Guided Reading Icons

Here is a guide to icons found in the guided reading lesson plans:

 Assessment opportunities occur throughout the lesson plans.

 ESL icons indicate activities that include movement, vocabulary development, or other strategies that work well for students acquiring English.

 Extra Help icons alert you to suggestions for additional support for students who need it.

 Challenging lessons are available for advanced students.

 Think Aloud icons show how you can demonstrate reading strategies to your students.

 See the **Literacy Center** icon for suggestions on how to use centers following the lesson.

 Find helpful tips and interesting background information where you see the **Teacher Tip** icon.

 See the **Technology** icon for suggestions on how to integrate *Paint, Write & Play!*™ into your instruction.

 Fun activities involve students and their families at the **School to Home and Back** icon.

 Students can reinforce important skills they have learned during the lesson with activities to take home.

SKILLS BANK

Select and teach skills from the Skills Bank during the "Teach Skills" step and following the guided reading lesson.

Phonological Awareness

Rhyming

■ Reread pages 2–3 to the children without showing them the text.

• **What are the two words that rhyme?** *(Biv/live)*

■ Repeat the process with pages 4–5 *(hair/wear)*, 13–14 *(Biv/live)*, and 15–16 *(know/rainbow)*.

Phonics

Vowel Digraph   *ai*

■ Reread pages 2–3 together. Write the word *rainbow* on the chalkboard.

• **Listen to the word *rainbow*. What sound does *ai* make?**

■ Show children several cards with words that have the *ai* digraph *(chain, main, gain)*. Together, read each word and say the sound *ai* makes.

Silent Consonant   *kn*

■ Together reread pages 15–16. Have students listen to the word *know*.

• **What do you notice about the word *know*? The *k* is silent when it is with the *n*.**

■ Write several other words beginning with *kn* *(knot, knife, knee)* and have students read them.

Vowel Digraph/Word Family   *-ow*

■ Have students reread page 3 and find a word in which the letters *ow* make the long *o* sound *(rainbow)*.

• **Can you find other *ow* words in the story that have the letters *ow* making the /ō/ sound?** *(yellow, know)*

CONTENT WRITING

Have children write a group story about some other things that Roy G. Biv might have that are colors of the rainbow. Have the group illustrate the story, bind it, and put it in the Big Book center.

■ Have students use magnetic letters or letter cards to add initial consonants, blends, or digraphs to the *-ow* word family to create additional words. Write their words on a vowel pattern chart.

 TEACHER TIP **If students suggest a word in which the letters *ow* make the vowel sound as in *town*, discuss the two sounds *ow* can make.**

Vocabulary

High-Frequency Word/Spelling   live

■ Have students reread page 3 and frame the word *live*.

■ Discuss the pronunciation and meaning of *live* with the short *i* sound and *live* with the long *i* sound. Point out that students will need to use the context of the sentence to determine the correct pronunciation and meaning of *live*.

■ Have students practice spelling *live* by writing it in large letters, small letters, and in colors.

Learning More

Roy G. Biv offers the following additional teaching opportunities:

Consonant Digraphs: *wh, sh*

Silent Consonant: *mb* (as in *comb*)

Compound Word: *rainbow*

High-Frequency Words: *here, where*

THE WRIGHT SKILLS™

For expanded instruction, see the following folders. (Skill is followed by folder number.)

FOCUS ON PREPHONICS:
Rhyming 2

PHONICS AND WORD STUDY, LEVEL B:
Vowel Digraph *ai* 25, *ow* 27; Word Family *-ow* 27; Initial Consonant Digraph *wh* 21, *sh* 18; Compound Words 44

 Give each student a take-home version of *Roy G. Biv* to assemble, color, and read, and then take home to share with family members.

THE STORY BOX®

Writing

STRUCTURE WRITING

Provide the following structure for students to complete and illustrate.

Jump, jump, _____.

Jump over the _____.

from *Jump, Jump, Kangaroo*, Set C

The guided reading lessons also provide a variety of writing connections to the stories. Writing activities include structure writing, journal writing, and content writing. A structure writing activity, for example, asks students to complete a structure or pattern from the story by adding their own words and then illustrating it. Journal writing activities might ask students to write about their feelings or reactions to the story, make personal connections to the story, change the story's ending, or write a sequel to the story. Content writing provides opportunities for students to research a topic and write about it. (For more on writing, see pages 18–27.)

2

BLUEBERRY MUFFINS by Sarah
2 cups of sugar
1 cup of flour

4 egg ◯ s
1/2 gallons of milk
12 blueberries
Mix the egreadis together and put it in the oven for 10 min. Eat them!

Take-Me-Homes

Give each student a take-home version of *Roy G. Biv* to assemble, color, and read, and then take home to share with family members.

from *Roy G. Biv*, Set G

The Take-Me-Homes for guided reading are blackline master reproductions of selected guided reading titles that students have read. Students are encouraged to assemble the Take-Me-Homes, color the illustrations, read the stories independently or to a partner, and then take the books home to share with their families. The Take-Me-Homes help children create their own at-home, independent reading library.

The additional reading practice involved in the Take-Me-Home component helps build fluency, comprehension, and skills acquisition as students reread books at their instructional and independent reading levels. Families also become more aware of their children's growth in reading as they see their children bring home books that are more and more challenging.

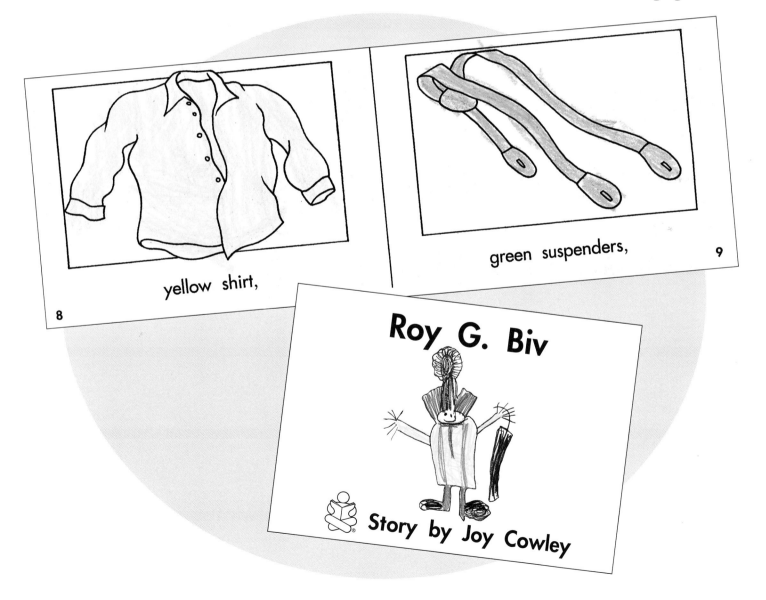

yellow shirt,

8

green suspenders, 9

Roy G. Biv

Story by Joy Cowley

Guided Reading in Your Classroom

Implementing guided reading in your classroom will involve arranging your room and schedule to accommodate small-group instruction. You will need to take the following steps to support guided reading in your classroom:

- Develop a community of learners.
- Create literacy centers.
- Establish a guided reading area.
- Determine what books are appropriate for students' reading levels.
- Create flexible guided reading groups.
- Develop a daily schedule.

Develop a Community of Learners

Before you begin a guided reading program in your classroom, you will want to lay a strong foundation in daily reading and writing activities. Children should participate daily in the following reading and writing activities:

- Shared reading, songs, read-alouds, and independent reading
- Talking about stories with others
- Responding to stories through reproductions, retellings, innovations, dramatic reenactments, and other artistic creations
- Reading familiar stories independently
- Writing in a wide variety of formats, such as stories, journals, diaries, letters, and logs
- Working on Daily News activities and other written language experiences

Create Literacy Centers

Literacy centers feature activities centered on reading, writing, listening, and speaking. Literacy centers provide opportunities for students to work cooperatively or independently while practicing and applying the skills they learn during the guided reading lessons. Students can work at different literacy centers while you work with guided reading groups. (For more on literacy centers, see pages 127–132.)

WHAT'S THE EVIDENCE?

Providing time for students to practice at literacy centers the skills they are learning is discussed by Christie, Enz, & Vukelich, 1997; Morrow, 1997; Fountas & Pinnell, 1996; and Routman, 1991.

Establish a Guided Reading Area

You will need to arrange a specific area in your classroom to conduct guided reading groups. Consider the following suggestions as you establish your guided reading area:

- Set aside a specific area for meeting with your guided reading groups. You might arrange yourself and students together at a table or on the floor, or you may prefer to sit in a chair with children sitting in front of you in a semicircle on the floor.

- If space is limited and you must place the guided reading area near a center, choose the center with the quietest activities.

- Position yourself so that you can observe the entire classroom as you conduct guided reading groups.

- Keep your guided reading books and materials in a convenient location for easy access.

Determine What Books Are Appropriate for Students' Reading Levels

Books selected for guided reading must be at the appropriate instructional level. Students should be able to read approximately 90 percent to 94 percent of the words in the story, based on the Assessment of Reading Behavior. The text should be challenging enough to require students to develop reading strategies and skills but not so difficult that they become frustrated in the process. The Assessment of Reading Behavior identifies three student reading levels:

- **Independent level:** 95 percent to 100 percent reading accuracy. Text read at this level is easy for students and doesn't require them to actually do any reading work. If students only read at an independent level, their reading ability doesn't develop as it should.

- **Instructional level:** 90 percent to 94 percent reading accuracy. Text read at this level best meets the reading needs of students. Students apply their reading strategies to decoding words and make use of the four cueing system.

- **Difficult level:** below 90 percent reading accuracy. Text read at this level presents too many challenges and prevents students from being effective readers. Books that are too difficult contain too many unknown words or concepts and cause children to become frustrated as they attempt to decode the text.

Create Flexible Guided Reading Groups

An ideal guided reading group consists of two to five children, with each child using his or her own copy of the book. Refer to your assessments and observations of the students to determine their ability levels. (For more on assessment, see The Story Box Assessment Kit.) Homogeneous groups are most appropriate at the emergent level because they allow you to focus on teaching specific, basic strategies and skills. Your grouping should be flexible and change as students' needs and abilities change.

Develop a Daily Schedule

During a typical day in your classroom, you can probably fit three to four guided reading groups into your reading time. Each guided reading group will require approximately fifteen to twenty minutes of instruction. While you are working with one group, the rest of the class should be occupied at literacy centers, doing related reading and writing activities. At the early emergent level, try to meet with your groups every day, whenever possible, especially with students who need extra help. (See pages 139–140 for more on daily schedules.

The Four Cueing System and Guided Reading

To effectively scaffold reading instruction for students, teachers need to know which strategies to focus on. Understanding the four cueing system and how children use each type of cue will help teachers determine these strategies. Good readers use all four cues simultaneously to gain information from the text. (The four cueing system is discussed in more detail in Chapter 2, on pages 37–38.)

The four types of cues are schema, semantic, syntactic, and graphophonic. When readers draw upon prior knowledge and experience, they use schema cues, which fundamentally relate to the three other types of cues. Students use semantic cues when trying to find meaning in a text and determining if what they read makes sense. Readers know if a text sounds right by using syntactic cues, which relate to the structure of language. Readers can decide if a text looks right by developing graphophonic cues, which involves focusing on the relationships between sounds and symbols and visual and spatial concepts.

Each major component of the guided reading lessons helps students develop and use the four cueing system. The following chart shows how the lessons support the four cueing system.

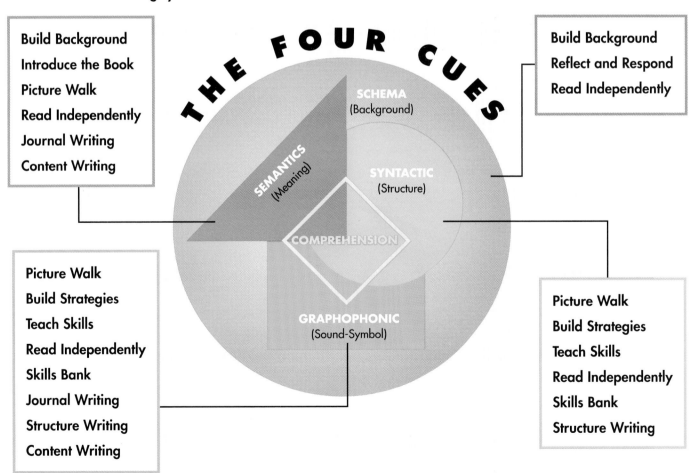

Build Background
Introduce the Book
Picture Walk
Read Independently
Journal Writing
Content Writing

Build Background
Reflect and Respond
Read Independently

Picture Walk
Build Strategies
Teach Skills
Read Independently
Skills Bank
Journal Writing
Structure Writing
Content Writing

Picture Walk
Build Strategies
Teach Skills
Read Independently
Skills Bank
Structure Writing

THE FOUR CUES

SCHEMA
(Background)

SEMANTICS
(Meaning)

SYNTACTIC
(Structure)

COMPREHENSION

GRAPHOPHONIC
(Sound-Symbol)

Schema Cues and Guided Reading

Schema cues are developed during the Build Background step and the Reflect and Respond step in the guided reading lesson. Asking students what they know about a topic and how they relate to it establishes a common ground for understanding a story. During the Reflect and Respond step of the lesson, comprehension questions require students to reflect on and make personal connections to the story to assist them in building schema. During Read Independently, students have opportunities to continue developing schema cues by rereading their guided reading books and other familiar books at their instructional levels.

Semantic Cues and Guided Reading

Students learn to use semantic cues to understand a story during the Build Background and Introduce the Book steps of the lesson, and the Picture Walk section of Introduce the Book. Students with limited experiences or language may require additional support to help them build background knowledge before reading a story. This support can come from things such as manipulatives, pictures, field trips, and dramatizations. After-reading discussion during the Reflect and Respond step and the Reading Independently step help students continue to develop semantic cues as they recall information from the story and respond to the story's events. In addition, students reflect their understanding of the meaning of the story during Content Writing and Journal Writing activities.

Syntactic Cues and Guided Reading

The guided reading process helps students develop and use syntactic cues by calling attention to language patterns and grammatical structures in the stories during the Picture Walk section of the Introduce the Book step, and in the Build Strategies step. Children can then use these structures to assist them in decoding words and to gain meaning from the story. Syntactic cues are also focused on in the Skills Bank and in the Structure Writing activities and Read Independently.

Graphophonic Cues and Guided Reading

The graphophonic cues are an integral part of the guided reading process. Students' attention is focused on graphophonic cues during the Picture Walk section of the Introduce the Book step, and during the Build Strategies step. In these steps, you might ask students to look at words from left to right, think of what sound or letter a word begins with, use knowledge of phonics and spelling patterns to decode, listen for sounds of rhyming words, and/or discuss the features of the text. The Teach Skills step and Skills Bank provide opportunities for teachers to explicitly teach and focus on the appropriate graphophonic skills of phonological awareness, concepts of print, phonics, and/or word structure that will meet the individual needs of the guided reading group. Students can continue to develop graphophonic cues as they practice decoding words, look for known parts of words and patterns in words, use what they know about a word to decode an unknown word, and reread material at their instructional levels during the Read Independently step. Finally, children demonstrate their understanding of phonics as they write during Journal Writing, Structure Writing, and Content Writing activities.

WHAT'S THE EVIDENCE?

The works of Share & Stanovich, 1995, and Adams, 1990, support the principle that students need to use all cues to support their reading. Support that the four cueing system should be an integral part of the guided reading process comes from P. Cunningham, 1995; Share & Stanovich, 1995; Robb, 1994; Adams, 1990; and Clay, 1979.

Guided Reading Planning Form

The guided reading lessons in The Story Box will assist you in planning your own daily guided reading lessons. Your guided reading lessons will be based on the strengths and needs your students demonstrate during the previous day's lesson and from your daily observations and assessments. You will need to select books that are at the appropriate instructional level, identify any concepts and vocabulary that are challenging for the students, determine which reading strategies your students need to work on, and identify specific skills that you plan to introduce or review.

On the following page, we have provided a sample, filled-out planning form that covers one week of guided reading lessons for a group of four students who read at the Set B instructional level. You may want to use a form like this one, which will help you monitor your students' progress; record comments, observations, and assessments done with the students; plan your own guided reading lessons; and record an entire week of completed lessons for future review. A blank blackline master of this form is provided at the back of the guide on pages 174–175.

Guided Reading Planning Form

Reading group Josh, Mia, Tina, Jorge

Date	Title	Set	Challenging concepts	Difficult vocabulary/ sentence structure
Monday 11/18	*The Tree House*	B	tree house	sentence structure on last page
Tuesday 11/19	*The Big Hill*	B	climb	sentence structure on last page
Wednesday 11/20	*Rat's Funny Story*	B	(none)	*ha-ha-ha pattern*
Thursday 11/21	*Mrs. Wishy-Washy's Tub*	B	tub (bathtub, bath)	*wishy-washy*
Friday 11/22	*The Bridge*	B	meanies	*bridge number words oh-oh*

A blank blackline master of this form can be found on pages 174–175.

Strategies	Skills	Comments	Assessments
• Point to words • Initial sounds	• z • short vowel /u/ • short u • up	Josh had trouble with last page. Others doing well with one-to-one correspondence.	Mia—92% on Assessment of Reading Behavior
• Directionality • Point to words	• r • review short u • review up	Directionality and one-to-one correspondence is coming along for all students.	Tina—93% on Assessment of Reading Behavior
• Return sweep	• review r • on	Focus on return sweep with Mia, Josh, and Jorge.	Josh—90% on Assessment of Reading Behavior
• Return sweep	• alliteration /w/ • w • short i • review short u • is, on	Group still doing well with one-to-one correspondence. Mia doesn't have return sweep yet.	Jorge—90% on Assessment of Reading Behavior
• Return sweep • Directionality	• segmenting and blending • final x • short i • on	Return sweep used on every page. Everyone is doing better.	Concepts of Print Checklist—shows all four students are developing one-to-one correspondence and directionality

Creating Your Classroom Environment

Providing an engaging classroom environment is an essential part of a successful balanced reading program. The environment you create should stimulate and support students' literacy development as they participate in a wide range of whole-group, small-group, and independent learning activities. This chapter provides numerous detailed suggestions for implementing and managing a rich, multifaceted reading environment.

As you establish literacy centers, content centers, and resource centers in your classroom, try to make the environment inviting and comfortable for students.

Provide items such as throw rugs, pillows, bean bag chairs, child-size overstuffed chairs or lawn chairs, rocking chairs, reading lamps, stuffed animals, and magazine or newspaper holders so that students feel at home as they enjoy reading and writing experiences. As you plan the physical layout of your room, consider its size, shape, and usable wall and floor space. Also consider the flow of movement and where it makes most sense to locate noisy activities and quiet ones.

As you teach skills and develop themes, take these opportunities to add relevant signs, charts, posters, wall murals, wall stories, word charts, and so on to your environment. Make sure to clearly label areas of the room so students can easily find literacy centers and materials.

The Layout of Your Classroom

Here is a list of features you might want to consider when determining your classroom layout:

- Areas for whole-class read-alouds, shared reading, presentations, and sharing time

- Areas for guided reading, small-group activities, and individual instruction

- A special chair for students to sit in when they do independent reading or read aloud their own stories, favorite stories, or poems

- Work space for other adults (teacher assistants, specialists, or volunteers) who are in the room on a regular basis

- Effective groupings of tables or desks for cooperative learning activities

- Effective placement of resource centers (reading, writing, art, computer, science, math)

- A quiet library or book corner with easily accessible books and comfortable seating

- Wall space at students' eye level for displaying their art and writing

- Ample chalkboard space

- Ways to hang things from the ceiling

- Extra bulletin boards

- Permanent fixtures (sink, shelves, cupboards, outlets, lighting) for different activities

- A good location for a teacher center (desk, materials, conferencing)

- Storage space for multiple sets of guided reading books, teacher reference books, and supplies that students don't need access to

- Easy student access to all of the resource areas

- A room arrangement that facilitates teacher monitoring of all activities

- A visually stimulating environment

- A print-rich environment

Centers are designated parts of your classroom where children can work on specific types of activities in small groups, with partners, or independently. Centers provide students with a variety of ways to engage in reading, writing, listening, and speaking experiences. Centers do not always have to contain tables and chairs or even be in a specific place in the room. A center may consist of a window ledge, a sink, a rug, or a portable box. Whatever form a center takes, it should foster literacy, be well organized, and provide easily accessible supplies.

Many of your centers will relate directly to the teaching you do, giving students opportunities to practice and apply what they learn. Literacy centers are those centers most closely related to reading and writing. They should support the skills and strategies students learn in shared reading and guided reading lessons. Content-area centers focus on subjects such as math, social studies, and science. These centers support an integrated approach to teaching, allowing you to connect lesson themes or topics to related disciplines. Resource centers provide specific types of resources that can engage students and support the activities of other centers.

Literacy Centers

The literacy centers most important for emergent readers and writers include independent reading centers, integrated language arts centers, and skill centers.

Independent Reading Centers

Independent reading centers are the areas in the classroom where students read on their own, with a partner, or with a small group of students. The independent reading centers include a Big Book center, a poetry center, a library center, a pocket chart center, an overhead center, a read the room center, and a book boxes center.

Big Book Center

This center contains books previously read during shared reading lessons, offering students opportunities to reread familiar stories. As you create class reproductions, innovations, and retellings over the school year, you may want to add them to the Big Book center for students to enjoy and read. Provide a pointer at the center for students to use to practice pointing to the words in the stories as they read.

Poetry Center

This center can contain poems you introduce in class, including those from Poems for Sharing used during shared reading time. Students can return to old favorite poems to read or dramatize. Be sure to provide a pointer for students to use as they reread the poems. They can also work with the sequencing images and activities that are provided in *Poems for Sharing Teacher Notes*.

A Big Book Center

A poetry center

127

Library Center

Perhaps one of the most important parts of your reading environment, the library center, should contain books and other reading materials that span a wide range of reading levels, from below to above the grade level you teach. Include single titles and multiple sets of some books. Organize the library so students can easily find materials.

The following is a list of suggested materials for your classroom library:

- Picture books
- Pupil-book versions of Big Books read during shared reading
- Books that you have read aloud
- Fiction books in a variety of genres
- Nonfiction books, magazines, newspapers
- Poetry and songs
- Dictionaries
- Encyclopedias
- Additional reference books, such as atlases and almanacs
- Tape recorder, headphones, and audiocassettes

Make the library an inviting place for students to read. Provide cozy furniture, such as bean bag chairs, rugs, pillows, and a rocking chair, and stuffed animals. Decorate with reading posters, wall charts on which children can record their favorite or new words, photos of authors and illustrators, illustrations, and student artwork.

Pocket Chart Center

Students can use the pocket chart center to practice sequencing stories and poems or creating innovations. They can match sentence strips and/or words from stories and poems, build word families using word cards, match illustrations to the text on sentence strips, or match letters or pictures to letters. Provide a pointer at this center for children to use while reading.

A pocket chart center

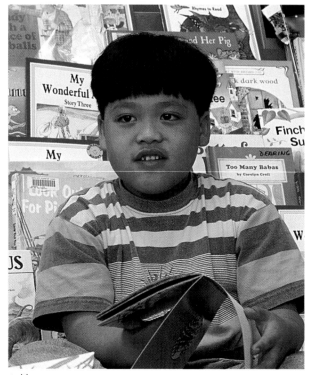

A library center

Overhead Center

This center might include stories or poems students have written, or ones you have written, on transparencies. Set the overhead projector on the floor or on a low counter or desk so that students can place transparency pages on the overhead and read from the wall. They can also use magnetic letters and clear plastic letter tiles to mix and make words, create word families, and practice blending and segmenting sounds and word parts. Include a pointer so students can track the print of the story as they read it.

Read the Room Center

On available wall space around your classroom, you can hang up wall stories and wall murals; reproductions, innovations, or retellings before they are turned into book format; word charts; posters; and so on. If possible, hang the print materials at the students' eye level. To make reading the room fun, you might provide students with, colorful or unusually shaped "read the room" glasses.

Book Boxes Center

At the book boxes center, students select books for independent reading. There should be several book boxes available, with each box containing books that are appropriate for specific reading levels. Clearly label the instructional level on each book box so that students know which box they are to select books from for paired and independent reading.

Set up the book boxes center after your students begin guided reading and you introduce a few guided reading books that you can place in each book box. Optimally, each box should contain from eight to ten different titles. Familiar read-aloud books or pupil books of shared reading Read-Together titles that you introduce may also be added to the boxes.

An overhead center

A read the room center

A book boxes center

129

Integrated Language Arts Centers

Integrated language arts centers stress reading-related activities that contribute to developing literacy. The integrated language arts centers include a writing and publishing center, a listening center, and a drama and music center.

A writing and publishing center

Writing and Publishing Center

In your writing and publishing center, provide ample materials that students can freely use for any of their writing and publishing activities. The following is a list of suggested materials for this center:

- Paper—various sizes, lined and unlined, colored, construction, drawing, class-designed, and stationery
- Mat boards, tagboard
- Writing tools, including pencils, pens, colored pencils, chalk, colored chalk, crayons, colored markers
- Envelopes
- Scissors, glue, paste, tape, rulers
- Dictionary
- Word charts that model rich language and vocabulary
- Literature books that provide good models for writing
- Storage units to hold writing folders
- Class-designed stickers or sheets for special book pages, including "Published by," "About the Author," and "Dedicated to"

Listening Center

The listening center contains audio equipment, audiocassettes, and copies of familiar books, poems, and songs that are introduced during shared reading. Students listen to recordings of the stories, poems, and songs, and follow along by reading the text. Provide blank tapes for students to record their favorite stories or poems or to practice reading a story independently or with a partner.

Drama and Music Center

This center could consist of a large box filled with props and old clothing that students can use for dressing up and playing make-believe, and for dramatizations, retellings, skits, and plays. You may also wish to keep a box of instruments and/or a piano or keyboard in this center for students to use to make sound effects for plays or to accompany the reading of stories, poems, and songs. You may wish to provide a tape recorder and blank cassettes for students to use to record their dramatizations, songs, and readings.

A listening center

A drama and music center

Skill Centers

Skill centers are the areas in which students practice skills related to reading. Skill centers include an alphabet center and a word study center, but there are many other possibilities for skill centers. You can create a center for any particular skill your students are developing.

Alphabet Center

In the alphabet center, students practice letter- and word-recognition skills through letter and word activities, such as sorting, classifying, and manipulating. Students might also practice writing, experimenting with sounds and letter symbols within the context of their own creations. You may want to make available the following materials:

- Alphabet charts
- Alphabet books
- Alphabet friezes
- Chalkboards, white boards
- Magnetic letters, letter cards
- Sand trays, tactile letters
- Paint brushes and small containers for water (for "painting" letters and words on the chalkboard)

Word Study Center

In the word study center, students experiment with building, comparing, and sorting words. Students can practice writing and spelling words; searching for words in magazines, newspapers, and books; and building word families or manipulating letters in words to make new words. The following materials might be found in a word study center:

- Magnetic letters, letter cards
- Magnetic boards or cookie sheets
- Pocket charts
- Word charts, vowel pattern charts
- Dictionary
- Newspapers, magazines, books
- Chalkboards, white boards
- Paper, pencils, crayons, markers
- High-frequency word lists

An alphabet center   A word study center

Content-Area Centers

In content-area centers, your students develop an integrated literacy because they see the applications of reading to all content areas. Content-area centers might include an art center, a math center, a science and discovery center, and a social studies center.

Art Center

The art center contains art supplies and materials for use in art or art-related projects. You may want to provide items such as the following in your art center:

- Different kinds of paper and cardboard
- Paints, paint brushes
- Crayons, markers, pencils
- Glue, scissors, tape
- Modeling clay
- Yarn, scraps of material, pipe cleaners
- Feathers, twigs
- Egg cartons, paper plates, paper cups
- Painting easels
- Old shirts or smocks to protect clothing

Math Center

The math center contains a wide range of materials for students to use in adding, subtracting, matching, patterning, constructing, graphing, and so on. The math center might include the following items:

- Found materials—buttons, shells, beans
- Commercially produced materials—blocks, jigsaw puzzles, small toys, magnetic boards
- A set of pan scales and objects to weigh, plus a means to record the measurements
- Tape measures, rulers, and yardsticks for measuring distances and sizes
- Clocks for learning to tell time
- Play money and a small cash register
- Monthly and weekly calendars, time lines
- Water or sand trays and containers of various sizes for experimentation with volumes and weights

An art center   A math center

Science and Discovery Center

A table near a window or a wide section of a window ledge makes an excellent science and discovery center. Decorate the area with charts or posters. The science center can be used for activities such as tracking the weather, growing plants, and conducting experiments. It can also be used for displaying things students bring to school, such as pine cones, shells, and rocks.

You may wish to have the science center close to the math center so materials can be shared. The water tray, for example, can be used to do flotation experiments at the science center and volume or weight experiments at the math center. You might wish to have materials such as the following in the science center:

- Magnifying glasses and a microscope
- Field glasses
- Aquarium and/or terrarium
- Thermometers for both indoor and outdoor temperatures
- Compass
- Nonfiction and fiction books and magazines on science
- Paper, pencils, and journals to record observations

Social Studies Center

Your social studies center should provide opportunities for students to explore their own community as well as other communities. Provide any of the following materials at the social studies center:

- Maps of the school, community, state, country, world
- Globes
- An atlas and almanac
- Stamps from other places
- State and national flags
- Time lines
- Photos of clothing, housing, and life in earlier times and from other cultures
- Nonfiction and fiction books and magazines about other communities and cultures

A social studies center

A science and discovery center

Resource Centers

Resource centers provide you and your students with the space and the tools to facilitate classroom learning, activities, and projects. These centers include a computer center, a block center, a simulation center, and a teacher resource center.

Computer Center

If you have computers in your classroom, arrange them so students have easy access to them and to the accompanying software. Label the software so children know which programs to use for reading, writing, math, and so on. If possible, provide a printer so that students can print out their stories, artwork, writing examples, and word lists. Display some of their computer graphics at the computer center.

Block Center

In this center, provide a variety of building materials for students to use to create three-dimensional projects. There should be blocks of different sizes, shapes, and colors. You may wish to include plastic toys, such as cars, animals, people, and scenery, so that students can create environments for their structures. Provide writing paper, pencils, and crayons for students to use to illustrate their constructions.

A computer center

A block center

Simulation Center

The simulation center is a place where students can create "real worlds" or settings that tie in with study topics they are learning in the other classroom centers. Settings might include a doctor's office, a pet store, a business office, a zoo, a grocery store, a farm, a factory, or a travel agency. Students not only help create but also run simulations, incorporating materials and features of many of the other centers, such as drama (role-playing and creating props and scenery), math (buying and selling), and science (making information cards). Simulations provide meaningful contexts for reading, writing, listening, speaking, observing, illustrating, experiencing, and doing.

Children dress up in a farm simulation center

Teacher Resource Center

It is helpful to have an area for yourself that students do not have access to, where you can store multiple copies of unread books to use for modeling or to introduce during shared and guided reading times. You might also store nonfiction and fiction titles that you can use later on during content-area studies, as well as your own teaching and information resources.

WHAT'S THE EVIDENCE?

The importance of developing a print-rich, engaging environment is supported by Morrow, 1997, 1992; Fountas & Pinnell, 1996; and Loughlin & Martin, 1987.

References cited in the "What's the Evidence?" boxes are listed in a bibliography at the end of this guide.

Managing Your Classroom

Once you have planned your classroom environment and before you implement your centers, make sure you have management strategies that you can use to establish clear expectations, rules, and responsibilities in the classroom. As students become accustomed to daily routines and signals, they will begin to move easily and quickly among activities, focus on their work, and become more independent learners.

Beginnings, Endings, and Transitions

You may wish to use some of the following strategies as children move from activity to activity during the school day:

- When students come into the room, have them read quietly for the first few minutes.

- Sing a special song; tell a short story; or recite a rhyme, poem, or chant to signal children to move on to the next activity, form a line, or clean up the centers.

- Use a brief movement exercise to help students regain their focus after an activity.

- Bring an activity or a day to closure by having the class summarize or share experiences.

Controlling Volume

The following strategies will help you quiet your students' voices:

- Whisper, and your students will quiet down to hear what you are saying.

- Have the class take a deep breath with you.

- Play some gentle music.

Gaining Attention

You can gain students' attention and help them focus by using any of the simple techniques listed below. At the beginning of the year, model the signals that you will use and the appropriate responses you will expect from students.

- Clap a rhythm.

- Ring a chime or bell.

- Sing a special song.

- Play some music.

- Use a hand signal such as raising your hand, or mime a signal.

- Designate a certain spot in the room for "Stop and Think." When you stand in that place, students should stop what they are doing and think about the activity they should do next or think about how they are behaving.

- Have the class take a deep breath with you.

Establishing Procedures and Routines

Help your students develop independence and learn to follow classroom procedures by discussing the following questions and modeling appropriate responses:

- Where do I go when I am finished?
- Where do I get supplies when I need them?
- Where do I put my things when I am finished?
- What is the clean-up signal?
- What is the signal to pay attention?

Housekeeping

Your students can learn to be responsible for their personal belongings and to help keep the classroom clean. When you set up your classroom and establish housekeeping procedures, include students in the process. Encouraging them to participate in the management and care of the classroom and its materials will deepen their sense of connection and responsibility to the environment. They can easily remember this three-part housekeeping principle:

- Students create it.
- Students care for it.
- Students clean it.

The following suggestions will help you manage classroom housekeeping:

- Discuss the need for students to be responsible for their personal items and storage areas.
- Show students where general supplies are stored, and discuss procedures for retrieving them.
- Assign students to clean-up teams or area-maintenance teams.
- Have students sing a clean-up song to let everyone know it is time to clean up.

Equipment and Materials

Discuss and model appropriate, safe ways to use equipment in the classroom. Students will need guidelines for using the following items:

- Chairs, desks, and tables
- Tape dispensers
- Staplers
- Sinks
- Pencil sharpeners
- Writing or art materials
- Overhead projector
- Cassette recorders
- VCRs
- Computers, CD-ROMs

Planning Your Day

At the beginning of the school year, you will want to gradually phase in the components of a balanced reading program. With early emergent students, the first six weeks of your language arts time may only consist of shared reading activities. Once you have established routines, you might spend the next six to eight weeks phasing in literacy and resource center activities, guided reading, and independent reading. The rest of your day would include content-area learning and thematic studies.

In a full-day kindergarten or first-grade classroom, you will have plenty of time each day to involve your students in a variety of literacy activities including guided reading instruction, writing, content-area studies, and integrated learning. If you have a half-day kindergarten classroom, it will be necessary to provide the best learning experiences possible for your students in the time you have. You will have to teach the same skills, strategies, and content areas as full-day kindergarten, but you will have less time for extended focus on the subject areas.

The following tables show sample schedules for full-day kindergarten, half-day kindergarten, and first grade.

Full-Day Kindergarten			
Morning	**Activity**	**Afternoon**	**Activity**
8:30–8:40	• Opening exercises (calendar, Daily News)	12:30–12:50	• Read-alouds • Sustained silent reading
8:40–9:15	• Poems for Sharing • Shared reading • Skills instruction • Language arts activities	12:50–1:30	• Math
9:15–10:15	• Guided reading • Independent reading • Skills instruction • Literacy centers	1:30–1:50	• Special classes (library, music, physical education)
10:15–10:30	• Recess	1:50–2:20	• Integrated studies
10:30–11:45	• Read-alouds • Model writing • Journal writing • Writer's workshop • Spelling skills and letter reproduction	2:20–2:30	• Sharing • Dismissal
11:45–12:30	• Lunch		

Half-Day Kindergarten

Morning	Afternoon	Activity
8:30–8:40	12:00–12:10	• Opening exercises (calendar, Daily News)
8:40–8:55	12:10–12:25	• Poems for Sharing • Shared reading • Skills instruction • Language arts activities
8:55–9:20	12:25–12:50	• Guided reading • Independent reading • Skills instruction • Literacy centers
9:20–9:45	12:50–1:15	• Modeled writing • Journal writing • Writer's workshop • Spelling and letter reproduction
9:45–10:05	1:15–1:35	• Read-alouds • Sustained silent reading
10:05–10:30	1:35–2:00	• Math • Integrated studies
10:30–10:50	2:00–2:20	• Special classes (library, music, physical education)
10:50–11:00	2:20–2:30	• Sharing • Dismissal

First Grade

Morning	Activity
8:30–8:40	• Opening exercises (calendar, Daily News)
8:40–8:55	• Poems for Sharing • Shared reading • Skills instruction • Language arts activities
8:55–10:15	• Guided reading • Independent reading • Skills instruction • Literacy centers
10:15–10:30	• Recess
10:30–11:45	• Read-alouds • Modeled writing • Journal writing • Writer's workshop • Spelling skills
11:45–12:30	• Lunch
Afternoon	
12:30–12:50	• Read-alouds • Sustained silent reading
12:50–1:30	• Math
1:30–1:50	• Special classes (library, music, physical education)
1:50–2:20	• Integrated studies
2:20–2:30	• Sharing • Dismissal

Meeting the Needs of All Students

The Story Box reading program is flexible, designed to meet the needs of all of the students in your classroom. Because of its gradually leveled stories, supportive language structures, and adaptable lesson plans, The Story Box can be effectively used with students who would not be considered typical learners. These include students who speak English as a second language (ESL), students with special needs who have difficulty functioning at grade level, and gifted students who require more challenging materials and activities. The lesson plans for both shared reading and guided reading indicate, with appropriate icons, which activities are best suited for ESL students, special needs students or students who need extra help, and gifted students. The Story Box is also effective at fostering the development of the multiple intelligences.

Working with ESL Students

Students who come from homes where English is spoken as a second language or not spoken at all face special challenges in the classroom. The Story Box emergent-level books help ESL students learn English through simple stories that model natural language patterns and engaging illustrations that support the text. By teaching English in meaningful contexts, The Story Box provides ESL students with a framework for building literacy understanding that can assist with their acquisition of other languages as well.

Through the shared reading and guided reading lessons, ESL students learn conventions of print, such as where print begins, the left-to-right directionality of print, and the concept that sentences begin with capital letters and end with periods or other end punctuation. They learn about proper word order, sentence construction, and grammar (syntax). They also become familiar with the sound of spoken English and increase their English vocabulary. As they learn particular skills, students absorb the underlying concept that, like their primary language, English conveys meaning (semantics), whether it is written or spoken.

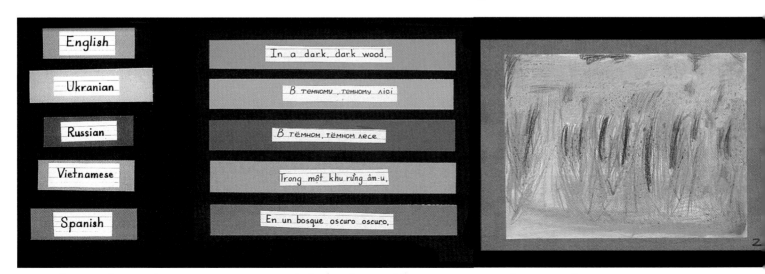

This reproduction of *In a Dark, Dark Wood* includes translations of languages represented in an ESL classroom.

The Stages of Language Acquisition

The Story Box assists ESL students at each of the five basic stages of language acquisition: (1) pre-production, (2) early production, (3) speech emergence, (4) intermediate fluency, and (5) advanced fluency. As students move naturally through these stages of language acquisition, their language proficiency improves. The Story Box assists you in teaching your ESL students about schema, graphophonic, syntactic, and semantic cues and strategies at each language proficiency level.

Pre-production: At this stage, students are nearly, if not totally, silent. They are acquiring a great deal of linguistic knowledge but are not yet able to verbalize that knowledge. Shared reading activities are wonderful for students at this level because they do not require students to participate until they are ready.

Early production: At this level of proficiency, students begin to contribute more orally. In shared reading, students recognize phrases and patterns in the story and begin to "chime in" after a couple of readings of a book. Students also can create their own adaptations of a story.

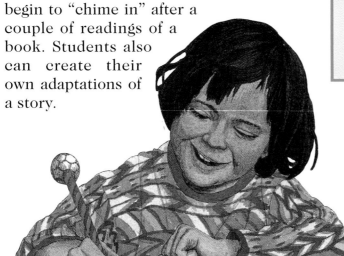

Speech emergence: Learners at this level of proficiency begin to communicate and tell stories about themselves. After brainstorming topics of interest, students can complete a related drawing or writing assignment.

Intermediate fluency: At this level, learners can begin to take more responsibility for their own language acquisition. You can use more guided reading activities in English to give students more independence. Students can read a favorite book, write to the author, or share their personal reactions to the book. They may also debate points of view or compare characters in a story.

Advanced fluency: At this level, students only need occasional assistance when, for example, they encounter an unfamiliar word or phrase. Once ESL students reach this level of proficiency, they are reading as well as native English speakers of the same age.

WHAT'S THE EVIDENCE?

From extensive research in language development, Terrell, 1977, determined five basic stages of language acquisition: preproduction, early production, speech emergence, intermediate fluency, and advanced fluency.

Selecting Books for ESL Students

To learn to read in English, ESL students need to be able to start off relying heavily on the English they already know. Choose books that contain the following five criteria: (1) common words; (2) clear spacing and font; (3) strong picture support; (4) repetition, rhyme, and pattern; and (5) clear meaning and story line.

Common words: Understanding most words is important for basic comprehension. Students don't have to be familiar with every word in a book but at the emergent level, if more than two or three words are unfamiliar, the book is probably too difficult. Books that contain nonsense words are likely to confuse and frustrate ESL readers.

Clear spacing and font: Since many students at the emergent level are working on recognizing letters and understanding basic concepts of print, it is important to select books with letters and words that are easy to see because of clear spacing and large font sizes.

Strong picture support: ESL students are more successful at reading books in which the pictures tell the story as clearly as the words do. Illustrations that carry the story line help teach new English vocabulary. Books with photographs can also be very helpful.

Repetition, rhyme, and pattern: Repetition and language patterns provide ESL students with support and allow them to use higher level skills of prediction while reading. Rhyme helps develop skills of phonological awareness, which can be much more difficult to master for ESL students because English sounds may be very different from sounds in the students' first language. When students reread, repetition, rhyme, and pattern provide them with opportunities to practice fluency and secure syntactic structures.

Clear meaning and story line: The meaning of the book needs to be clearer and more explicit for ESL students than it does for native English speakers. At the early emergent level, meaning can be conveyed with just a few words. Books at the upper emergent level have more developed story lines and a sense of beginning, middle, and end. Books that have nonsense words make reading more difficult for ESL students because they cannot use meaning and structure to figure out the words.

Many of the Story Box Read-Togethers and guided reading titles meet these criteria. See the table on the next two pages for a list of the titles recommended for use with ESL students. Some of these titles may have difficult or unknown vocabulary, but the illustrations and/or text structure will support the students during reading.

WHAT'S THE EVIDENCE?

Books that show the complex system of English in natural, meaningful ways support language acquisition in ESL students. ESL students benefit from the use of rhyme, predictability, pattern, and colorful use of the English language. Providing this structure for ESL students is supported by Braunger & Lewis, 1997; Fitzgerald, 1995; Krashen, 1981; and Terrell, 1977.

Recommended Story Box Books for ESL Students

Early Emergent Readers

Read-Togethers 1

The Farm Concert
In a Dark, Dark Wood
The Jigaree
The Monsters' Party
Mrs. Wishy-Washy
Sing a Song

Read-Togethers 2

Dan, the Flying Man
Meanies
The Red Rose
Who Will Be My Mother?

Guided Reading Set A

Brenda's Birthday
The Chocolate Cake
The Ghost
In the Mirror
Painting
A Party
Shoo, Fly!
Snowman
The Surprise
Swing
Waiting

Guided Reading Set B

The Bicycle
The Bridge
Chick's Walk
Fishing
The "Gotcha" Box
Green Grass
A Monster Sandwich
Mrs. Wishy-Washy's Tub
Rat's Funny Story
Salad
The Storm
The Tree House
Who's Going to Lick
  the Bowl?

Guided Reading Set C

Come with Me
Dan Gets Dressed
Going to School
Halloween
Jump, Jump, Kangaroo
Look Out, Dan!
Mouse Train
My Picture
Nighttime
Round and Round
What Can Jigarees Do?
What's for Lunch?

Guided Reading Set D

The Boogie-Woogie Man
Copycat
The Gifts
Happy Birthday, Frog
Houses
How to Make a Hot Dog
Ice-Cream Stick
Microscope
On a Chair
Silly Old Possum
Sunflower Seeds
Tick-Tock

Recommended Story Box Books for ESL Students

Upper Emergent Readers

Read-Togethers 3

The Hungry Giant
Lazy Mary
Obadiah
One Cold, Wet Night

Read-Togethers 4

Caterpillar's Adventure
Gloves
Milwaukee Cows
The Mirror
The Scrubbing Machine

Guided Reading Set E

The Bears' Picnic
The Bee
Flying
Little Hearts
Little Meanie's Lunch
Lost
My Home
No, No
Plop!
Stop!
Umbrella
Valentine's Day
Who Can See the
   Camel?
Who Lives Here?

Guided Reading Set F

Ducks
Ebenezer and the Sneeze
How to Make Can Stilts
I Love Chickens
Little Pig
Look for Me
My Brown Cow
Roberto's Smile
What a Mess!

Guided Reading Set G

The Fantastic Cake
Grumpy Elephant
Horace
How Many Hot Dogs?
My Mom and Dad
Oh, Jump in a Sack
Pet Shop
Roy G. Biv
Teeth
Two Little Dogs
Where Is Skunk?

Guided Reading Set H

The Best Children in the
   World
The Giggle Box
Gulp!
The Hungry Giant's Lunch
Tittle-Tattle Goose

Working with Special Needs Students

Many children start school without the necessary skills to make them successful readers. As a teacher, you need to be aware of your students' social, economic, and cultural backgrounds. Certain students may lack life experiences that would help them link new information to their prior knowledge, some may lack the language proficiency necessary for understanding the reading process, and others may not be able to attend to typical learning situations.

Like all students, special needs students require the opportunity to learn in a classroom that integrates oral and written language skills instruction and cross-curricular instruction. Such students need to experience the same exciting interactions with language and print as their peers do. While special needs students may require some specialized instruction in phonological awareness, concepts of print, phonics, and the development of reading strategies, their instruction, like that of other students, should be centered around appropriate text and engaging activities that facilitate their learning.

The Story Box guided reading titles are ideal for supporting struggling readers because of the books' gradually leveled and sequential text, predictability, picture support, natural language structures, and strong skill lessons. Because the guided reading titles are used at each student's instructional reading level, which is between 90 percent and 94 percent accuracy, even special needs readers can be successful in unlocking new words and building on previously learned skills.

The books you use with students who require extra support should

- be at the children's instructional reading level;
- challenge students to develop and use effective reading strategies;
- be gradually leveled to ensure time to practice and learn reading strategies;
- relate to ideas that students can understand;
- provide many opportunities for students to practice skills; and
- engage children in the reading process.

Developing a Special Needs Intervention Program

Students who are struggling in reading and writing and are lagging behind their classmates will benefit from an intervention program either implemented by you, the classroom teacher, or by a school specialist. By intervening at an early stage, you will be able to respond to and monitor any difficulties or confusions that your students might be experiencing in reading and writing. Early intervention prevents incorrect or unproductive reading and writing behaviors from becoming habitual.

The main objective of an intervention program is to bring struggling readers to grade level in reading and writing skills. These students need explicit instruction in phonological awareness, letter recognition, concepts of print, and phonics skills. Students with limited oral vocabularies and little experience with written stories need extra practice learning to use semantic (meaning) cues in reading and will benefit from read-alouds, shared reading, and supportive guided reading experiences. Students who don't know the alphabet and/or haven't made the mental link between sounds and symbols are unable to access graphophonic (sound-symbol) cues. They need explicit instruction in sound-symbol relationships and practice using their phonics skills in shared reading and guided reading situations. Students who are English language learners, who speak a dialect, or have had little exposure to book language may have difficulty using syntactic (structure) cues in reading. These children will also benefit from read-alouds, shared reading, and guided reading experiences that develop their language.

Meeting the needs of your struggling students requires careful planning and commitment on your part. In an intervention program, you need to spend more time with your struggling readers than you normally allot for your reading groups. Research shows that children having problems with reading need more time for reading instruction and practice but typically receive less teacher attention than their peers do.

You will need to determine the best location in your classroom to work with struggling readers, either in a small group or one-on-one. This area should be as free from distraction as possible and provide ample space for books, materials, and student involvement.

Special needs groups should be fluid and flexible, with each student receiving additional support only for as long as necessary. Observe each student's reading and writing behavior and conduct ongoing diagnostic assessments to monitor student progress. Use your observations and assessments to adapt your teaching. The assessments provided in The Story Box Assessment Kit are appropriate for all students, including those with special needs.

WHAT'S THE EVIDENCE?

Children with special needs in reading benefit from interventions that focus on developing and strengthening their reading and writing skills. The importance of meeting the needs of these children is supported by Braunger & Lewis, 1997; Iversen & Bancroft, 1997; Honig, 1996; Spear-Swerling & Sternberg, 1996; Torgesen, 1997/98; Allington & Walmsley, 1995; Shanahan & Barr, 1995; Hiebert & Taylor, 1994; Juel, 1994; and Iverson & Tunmer, 1993.

Tips for Helping Struggling Readers

- Provide a successful, supportive, learning experience that includes a wide variety of reading materials.

- Teach skills and strategies within the context of meaningful reading and writing.

- Provide instruction that focuses on gaining meaning through knowledge of words, letters, and spelling patterns.

- Help students develop fluency in their reading.

- Monitor and guide students' reading behaviors and development.

- Help students acquire strategies that move them toward independent reading.

- Provide writing opportunities that focus on necessary skills.

- Help students see themselves as readers and writers.

- Provide ample time to engage in reading a wide variety of books.

Schedules for Intervention Groups

To provide the instruction and support that students in an intervention group need, you should plan on spending 25–30 minutes each day with them. A sample one-day schedule might look like the following chart:

Sample One-Day Schedule

5 minutes	Read familiar books and do an Assessment of Reading Behavior on one student each day.
10 minutes	Introduce and practice reading a new guided reading book.
7 minutes	Teach specific skills and strategies.
8 minutes	Do a writing activity, which is often based on the story just read.

You may wish to try a two-day lesson format using a guided reading book. Your two-day schedule might look like this chart:

Sample Two-Day Schedule

	Day 1		Day 2
5 minutes	Read familiar books.	5 minutes	Read familiar books. Do an Assessment of Reading Behavior with the guided reading book from Day 1 with one student each day.
10 minutes	Introduce and practice reading a new guided reading book.	5 minutes	Reread the guided reading book from the previous day together.
10 minutes	Teach specific skills and strategies.	10 minutes	Have the group write about the guided reading book from Day 1.
		5 minutes	Teach specific skills and strategies.

Working with Gifted Students

Children who are gifted learners have talents that far surpass the expectations for their grade level. They are quite capable of using higher-level thinking skills, such as inferring, generalizing, and recognizing diverse relationships and patterns. Consequently, they need opportunities to ask and answer questions, think critically, and evaluate the results of their inquiry.

Gifted students can often pose tough but exciting challenges for you. A well-planned, integrated program of instruction can provide gifted students with the support, challenge, and freedom they need to fulfill their learning potential.

Working in cooperative learning groups helps gifted learners develop interpersonal relationships and enables them to make significant contributions to the class. Gifted students also need frequent opportunities to work on their own after they have been guided through the various processes of reading and writing. Typically, such students are highly confident in their ability to influence their own success or failure, making it possible for you to increasingly put them in charge of their own learning.

The Story Box Enrichment Readers

The Story Box Enrichment Readers are books that provide challenges in reading and offer writing opportunities for students in your classroom who are reading above the upper emergent level. The stories, plays, and poems in the Enrichment Readers provide a transition from more supportive guided reading groups to more independent, literature-circle discussion groups.

A sampling of Enrichment Readers

The Story Box Enrichment Readers have the following features:

- Complex story lines involving different cultures, times, and settings
- Well-developed characters and plots
- Complex literary elements
- New challenges in language usage, such as similes and metaphors
- Paragraphs in stories
- Detailed illustrations that support story meaning and create story atmosphere
- Illustrations that can be used for confirming the text rather than predicting it
- Illustrations that represent the concepts of the story instead of the exact words

The Enrichment Readers in The Story Box can be used by your gifted learners in small-group literature circles, paired reading, and independent reading. These books invite rereading and reflection and provide many opportunities for related activities. Here are some possible follow-up activities that will challenge students:

- Listen to recordings of the stories on the Enrichment Readers audiocassettes at the listening center.
- Make a poster that relates to the book.
- Write a script for a play based on a story. Use the story's dialogue and characters to write the play.
- Make innovations to a story, poem, or play by changing the characters, setting, events, and/or plot.
- Write about personal experiences and how they relate to the book.
- Write a new ending or sequel to the story, poem, or play.
- Write a poem based on the story and then a story based on the poem.
- Research a topic from the book.
- Make "wanted" posters of characters from the book.
- Tape record a reading of the book for others to listen to.
- Make puppets and put on a puppet show for classmates.
- Compare a story to other versions of the same story.
- Write a book review that encourages others to read the book.

Literature Circles

A literature circle is a small group of students who meet with the teacher to discuss a story they have read. Students may all discuss the same book or different books. A literature circle provides an arena in which students can articulate their views, reactions, and insights about literature and thereby begin to experience literature on a deeper level. Students have opportunities to savor language, explore an author's craft, and engage in discussions to construct meaning. More specifically, students may compare different books and books by the same author or in the same genre, analyze characters and themes in books, and discuss specific literary elements in books. Literature circles also encourage cooperation and help students become aware of diverse thinking and experiences.

The first step in creating a productive, rewarding literature circle in your classroom is to develop group ground rules. You may want to have your students help determine the rules for running the circle. In one class, the students came up with the "Five *T*s to Terrific Teamwork":

1. Take turns (share the work).
2. Tune in your ear (listen carefully).
3. Task—stay on it (do the work).
4. Take all ideas (accept others' ideas).
5. Treat each person with respect (be kind and considerate of others).

As your students begin to work in a literature circle, it is your role to model the processes and behaviors you expect from them. You may choose to start your literature circle slowly, allowing students a chance to get used to sharing and exchanging ideas before actually discussing books they have read.

How you run your literature circle will depend on the abilities of the gifted learners in your class. If your gifted students still need some support, you may wish to follow a format similar to that of silent guided reading, in which students silently read sections of a book to find literary elements, such as character, setting, and plot, and then discuss their findings. If your gifted learners are reading fluently and developing confidence in independent reading, encourage them to read books individually before meeting with you and the rest of the group. Your literature discussions can then focus on students' reactions to books and the literary elements.

Students make a character traits web for "Silly Mr. Fox" from the Enrichment Reader *Just Like Me*.

Graphic Organizers

As students respond to books during literature circles, involve them in using graphic organizers to analyze characters, plot lines, genres, and other key literary elements. To help you teach key elements in all types of literature, use the following charts, webs, and maps. These items can be modified for students of all ability levels and used across content areas.

Story structure charts include literary elements, such as the title, characters, setting (time and place), events, problem, solution, and ending of a story. Students can record summary statements about the book in each category of the chart. Once students have read several stories and recorded information about them in the story structure chart, they can begin to compare books in terms of their literary features.

Genre charts have the same categories as story structure charts but contain information about different stories in a single genre. This type of chart helps students examine the elements common to a genre and make generalizations about genres.

Genre Matrix for Fairy Tales

Title	Setting	Characters	Problem	Events	Ending
"The Three Little Pigs" from Let Me In	long ago in the country	three pigs Mr. Wolf	Mr. Wolf wanted to get in each pig's house.	• The three pigs left home and each built their own home. • Mr. Wolf blew the straw house and the stick house in. • Mr. Wolf tried to blow in the brick house.	The three pigs caught Mr. Wolf in a pot and ate him up.
"Hot Water" from Well I Never	daytime in Little Pig's house	Little Pig Mr. Wolf	Mr. Wolf said that he wanted to get in Little Pig's house because he was cold.	• Little Pig let Mr. Wolf in his house a little bit at a time. • Little Pig tied Mr. Wolf in a sack, but he got out. • Ten wolves came and tried to get Little Pig.	Little Pig scared the wolves off with hot water and lived happily ever after.

Story Structure Chart

Title	Setting Time & Place	Characters	Problem	Solution	Ending
Wet Grass	daytime a field	Ned Lottie Mom	Ned didn't want to walk in the wet grass.	Lottie and Mom talked Ned into coming with them.	Ned decided he loved the wet grass.
Yum and Yuck	morning a farm	children hen Mom	The hen didn't want eggs for breakfast.	The hen took the children to the hen house to eat worms.	The children didn't eat the hen's worms, but the hen was happy.

Semantic maps are a way to visually represent the elements, structures, and meanings of stories or poems. To make a semantic map, or mind map, students draw a circle in the center of a piece of paper and write the title of the book inside it. They add lines branching out from the circle and write in key information, such as character names or events, on the lines. Different colors may be used to represent different events, details, or hierarchies of meaning.

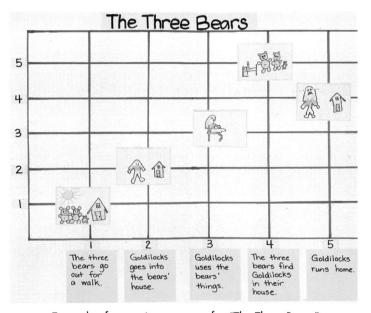

Example of an excitement map for "The Three Bears" in the Enrichment Reader *Let Me In*

Excitement maps help children understand the climax of a story. The students discuss the events in a story and, together, write a brief summary of each event. The children then draw a small illustration of each event. Next, the children place the summaries at the bottom of a large grid in sequential order and number them. The vertical axis of the grid is numbered from one to five, starting at the bottom. The students discuss the events and decide which one is the most exciting. They then place the illustration for the most exciting event above the appropriate text at the highest level (next to the number five). Then they discuss and place the illustrations for other events, one by one, in relation to the most exciting event.

Character traits webs help students identify the qualities or traits of characters that are evident through their actions in stories. On a piece of paper, students write the name of a character in a circle or draw the character in the center. They add lines branching out from the circle or drawing and write the character's traits on the lines. Then they add more lines and write examples of the character's actions in the book that reveal those traits.

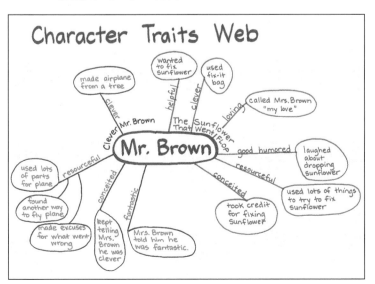

WHAT'S THE EVIDENCE?

Literature circles allow students to respond to books that they have read and learn more about the features of good stories. The works of Au, Carroll, Scheu, 1997; Christie, Enz, & Vukelich, 1997; Morrow, 1997; Fountas & Pinnell, 1996; and Daniels, 1994, promote the use of literature circles in helping students develop an ownership of literacy as they learn about the elements of literature.

Working with Multiple Intelligences

As you strive to meet the needs of all the students in your class, consider their different learning modalities. Howard Gardner (1983) argues that people have different ways of learning and representing knowledge and that everyone has capabilities that can be developed and enhanced in the right learning environment. Gardner has identified eight intelligences: (1) linguistic-verbal, (2) logical-mathematical, (3) musical, (4) visual-spatial, (5) bodily-kinesthetic, (6) interpersonal, (7) intrapersonal, and (8) naturalist. The learning environment in your classroom should accommodate all of the intelligences.

Linguistic-verbal: This type of intelligence is the capacity to use words effectively, either orally or in writing. People with developed linguistic-verbal intelligence can verbally convince others of a course of action, convey feelings and concepts, and remember information they have heard.

Logical-mathematical: This type is the capacity to use numbers and patterns effectively and to reason well. Logical-mathematical intelligence creates the ability to pursue linear thought patterns and explore and understand abstract systems of thought.

Musical: As suggested by its name, musical intelligence is the capacity to perceive, discriminate, transform, and create musical forms. Musical intelligence emerges earlier than all other intelligences.

Visual-spatial: This intelligence is the capacity to perceive the visual world and re-create or recognize it in other forms. Visual-spatial intelligence enables a person to form mental images and produce or manipulate a concrete representation of those images.

Bodily-kinesthetic: People with this intelligence have the capacity to use the whole body to express ideas and feelings and to use their hands to produce or transform objects. Bodily-kinesthetic intelligence includes a sense of timing, smoothness of movement, and the ability to combine the actions of mind and body.

Interpersonal: This is the capacity to perceive and make distinctions in the moods, intentions, motivations, and feelings of other people. This intelligence can include sensitivity to facial expressions, voice, and gestures. People with this ability can influence and direct others.

Intrapersonal: Intrapersonal intelligence is the capacity to develop self-knowledge and an understanding of self-motivation and emotions. This intelligence includes having an accurate picture of personal strengths and limitations and the ability to use self-discipline to change actions and perceptions.

Naturalist: This is the ability to recognize the characteristics, value, purpose, and interrelationships of plants and animals in one's enviroments.

WHAT'S THE EVIDENCE?

The importance of meeting the individual needs of students is discussed by Campbell, 1992, and Gardner, 1983.

Creating Theme and Topic Studies

Theme and topic studies are a form of inquiry in which students find answers to their questions through integrated learning experiences. Themes are the big ideas that give structure to content and build connections between different topic studies. A theme and topic study approach to teaching and learning is motivating for students because it is built around the students' interests, it allows them to participate through a variety of learning modalities, and it increases students' active participation in their own learning. Theme and topic studies

- integrate reading, writing, listening, and speaking into content-area instruction;
- help create a collaborative and cooperative environment;
- engage students in problem-solving, constructing meaning, and critical and creative thinking;
- increase students' comprehension and vocabulary;
- help develop skills and establish a purpose for learning;
- meet the needs and interest levels of all students through whole-group, small-group, and independent activities;
- promote inquiry and investigation of ideas and concepts;
- relate learning to real-life situations;
- make connections between the school, home, community, and cultural backgrounds; and
- develop a community of learners.

If you adopt a theme and topic study approach to teaching and learning, you can use the Story Box shared reading lesson plans as a resource. Thematic links, such as change, cycles, or relationships, and topic studies, such as friends, family, and pets are suggested in each shared reading lesson plan. Many of the integrating language arts and cross-curricular activities will help you develop theme and topic studies. The Bookshelf, a bibliography of related literature that appears at the end of the lesson plan, will assist you in collecting resources.

A complete list of the themes and topics identified for the Story Box Read-Together books begins on page 177. The list also includes the Story Box guided reading books and other books published by The Wright Group that may be used with each theme or topic.

WHAT'S THE EVIDENCE?

The integration of reading and writing across the content areas is supported by Guillaume, 1998; Morrow, 1997; Armbruster, 1992; Olson & Gee, 1991; and Ogle, 1986.

Using the KWHL Process to Create a Theme and Topic Study

How do you generate a theme and topic study? One of the best ways is to use an expanded KWL process. The KWL inquiry process allows students to focus on questions that form the structure for the area of study. The expanded inquiry process, KWHL, adds a new component—the *how* of learning:

- K–What do you *know* about a topic?
- W–What do you *want* to know?
- H–*How* will you learn about it?
- L–What did you *learn?*

The following table explains the four steps of the KWHL inquiry process and teaching strategies for each step.

KWHL Strategies and the Inquiry Process

Launching the Inquiry (activate schema and set a purpose for learning)	Exploring the Theme and Topic (refine and rethink ideas and information)	Celebrating the Inquiry Process (summarize and evaluate as meaning is reconstructed)
1. What do you know? (K) • Make language experience charts. • Scaffold information. • Make charts and webs. • Brainstorm ideas. • Provide hands-on experiences. • Have students draw what they know. **2. What do you want to know? (W)** • Organize questions • Categorize questions. • Determine areas of interest.	**3. How will you learn about it? (H)** • Provide multiple resources (fiction, nonfiction, poetry, newspapers, magazines, computer access, films, parents, community members). • Use whole-group, small-group, partner, and independent activities. • Use read-alouds. • Use shared reading. • Create graphic organizers. • Teach note-taking. • Engage students in dramatizations and creative movement. • Have students illustrate what they're learning. • Have students write captions. • Provide hands-on experiences. • Engage students in activities to develop vocabulary and comprehension. • Create centers to promote additional learning experiences. • Provide journals for observing, illustrating, and recording information.	**4. What did you learn? (L)** • Reach conclusions, make predictions, and ask more questions. • Create displays and projects. • Make Big Books and wall murals. • Have students write about it. • Have students discuss with others. • Expand charts, webs, and maps. • Make links to personal experiences. • Have students give presentations. • Extend learning to new topics and themes.

Launching the Inquiry

Begin the KWHL inquiry process by selecting a topic or theme. Your curriculum may have topics and themes that you are required to use. Other topics may arise from a shared experience such as a field trip, a classroom visitor, community events, or an assembly. The interests of the children in your class will also lead you to interesting topics for inquiry

After you have selected a topic or theme of study, begin by asking the children, *"What do you know?"* Prompt children to tell you what they know and record their answers. By finding out what the children already know about a topic, you can find out who the "class experts" are and who might be a bit confused about the topic.

The second step in the KWHL inquiry process is to ask the children, *"What do you want to know?"* One type of teaching strategy involves giving the children 3"x 5" cards on which to write any questions they have about the topic. Write some questions of your own.

Place the students' questions that ask about similar areas of interest in a column on a wall chart. Start new columns for each new area of interest. Often the children will be inspired to contribute additional questions after they see the questions their classmates have about the topic.

Next, help the children create headings for each group of questions. You might introduce specialized vocabulary at this point, such as the scientific terms *behavior, physical features,* and *habitat.* New vocabulary can be learned easily through repeated use within the context of the inquiry.

Exploring the Theme and Topic

The next step in the KWHL inquiry process is to brainstorm ideas for a *"How will you learn about it?"* chart. Encourage students to list as many ways that they might be able to learn about their topic as possible. Make sure students consider local experts and other people who can serve as valuable resources. Parents can be very helpful, sharing artifacts and contacting resource people if you keep them advised of the topics of study. Maintain an ongoing list of ways to learn so that children can refer to it often and add to it when they think of new strategies.

Many nonfiction books are too difficult for emergent readers to read independently, so you will need to read aloud to the children. Model how to use a table of contents, an index, captions, and a glossary by thinking aloud as you read. Highlight for children any features of the text that make reading and understanding the text easier such as headings, bold print, and diagrams. By showing them how to use nonfiction texts, you will build the foundation for independent use when children become more fluent readers.

Child learning about the features of nonfiction books

Children also need to be shown how to record information efficiently. Use each of the headings from the *"What do you want to know?"* questions chart to create headings for note-taking charts or for a large wall web on the topic. Make sure that the children understand that the information recorded on the class web is directly related to the questions they have asked about the topic.

When you read aloud a book to the students, pause frequently to allow students to think about and discuss the new information. Children should be encouraged to listen for information that will answer their questions. Ask students to tell you what they heard that might answer one of the class questions about the topic. Add to your class web or note charts as you and the children locate information. Have the children tell you where the information should be recorded by describing why it belongs under a particular category heading. Guide students to help you record only the most important words in note format, never whole sentences. Have student volunteers add words to the web whenever feasible to make this an interactive shared writing opportunity.

Often you'll find interesting facts that don't fit under any of the category headings your class has on the questions chart. You may want to add a section to your class web or note pages titled "Other Interesting Facts."

During your read-aloud and shared reading sessions, you will come across important words that may be new to the children. Create a class vocabulary chart to record new or important words. Invite the children to illustrate the words. Add to the chart whenever you discover words that are integral to the theme or topic study. This chart will serve as an important spelling resource for the children. It will also be a valuable tool for emergent readers and ESL learners.

Continue to read aloud from nonfiction and fiction titles and use other media to gather information. Create a chart that displays the book covers of each book you read. Have children volunteer to illustrate book covers and attach their illustrations to the chart under the headings *Nonfiction* or *Fiction.* This type of classifying activity will help children begin to understand the different conventions of genres and learn which types of books are more useful during inquiry.

Teachers often have children dramatize fiction stories. Nonfiction lends itself to drama quite readily. Students love to act out concepts that they are learning. Provide many opportunities for children to show you what they have learned with role-playing, skits, and creative movement.

Another way to engage students in their learning is to have them illustrate what they are learning. Each child could draw on individual chalkboards as you read aloud books on the topic of inquiry. Pause to let students share their drawings and explain to each other what they learned. Have children work together to create posters, models, or other displays that illustrate important concepts. Use shared, interactive writing activities, such as writing captions for illustrations. As a class, revise and edit the captions.

Celebrating the Inquiry Process

The third stage of the KWHL inquiry process is the celebratory stage. Students are asked to reach conclusions and make predictions about the topic or theme. They can also create displays, make Big Books and murals, and expand on the information already recorded on charts, webs, and maps. Students share what they have learned with each other and with visiting students, friends, and family. Help the students organize and plan a culminating activity, make invitations or flyers, and practice for their presentations.

A wall chart displaying illustrated book covers of books that the children read during a topic study about ducks

Sample Early Emergent Theme and Topic Study

Read-Together: *Three Little Ducks*

Theme: Cycles

Topics: Ducks, Growth, and Ponds

The following is a sample theme and topic study built around the early emergent Read-Together *Three Little Ducks* and based on the KWHL inquiry process. The featured theme is Cycles and the topics are Ducks, Growth, and Ponds. This study was developed to meet the needs and interests of the students. It is important to remember this model is meant as a guideline for your own creative development of activities for theme and topic studies.

Launching the Inquiry

Begin by finding out what the children already know about the life cycle of ducks. Give each child a blank speech bubble and invite the students to write a sentence about ducks in the speech bubble. Then have the children draw a picture of themselves. Create a wall chart with the children's portraits and speech bubbles, and label the chart "What do you know about ducks?"

Next, ask the children what they want to learn about ducks. Give the students 3" x 5" cards and ask them to write one question that they have about ducks. Then group the questions together by subject and create headings for each subject area. Make another wall chart titled "What do you want to learn about ducks?" with the headings and questions.

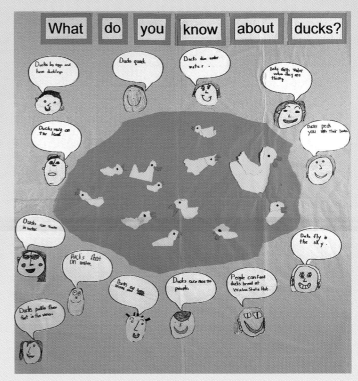

"What do you know about ducks?" wall chart

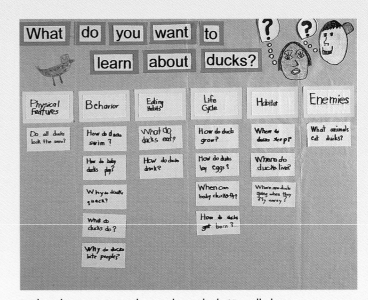

"What do you want to learn about ducks?" wall chart

Exploring the Theme and Topics

Look at the wall chart "What do you want to learn about ducks?" and at the questions that are listed under the subject header "Life Cycle." Ask the children how they can learn about ducks and their life cycle. Encourage them to think of all the different resources available to them, such as fiction and nonfiction books from the library, pictures, films or videos, the Internet, and other people. Have the children write their ideas at the top of a blank sheet of paper and illustrate the sentence. Then place the sentences and drawings on a wall chart labeled "How can we learn about ducks?"

After the students identify the ways that information can be located, begin the research process on the life cycle of ducks using the resources that the children identify in the activity above. The children will need your help and guidance, especially with any nonfiction books that might be too difficult for emergent readers to read independently. On a large wall web, write and record summary statements about the information that the children learn.

Once students have an understanding of the life cycle of ducks, expand the learning to include other animals that hatch from eggs. Ask the children to find out what other kinds of animals hatch from eggs and then list the different animals on a chart.

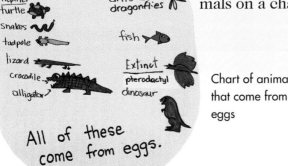

Chart of animals that come from eggs

Invite the children to draw a picture of each animal next to the word on the chart. You can also continue the research to find out the size and color of the different eggs, the environment that they hatch in, and how long it takes to hatch the eggs.

Encourage the students to continue their research on ducks in an effort to answer their other questions. Have the children refer to the wall chart "What do you want to learn about ducks?" to see their questions regarding ducks' physical features, behavior, eating habits, habitat, and enemies.

To learn the different physical features of ducks, ask the children to select a favorite duck to research. Have the students write summary statements about what they learn about the ducks and draw pictures of the ducks. Attach the pictures and summary statements to a wall mural to show the varieties of ducks studied.

Wall mural of varieties of ducks

To learn about one kind of habitat for ducks, lead a topic study on ponds. Provide resources for the children, including inviting a nature expert to talk to them about ponds and the wildlife around or in ponds. Then take a class field trip to a pond. Collect a sample of pond water to bring back to the classroom for the students to examine with a magnifying glass, microscope, or flashlight. Encourage the students to keep observation journals to record or illustrate what they see and learn about ponds. Create a wall chart that depicts all of the living and nonliving things that are found in or around a pond. Have the children write the words on the chart, along with small pictures of the words.

Wall chart of living and nonliving things in or around a pond

Celebrating the Inquiry Process

At the end of the theme study, ask the children to write a summary statement of one fact that they learned about ducks, and then invite them to draw a picture to go with their sentence. With the sentences and pictures, create a large wall chart titled "What did you learn about ducks?"

Next, with your students help, create a Duck Museum for parents and other classes to visit. Begin by brainstorming a list of things that visitors to the Duck Museum could do at the exhibit. Include activities like poetry readings of "Six Little Ducks" at the poetry center, a display of duck books in the library center, and a tape recording of "Three Little Ducks" at the listening center. Have the students make word cards for a duck innovation on the poem "To Market, to Market" and place

those at the pocket chart center for the guests to recreate. At the computer center, allow guests to look at the information available on ducks on a CD-ROM encyclopedia. If you have other monitors, display computer drawings of ducks that the children make.

Gather the charts and artwork from the theme study and display those on the classroom walls. To add a humorous touch to the classroom, ask the children to bring in their rubber duckies and place them in the Duck Museum. Then determine the different job duties, including museum docents. Allow the children to alternate their jobs during the "show."

"What did you learn about ducks?" wall chart

Sample Upper Emergent Theme and Topic Study

Read-Together:
Gloves

Theme: Environments

Topic: Woodland Animals

The following is a sample theme and topic study built around the upper emergent Read-Together *Gloves* and based on the KWHL inquiry process. The featured theme is Environments and the topic is Woodland Animals. This study was developed to meet the needs and interests of the students. It is important to remember this model is meant as a guideline for your own creative development of activities for theme and topic studies.

Launching the Inquiry

As you begin the study, have the children share all that they know about each of the animals—beetle, centipede, spider, caterpillar, frog, and mouse—in the book *Gloves*. Create a wall chart titled "What do you know about woodland animals?" with summary statements that the children write about the animals. Invite them to draw pictures of the animals and place those on the wall chart as well.

For the next step, ask the children what they want to know about woodland animals. Give each of the children 3" x 5" cards and invite them to write one question that they have about any of the animals in *Gloves*. Then determine the different subjects that the questions relate to, and create headings for each subject area. Finally, make a wall chart titled "What do you want to know about woodland animals?" with the children's questions placed under the appropriate subject headings.

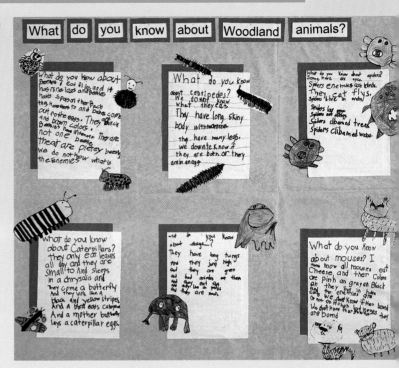

"What do you know about woodland animals?" wall chart

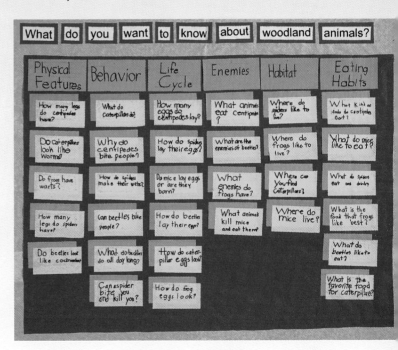

"What do you want to know about woodland animals?" wall chart

Exploring the Theme and Topic

Refer to the wall chart "What do you want to know about woodland animals?" Notice the different themes and topics the students are interested in. For this study, the theme of Environments is explored in connection with the topic Woodland Animals. Ask the children how they can learn about woodland animals. Write the children's responses on a wall chart labeled "How can we learn about woodland animals?"

How Can We Learn about Woodland Animals?
- read books
- watch real animals
- ask our parents
- look on the CD-Rom encyclopedia
- talk to a scientist
- look on the INTERNET
- watch a video
- think about times we saw these animals before

Wall chart that lists the different ways to learn about woodland animals

Then begin the research process by reading fiction and nonfiction books about different woodland animals to the students. Provide several resources the students will need to do their research, including additional fiction and nonfiction books, pictures, films or videos, the Internet, and other people. Introduce students to real woodland animals by bringing in mice for students to observe, providing observation boxes of insects, and taking a nature walk in a forest. Also, invite a nature expert to the class to discuss woodland areas and the animals found there. Encourage the children to keep an observation or nature journal to record and illustrate what they see and learn.

Next, ask the students to work with a partner, in a small group, or independently to research one of the woodland animals from *Gloves*. Encourage them to investigate the physical features of the animal, what types of shelter the animal needs, the animal's enemies, what the animal eats, the life cycle of the animal, and any other related information. Then ask the children to draw a picture of their animal and use the computer center to write summary statements of what they learned about the animal. Place the information about the animals on a wall chart so the students can see what their classmates researched and learned about all the woodland animals in *Gloves*.

Individual research projects on woodland animals

Have the students also create a data chart with their information that shows all the different woodland animals' characteristics.

Data Chart

	Beetle	Centipede	Spider	Caterpillar
Physical Features	• wings • 6 legs • head, thorax and abdomen	• two antennaes • many pairs of legs • long, skinny body	• 8 legs	• long body • short fat legs
Behavior	• can fly • can swim • burrow in wood	• active at night	• build webs	• eat all day long • crawl
Life Cycle	• lay eggs • larvae • pupae • adult beetle	• lays eggs	• lays eggs	• egg • caterpillar • chrysalis • butterfly
Enemies	• other beetles • humans • birds	• humans • birds	• birds, toads • snakes • lizards	• birds
Habitat	• on trees • on plants • under logs & rocks • in water	• under stone • under logs	• holes underground • in plants • in houses	• on plants
Eating Habits	• roots • bark • wood	• meat from other animals	• grasshoppers • insects • other spiders	• leaves

Data chart of woodland animals' characteristics

For the information the children collect about the life cycles of woodland animals, have them draw pictures that show the stages of life each animal goes through. Then have the students place the images in a circle and label the development stages, as well as the type of animal cycle. Place all of the cycles together on a class wall chart.

Class wall chart of animal life cycles

Encourage the children to continue to research the habitats or environment of woodland animals by inviting them to create a wall mural that shows the four seasons of a woodland environment. Divide the chart into four sections, with one section for each season. Have the children draw what each season looks like in a woodland environment, as well as the animals and their different types of shelter.

Also create an innovation on *Gloves*, changing the setting and characters. To determine the new setting and animals that live there, have the children research other environments such as oceans, fields, and deserts. In this study, the children choose a desert environment with a roadrunner, a scorpion, a tarantula, and a Gila monster all looking for a new home in an old cowboy boot.

Finally, have the children compare their own environment to the woodland environment. Encourage them to consider the types of shelter they live in and the different kinds of people that live there. Invite the students to also learn about the different environments that people live in all around the world.

Celebrating the Inquiry Process

Once the students have completed their study of woodland animals and environments, encourage them to share what they have learned. Turn your classroom into a woodland, with large, construction-paper trees; paper leaves on the floor; and shelters for animals. Remember to display all the charts and artwork from the theme study around the classroom. Invite parents, guardians, and other classes to visit. During their visit, have the students do presentations on the woodland animals they researched. Invite them to make animal headbands that they can wear during the presentation and while they guide the visitors through the "woodland."

Make sure that you have activities for the guests at the classroom centers. Display books and pictures of woodland animals at the library center, show stories that the students write about their woodland animals at the writing center, and provide an audiocassette and copy of the book *Gloves* at the listening center. Have the students do a choral reading of the Poems for Sharing poster "Hear Those Baby Mice" at the poetry center, and show the computer center that the children use when writing reports like the one they wrote on woodland animals.

Developing the School-Home Connection

Parents and caregivers are your students' first teachers. A parent's or guardian's influence is the most important factor in early childhood development, behavior, and motivation to read; and home language, culture, and literary experiences are the basis for literacy. Good family literacy habits promote positive attitudes toward reading and writing.

A child's success in school depends a great deal on his or her early literacy experiences in the home, the most important of which is regular and interactive storybook reading. When family members read to their children at home, they build a love of stories and language, background knowledge, phonological awareness, vocabulary, and an understanding of print concepts and sound-symbol relationships. For families and teachers to effectively work together to support children, there must be open lines of communication between the home and school and a level of trust that allows families to become actively involved in children's school education.

The table at right shows teacher and family responsibilities in this crucial school-home connection.

The School-Home Learning Connection

The Teacher's Role

- Keep families informed on a regular basis of what is happening in the classroom.

- Let families know what students are studying.

- Tell families how you want to handle homework.

- Inform families how you are teaching subject areas and skills.

- Explain to families how they can become involved in the classroom.

- Share school policies, current trends, and research to help families understand your teaching philosophies.

- Include families in the learning process.

- Invite families to share aspects of their culture, jobs, travels, and so on.

- Invite parents or guardians to volunteer in the classroom.

- Make home visits a few times a year.

- Develop family workshops for

  - using reading, writing, and spelling strategies at home;

  - doing math activities at home;

  - making books together at home; and

  - building an understanding of how to enhance phonological awareness and phonics at home.

- Explain programs and ideas clearly, without using teacher jargon.

- Send home weekly newsletters.

- Involve families in filling out home surveys and questionnaires.

- Telephone parents or guardians to discuss positive comments about their children.

- Organize a parent information night.

- Sponsor a class mascot that makes a family visit each weekend; family members can help the child write about the mascot's visit.

- Place bookmarks with a special message in books that students take home so parents know what to expect of their child. You can choose from the following messages: "I can read this book by myself. I would love to read it to you," "I can read most of this book, but you may need to help me," or "I can't read this book all by myself, but I'd love to have you read it to me." All of these bookmarks are available as reproducibles on page 176.

The Family's Role

- Set realistic expectations for your child.

- Create a home environment that supports learning.

- Be aware of what is happening at school.

- Attend programs, performances, open houses, and conferences.

- Volunteer in the classroom and provide teaching assistance at home.

- Read to your child every day.

- Listen to your child read every day.

- Write to and with your child every day.

- Ask daily questions about your child's experiences in school.

- Be involved in your child's education.

Supporting Learning at Home

Parents and guardians often ask teachers what they can do at home to support their child's learning. Presented on the following pages are some quick reading and writing reminders that can be sent home to help family members become involved in their child's reading and writing development. You may want to send these reminders home throughout the first few weeks of school or include them periodically in your weekly newsletters for parents and guardians.

Ways to Support Learning at Home

Read to Your Child

- Read bedtime stories, stories while traveling, letters from relatives and friends, and any interesting items or articles from newspapers and magazines.
- Post a funny cartoon on the refrigerator and read it with your child.
- Take books to read to your child while you wait at the doctor's office, in the car, or whenever you have a few spare minutes.
- Keep books accessible and in common places, such as in the car, in the kitchen, and near the television.
- Encourage your child to enjoy a book instead of watching television.
- Make sure your child has a special place to keep his or her own books.
- Provide space and materials at home that will encourage your child to read and write.
- Designate a family reading night once a week.
- Read nursery rhymes and poetry and sing songs together.
- Play word games.
- Help your child look for words and/or letters that he or she knows in the print world around you.
- Talk about letters, sounds, and words.

Tell Stories Together

- Make up stories that involve your child as a character or tell stories about your childhood or other family members.
- Encourage your child to tell stories to you and other family members.
- Ask your child to tell you the plot of a book or movie. (Retelling aids retention and summarizing skills.)

Encourage Your Child to Write

- Encourage your child to write thank-you notes and letters to relatives.
- Make holiday or birthday cards with your child.
- Give your child materials to make a special book to give as a gift.
- Suggest that your child write a letter to someone special or important.
- Encourage your child to keep a daily journal. A blank book or diary makes a special gift for your child.
- Invite your child to help you make lists.
- Encourage your child to write about memorable experiences and share them with you.

Encourage Your Child to Read

- Ask your child to read to you or to another family member.
- Encourage your child to read to you while you are cooking, driving, or waiting for appointments.
- Listen carefully and appreciatively when your child reads to you.
- Read alternate pages with your child: you read one page and they read the next page.
- Have your child read just the dialogue for one character in a story, perhaps the main character, while you read the rest of the book.
- A few children's television programs, such as "Reading Rainbow" and "Wonderworks" on PBS, are worthwhile and can be springboards to reading.

Visit the Public Library

- Take your child to the library to check out books, magazines, audiocassettes, and videos.
- Attend library programs and participate in summer reading programs.
- Spend time at the library on a rainy Saturday.
- Help your child research a topic of special interest to him or her.
- Put new children's books on hold if they are not available to check out.

Turn Off the TV and VCR

- To make your child a better reader and writer, any kind of creative play, trips to the store or library, or family discussions are better than watching television. When children are watching television or videos, they are not reading, writing, using their imaginations, or socializing.

- If books and writing and drawing materials are always handy, your child will always have something to do besides watching television or videos.

Let Your Child See You Read and Write

- Make sure your child sees you reading and writing at home so that he or she doesn't conclude that these are just things that are done at school. Show them that these activities are useful and enjoyable and have real-life purposes.

- Talk about interesting newspaper or magazine articles you have read. Show your child what a headline is, where the comics are, and how readers decide which articles they want to read.

- Show your child the books you read. Tell a little about the characters and the plot and why you like or don't like certain books.

- Share the magazines you read and explain why you subscribe to them.

- Talk about the ways you use reading and writing in your own job or daily routine.

Write to Your Child

- Post job lists on the refrigerator, tuck a note in your child's lunch box, or write a letter telling how proud you are of him or her.

- Write a short letter to your child, sharing your feelings about a problem, asking for help, or saying, "I'm sorry."

- Make shopping lists together.

- Write reminder notes to each other.

- Write to your child when you have trouble reaching him or her. Written words have their own special power.

Using Take-Me-Homes Stories and Activities

The Story Box reading program includes take-home stories and activities to help create a strong reading and writing link between school and home. Known as Take-Me-Homes, these activities correspond to the shared reading Read-Togethers and selected guided reading titles, giving students a way to share with family members the reading experiences they are having in school.

Once the Take-Me-Homes have been shared with family members, children can keep them as part of their home library. Students can store their Take-Me-Homes in things like empty shoe boxes, cereal boxes, baskets, or on bookshelves. Then they can return to them again and again to practice reading skills.

The Take-Me-Homes provide opportunities for students to

- behave as successful readers;
- read independently and fluently;
- read to parents, siblings, dolls, stuffed animals, and so on;
- create a home reading library; and
- bring family members together to support them in their beginning reading.

WHAT'S THE EVIDENCE?

The home environment and how teachers interact with families affect how children learn. The importance of supporting a strong home-school connection has been discussed by Genisio, 1998; Strickland, 1998a; Christie, Enz, & Vukelich, 1997; Morrow, 1997; Moustafa, 1997; Honig, 1996; Routman, 1996; Morrow & Paratore, 1993; and Adams, 1990.

Poor Old Polly

by STACIA

Teacher Instructions: Have each child write his or her name in the blank and illustrate this page to make a cover. Then have the children fill in the blanks on the next page and illustrate the page. Help students staple the pages together along the left side. Copy the next page multiple times to make a longer booklet. Invite the children to read their booklets.

Permission is given to teachers who purchase Story Box pupil editions to reproduce these pages for classroom and take-home use only. ©1999 Wright Group Publishing, Inc.

33

Old Polly found a HOUS_____;
she swapped it for a ____mous____.

32

Old Polly found a HAT_____;
she swapped it for a BAT.

32

Shared Reading Planning Form

A Week with _____   Date _____

Day	Sharing the Reading	Skills Bank	Integrating Language Arts	Comments/ Observations/ Assessments
Day 1				
Day 2				
Day 3				
Day 4				
Day 5				

For more information about this form, see pages 84–85.

Guided Reading Planning Form

Reading group _____

Date	Title	Set	Challenging concepts	Difficult vocabulary/ sentence structure

For more information about this form, see pages 121–123.

Strategies	Skills	Comments	Assessments

THE STORY BOX

I can read
this book
by myself.
I would
love to
read it
to you.

THE STORY BOX

I can read
most of
this book,
but you
may have
to help
me.

THE STORY BOX

I can't
read this
book all
by myself,
but I'd
love to
have you
read it to
me.

For more information about these bookmarks, see page 167.

Use this list to help you develop theme and topic studies. The Story Box Read-Togethers, as well as Story Box guided reading titles and other books published by The Wright Group, are organized by theme and topic.

Themes

Celebrations

The Birthday Party (SUNSHINE™, Set AA)

Eating Out (SUNSHINE™ Community Books, Set 1)

Happy Birthday, Frog (The Story Box®, Set D)

Monster Party (The Song Box®, Set C)

The Monsters' Party (The Story Box® Read-Togethers 1)

My Birthday Party (Visions™, Set C)

She'll Be Comin' 'Round the Mountain (The Song Box®, Set D)

Community

And the Sidewalk Went All Around (The Song Box®, Set C)

The Bus (TWiG® Books, Set CC)

Call 911 (TWiG® Books, Set D)

City Lights (Visions™, Set A)

Come with Me (The Story Box®, Set C)

Down to Town (SUNSHINE™, Set A)

Garbage (Wonder World™, Set D)

Going to School (The Story Box®, Set C)

Our Street (SUNSHINE™, Set D)

"To Market, to Market" (Heritage Readers™, Book AA)

To Town (The Story Box® Read-Togethers 1)

Creativity

At School (SUNSHINE™, Set BB)

The Circus (Wonder World™, Set D)

Down by the Bay (The Song Box®, Set B)

I Found a Can (TWiG® Books, Set DD)

I Write (SUNSHINE™, Set CC)

Monster Party (The Song Box®, Set C)

The Monsters' Party (The Story Box® Read-Togethers 1)

My Picture (The Story Box®, Set C)

My Story (Wonder World™, Set A)

Painters (TWiG® Books, Set C)

Painting (The Story Box®, Set A)

To Town (The Story Box® Read-Togethers 1)

Cycles

"The House that Jack Built" (Heritage Readers™, Book AA)

Making Patterns (TWiG® Books, Set CC)

The Migration (Wonder World™, Set D)

Nighttime (The Story Box®, Set C)

Poor Old Polly (The Story Box® Read-Togethers 2)

The Snow (SUNSHINE™ Community Books, Set 1)

Three Little Ducks (The Story Box® Read-Togethers 2)

"The Ugly Duckling" (Heritage Readers™, Book AA)

Water (SUNSHINE™ Nonfiction, Set C)

What Season Is This? (Wonder World™, Set A)

Where Is Water? (TWiG® Books, Set CC)

Who Will Be My Mother? (The Story Box® Read-Togethers 2)

Environments

Chick's Walk (The Story Box®, Set B)

City Lights (Visions™, Set A)

The Divers (Wonder World™, Set C)

The Farm (SUNSHINE™, Set CC)

Grandpa, Grandpa (The Story Box® Read-Togethers 2)

In My Backyard (Visions™, Set A)

In the Mountains (TWiG® Books, Set AA)

In the Sea (SUNSHINE™ Nonfiction, Set B)
My Apartment (Visions™, Set A)
Nests (Wonder World™, Set A)
Underground (TWiG® Books, Set D)

Exploration: Discovery

And the Sidewalk Went All Around (The Song Box®, Set C)
Bug-Watching (TWiG® Books, Set B)
Dan, the Flying Man (The Story Box® Read-Togethers 2)
I Like to Find Things (SUNSHINE™ Nonfiction, Set B)
In a Dark, Dark Wood (The Story Box® Read-Togethers 1)
The Jigaree (The Story Box® Read-Togethers 1)
Microscope (The Story Box®, Set D)
Under Water (TWiG® Books, Set C)
What's That? (SUNSHINE™, Set DD)

Relationships

Big Sister (Visions™, Set D)
Down by the Bay (The Song Box®, Set B)
Grandpa, Grandpa (The Story Box® Read-Togethers 2)
Hairy Bear (The Story Box® Read-Togethers 2)
How Many Kittens? (TWiG® Books, Set DD)
The Jigaree (The Story Box® Read-Togethers 1)
Little Brother (The Story Box®, Set B)
Love Is (Visions™, Set C)
The More We Get Together (The Song Box®, Set B)
Poor Old Polly (The Story Box® Read-Togethers 2)
The Red Rose (The Story Box® Read-Togethers 2)
Three Little Ducks (The Story Box® Read-Togethers 2)
Who Will Be My Mother? (The Story Box® Read-Togethers 2)
Wood (TWiG® Books, Set D)

Relationships: Conflict

Copycat (The Story Box®, Set D)
Fee-Fie-Foe-Fum (The Song Box®, Set C)
"The Little Old Woman and Her Pig" (*Heritage Readers*™, Pocketful of Posies)
Look Out! (SUNSHINE™, Set C)
Meanies (The Story Box® Read-Togethers 2)
Mrs. Wishy-Washy (The Story Box® Read-Togethers 1)
No, You Can't! (SUNSHINE™, Set D)
"Three Billy Goats Gruff" (*Heritage Readers*™, Book AA)
Who's Going to Lick the Bowl? (The Story Box®, Set B)

Relationships: Cooperation

"Androcles and the Lion" (*Heritage Readers*™, Book AA)
Basketball (Wonder World™, Set A)
Cookies (TWiG® Books, Set A)
The Farm Concert (The Story Box® Read-Togethers 1)
Helping Dad (SUNSHINE™, Set B)
I Can Do Anything! (SUNSHINE™, Set B)
Making Music (Wonder World™, Set B)
Meanies (The Story Box® Read-Togethers 2)
Sing a Song (The Story Box® Read-Togethers 1)
Tossed Salad (TWiG® Books, Set DD)
Yes, Ma'am (The Story Box® Read-Togethers 1)

Relationships: Responsibility

Big Sister (Visions™, Set D)
Little Brother (SUNSHINE™, Set B)
The Nest (The Story Box®, Set C)
Old MacDonald Had a Farm (The Song Box®, Set A)
Yes, Ma'am (The Story Box® Read-Togethers 1)

Topics

Animals

The Animal Fair (The Song Box®, Set A)
Chick's Walk (The Story Box®, Set B)
The Farm (SUNSHINE™, Set CC)
In the Sea (SUNSHINE™ Nonfiction, Set B)
Legs, Legs, Legs (Wonder World™, Set B)
Old MacDonald Had a Farm (The Song Box®, Set A)
Poor Old Polly (The Story Box® Read-Togethers 2)
Sing a Song (The Story Box® Read-Togethers 1)
"The Traveling Musicians" (*Heritage Readers*™, Book AA)
Underground (TWiG® Books, Set D)
Who Lives in This Hole? (TWiG® Books, Set C)
The Zoo (Wonder World™, Set B)

Baby Animals

Big and Little (SUNSHINE™, Set C)
Closer and Closer (TWiG® Books, Set B)
How Many Kittens? (TWiG® Books, Set DD)
My Puppy (SUNSHINE™, Set B)
The Nest (The Story Box®, Set C)
Three Little Ducks (The Story Box® Read-Togethers 2)
"The Ugly Duckling" (*Heritage Readers*™, Book AA)

Bears

"A Bear Went over the Mountain" (*Heritage Readers*™, Pocketful of Posies)
The Bicycle (The Story Box®, Set B)
Big and Little (SUNSHINE™, Set C)
Bigger and Bigger (TWiG® Books, Set DD)
Hairy Bear (The Story Box® Read-Togethers 2)
Who Likes the Cold? (TWiG® Books, Set D)

Behaviors (Good and Bad)

Fee-Fie-Foe-Fum (The Song Box®, Set C)
Gary the Ghost (The Song Box®, Set C)
I Want Ice Cream (The Story Box®, Set A)
Little Brother (SUNSHINE™, Set B)
Meanies (The Story Box® Read-Togethers 2)
Shoo! (SUNSHINE™, Set C)
Sometimes (Wonder World™, Set A)

Chores

Garbage (Wonder World™, Set D)
Mrs. Wishy-Washy's Tub (The Story Box®, Set B)
My Room (TWiG® Books, Set AA)
Yes, Ma'am (The Story Box® Read-Togethers 1)

Ducks

Three Little Ducks (The Story Box® Read-Togethers 2)
Time for Sleep! (SUNSHINE™, Set C)
"The Ugly Duckling" (*Heritage Readers*™, Book AA)

Families

Bath Time (Wonder World™, Set A)
Big Sister (Visions™, Set D)
"The Farmer in the Dell" (*Heritage Readers*™, Pocketful of Posies)
Hairy Bear (The Story Box® Read-Togethers 2)
How Many Kittens? (TWiG® Books, Set DD)
I Love My Family (SUNSHINE™, Set C)
Little Brother (The Story Box®, Set B)
My Family (SUNSHINE™, Set CC)
My Mama (Visions™, Set A)
She'll Be Comin' 'Round the Mountain (The Song Box®, Set D)
Sing a Song (The Story Box® Read-Togethers 1)
Who Will Be My Mother? (The Story Box® Read-Togethers 2)

Fantasy Character

Chinese Kites (TWiG® Books, Set A)

Dressing Up (SUNSHINE™, Set AA)

Fee-Fie-Foe-Fum (The Song Box®, Set C)

If You Meet a Dragon… (The Story Box®, Set A)

Meanies (The Story Box® Read-Togethers 2)

Monster Party (The Song Box®, Set C)

The Monsters' Party (The Story Box® Read-Togethers 1)

What Can Jigarees Do? (The Story Box®, Set C)

Farm Animals

The Farm (SUNSHINE™, Set CC)

Father's Old Gray Whiskers (The Song Box®, Set B)

Green Grass (The Story Box®, Set B)

How Many Kittens? (TWiG® Books, Set DD)

Mrs. Wishy-Washy's Tub (The Story Box®, Set B)

Old MacDonald Had a Farm (The Song Box®, Set A)

Time for Sleep! (SUNSHINE™, Set C)

Who Will Be My Mother? (The Story Box® Read-Togethers 2)

Yes, Ma'am (The Story Box® Read-Togethers 1)

Farms

The Farm (SUNSHINE™, Set CC)

The Farm Concert (The Story Box® Read-Togethers 1)

How Many Kittens? (TWiG® Books, Set DD)

Mrs. Wishy-Washy (The Story Box® Read-Togethers 1)

Old MacDonald Had a Farm (The Song Box®, Set A)

Shoo! (SUNSHINE™, Set C)

Feelings

At School (SUNSHINE™, Set BB)

Fee-Fie-Foe-Fum (The Song Box®, Set C)

Hairy Bear (The Story Box® Read-Togethers 2)

I Like… (SUNSHINE™, Set BB)

I Want Ice Cream (The Story Box®, Set A)

In a Dark, Dark Wood (The Story Box® Read-Togethers 1)

Jack-o'-Lantern (TWiG® Books, Set D)

My Day (SUNSHINE™ Nonfiction, Set A)

Sometimes (Wonder World™, Set A)

"The Ugly Duckling" (*Heritage Readers*™, Book AA)

Yankee Doodle (The Song Box®, Set D)

Flying

The Airplane (SUNSHINE™, Set DD)

Dan Gets Dressed (The Story Box®, Set C)

Dan, the Flying Man (The Story Box® Read-Togethers 2)

Flight Deck (Wonder World™, Set D)

Helicopter over Hawaii (TWiG® Books, Set A)

I Can Fly (SUNSHINE™, Set A)

The Migration (Wonder World™, Set D)

Would You Like to Fly? (TWiG® Books, Set C)

Friends

Come and Play, Sarah! (SUNSHINE™ Nonfiction, Set D)

Come with Me (The Story Box®, Set C)

"Friends" (*Heritage Readers*™, Book AA)

The Jigaree (The Story Box® Read-Togethers 1)

The More We Get Together (The Song Box®, Set B)

My Birthday Party (Visions™, Set C)

My Friend at School (Visions™, Set C)

The Playground (TWiG® Books, Set AA)

Snowball Fight! (Wonder World™, Set B)

The Surprise (The Story Box®, Set A)

Team Sports (TWiG® Books, Set BB)

Gardening

Goober Peas (The Song Box®, Set D)
The Red Rose (The Story Box® Read-Togethers 2)
Sunflower Seeds (The Story Box®, Set D)

Geography/Landscape

Dan, the Flying Man (The Story Box® Read-Togethers 2)
Dinner! (SUNSHINE™, Set A)
Helicopter over Hawaii (TWiG® Books, Set A)
The Migration (Wonder World™, Set D)
My Three-Wheeler (Visions™, Set D)
Nature Hike (TWiG® Books, Set DD)

Geography/Mapping

Dinner! (SUNSHINE™, Set A)
In a Dark, Dark Wood (The Story Box® Read-Togethers 1)
Nature Hike (TWiG® Books, Set DD)
There Is a Planet (SUNSHINE™, Set C)

Gifts

The Birthday Party (SUNSHINE™, Set AA)
The Gifts (The Story Box®, Set D)
My Birthday Party (Visions™, Set C)
The Red Rose (The Story Box® Read-Togethers 2)

Grandparents

The Bus (TWiG® Books, Set CC)
The Gifts (The Story Box®, Set D)
Grandpa, Grandpa (The Story Box® Read-Togethers 2)
The Letter (TWiG® Books, Set BB)
My Letter (Wonder World™, Set C)
Our Grandad (SUNSHINE™, Set BB)
Our Granny (SUNSHINE™, Set B)
She'll Be Comin' 'Round the Mountain (The Song Box®, Set D)
This Old Man (The Song Box®, Set B)

Growth

Beautiful Flowers (Wonder World™, Set B)
Big and Little (SUNSHINE™, Set C)
The Flower Box (TWiG® Books, Set AA)
I Can (Visions™, Set B)
The Seed (Wonder World™, Set A)
Sunflower Seeds (The Story Box®, Set D)
Three Little Ducks (The Story Box® Read-Togethers 2)
Trees (TWiG® Books, Set B)
"The Ugly Duckling" (*Heritage Readers*™, Book AA)

Health Care

Bare Feet (Visions™, Set B)
Cleaning Teeth (Wonder World™, Set C)
Ice Cream (SUNSHINE™, Set D)
Mrs. Wishy-Washy (The Story Box® Read-Togethers 1)
Shopping (SUNSHINE™, Set AA)

Health/Cleanliness

Bare Feet (Visions™, Set B)
Bath Time (Wonder World™, Set A)
Bubbles (SUNSHINE™, Set BB)
Cleaning Teeth (Wonder World™, Set C)
Father's Old Gray Whiskers (The Song Box®, Set B)
Ice Cream (SUNSHINE™, Set D)
The Laundromat (Visions™, Set B)
Mrs. Wishy-Washy's Tub (The Story Box®, Set B)
Sing a Song (The Story Box® Read-Togethers 1)

Math

The Ants Go Marching (The Song Box®, Set A)
The Farm (SUNSHINE™, Set CC)
Grandpa, Grandpa (The Story Box® Read-Togethers 2)
Measure It (TWiG® Books, Set DD)
One Bird Sat on the Fence (Wonder World™, Set B)

One, One, Is the Sun (The Story Box®, Set D)

"One, Two, Three, Four, Five" (*Heritage Readers*™, Book AA)

Rainy Day Counting (TWiG® Books, Set CC)

This Old Man (The Song Box®, Set B)

Uncle Buncle's House (SUNSHINE™, Set C)

Movement

The Ants Go Marching (The Song Box®, Set A)

At the Playground (Visions™, Set C)

Basketball (Wonder World™, Set A)

Getting Fit (Wonder World™, Set A)

I Can Jump (SUNSHINE™, Set D)

I Go, Go, Go (SUNSHINE™, Set DD)

"Itsy Bitsy Spider" (*Heritage Readers*™, Pocketful of Posies)

The Jigaree (The Story Box® Read-Togethers 1)

Jump, Jump, Kangaroo (The Story Box®, Set C)

The Playground (TWiG® Books, Set AA)

This Old Man (The Song Box®, Set B)

Music

The Farm Concert (The Story Box® Read-Togethers 1)

Happy Birthday, Frog (The Story Box®, Set D)

Making Music (Wonder World™, Set B)

Sing a Song (The Story Box® Read-Togethers 1)

This Old Man (The Song Box®, Set B)

"The Traveling Musicians" (*Heritage Readers*™, Book AA)

Ocean

The Divers (Wonder World™, Set C)

Down by the Bay (The Song Box®, Set B)

Grandpa, Grandpa (The Story Box® Read-Togethers 2)

In the Sea (SUNSHINE™ Nonfiction, Set B)

Look Out, Dan! (The Story Box®, Set C)

Ocean Waves (TWiG® Books, Set BB)

Under Water (TWiG® Books, Set C)

Water (SUNSHINE™ Nonfiction, Set C)

Parties

The Birthday Party (SUNSHINE™, Set AA)

Monster Party (The Song Box®, Set C)

The Monsters' Party (The Story Box® Read-Togethers 1)

My Birthday Party (Visions™, Set C)

The Pajama Party (SUNSHINE™, Set B)

A Party (The Story Box®, Set A)

Paths

And the Sidewalk Went All Around (The Song Box®, Set C)

Dinner! (SUNSHINE™, Set A)

In a Dark, Dark Wood (The Story Box® Read-Togethers 1)

Performing Arts

The Boogie-Woogie Man (The Story Box®, Set D)

Magic! (TWiG® Books, Set C)

Moccasins (TWiG® Books, Set A)

The Monsters' Party (The Story Box® Read-Togethers 1)

To Work (SUNSHINE™, Set B)

Pet Care

Bath Time (Wonder World™, Set A)

Going to the Vet (SUNSHINE™, Set D)

Mrs. Wishy-Washy (The Story Box® Read-Togethers 1)

Mrs. Wishy-Washy's Tub (The Story Box®, Set B)

My Cat (SUNSHINE™ Nonfiction, Set B)

Wood (TWiG® Books, Set D)

Predators

Chick's Walk (The Story Box®, Set B)
I Like to Eat… (SUNSHINE™, Set C)
Look Out! (SUNSHINE™, Set C)
One Bird Sat on the Fence (Wonder World™, Set B)
The Red Rose (The Story Box® Read-Togethers 2)
"Sheep and Coyote" (*Heritage Readers™*, Pocketful of Posies)
Underground (TWiG® Books, Set D)
What's for Lunch? (The Story Box®, Set C)

Safety

Call 911 (TWiG® Books, Set D)
Grandpa, Grandpa (The Story Box® Read-Togethers 2)
Look Out, Dan! (The Story Box®, Set C)
Nature Hike (TWiG® Books, Set DD)
"One, Two, Three, Four, Five" (*Heritage Readers™*, Book AA)
Stop! (Wonder World™, Set C)
To Town (The Story Box® Read-Togethers 2)

Sound

Hello, Hello, Hello (SUNSHINE™, Set D)
Listen (Visions™, Set D)
Old MacDonald Had a Farm (The Song Box®, Set A)
She'll Be Comin' 'Round the Mountain (The Song Box®, Set D)
The Storm (The Story Box®, Set B)
Time for Sleep! (SUNSHINE™, Set C)
To Town (The Story Box® Read-Togethers 1)
Walking, Walking (TWiG® Books, Set D)
The Wind (Wonder World™, Set D)

Space

Gravity (Wonder World™, Set D)
The Jigaree (The Story Box® Read-Togethers 1)
Night Sky (TWiG® Books, Set BB)
Space Journey (SUNSHINE™, Set BB)
The Space Shuttle (SUNSHINE™ Nonfiction, Set D)
What Can Jigarees Do? (The Story Box®, Set C)

Trading

Poor Old Polly (The Story Box® Read-Togethers 2)
"To Market, to Market" (*Heritage Readers™*, Book AA)
"Where I Can Dance" (*Heritage Readers™*, Book AA)

Transportation

The Airplane (SUNSHINE™, Set DD)
And the Sidewalk Went All Around (The Song Box®, Set C)
Dan, the Flying Man (The Story Box® Read-Togethers 2)
Flight Deck (Wonder World™, Set D)
Getting There (Wonder World™, Set B)
Going to School (The Story Box®, Set C)
Helicopter over Hawaii (TWiG® Books, Set A)
I've Been Working on the Railroad (The Song Box®, Set D)
My Uncle's Truck (Visions™, Set D)
Our Car (SUNSHINE™, Set C)
To Town (The Story Box® Read-Togethers 1)

Water and Mud

Baby Gets Dressed (SUNSHINE™, Set A)
Bare Feet (Visions™, Set B)
Just Look at You! (SUNSHINE™, Set AA)
Mrs. Wishy-Washy (The Story Box® Read-Togethers 1)

Woods

In a Dark, Dark Wood (The Story Box® Read-Togethers 1)
In the Forest (TWiG® Books, Set D)
Nature Hike (TWiG® Books, Set DD)

Use this list to help you develop theme and topic studies. The Story Box Read-Togethers, as well as Story Box guided reading titles and other books published by The Wright Group, are organized by theme and topic.

Themes

Celebrations

Birthdays (SUNSHINE™ Read-Togethers, Set 1)

Bunny Hop (The Song Box®, Set H)

"Humpty Dumpty and Alice" (*Heritage Readers™*, Book A)

The Hungry Giant's Birthday Cake (The Story Basket®, Set C)

Masks (Wonder World™, Set E)

Milwaukee Cows (The Story Box® Read-Togethers 4)

Our Tree House (TWiG® Books Read-Togethers, Set 1)

Party Time at the Milky Way (SUNSHINE™, Set I)

The Pirate Feast (The Story Basket®, Set B)

Who's There? (The Story Box® Read-Togethers 4)

Will It Rain on the Parade? (Wonder World™, Set J)

Change

Boring Old Bed (SUNSHINE™, Set J)

Cowboy Jake (SUNSHINE™, Set H)

Milwaukee Cows (The Story Box® Read-Togethers 4)

Miss Mary Mack (The Song Box®, Set G)

Obadiah (The Story Box® Read-Togethers 3)

Community

"The Boy Who Cried Wolf" (*Heritage Readers™*, Book A)

Busy Bees (The Song Box®, Set F)

City Senses (TWiG® Books, Set FF)

Communities (Wonder World™, Set F)

Going to the Park with Granddaddy (Visions™, Set F)

The Marketplace (Visions™, Set G)

Mr. Beekman's Deli (The Story Basket®, Set B)

The Night Train (The Story Box®, Set G)

People Can Build (SUNSHINE™ Nonfiction, Set E)

The Scrubbing Machine (The Story Box® Read-Togethers 4)

Will It Rain on the Parade? (Wonder World™, Set J)

Creativity

A Bottle Garden (Wonder World™, Set F)

Ballyhoo! (The Story Basket®, Set B)

"Block City" (*Heritage Readers™*, Book A)

The Jumbaroo (The Story Basket®, Set A)

The Magic Store (SUNSHINE™, Set J)

Masks (Wonder World™, Set E)

Milwaukee Cows (The Story Box® Read-Togethers 4)

Mix It Up (TWiG® Books, Set EE)

Mud Soup (The Song Box®, Set H)

A Name Garden (SUNSHINE™ Nonfiction, Set H)

Our Tree House (TWiG® Books Read-Togethers, Set 1)

Smarty Pants (The Story Box® Read-Togethers 3)

Cycles

Caterpillar's Adventure (The Story Box® Read-Togethers 4)

Day and Night (TWiG® Books, Set F)

Fall (SUNSHINE™ Community Books, Set 2)

Frog on a Log (The Song Box®, Set F)

Munch, Munch, Munch! (The Song Box®, Set E)

No, No (The Story Box®, Set E)

One Cold, Wet Night (The Story Box® Read-Togethers 3)

Spring (SUNSHINE™ Community Books, Set 2)

To the Ocean (TWiG® Books, Set EE)

When the Sun Goes Down (Wonder World™, Set H)

Where Are the Seeds? (Wonder World™, Set E)

Environments

Camouflage (SUNSHINE™ Nonfiction, Set F)

Don't Throw It Away! (Wonder World™, Set G)

Gloves (The Story Box® Read-Togethers 4)

A House for Me (TWiG® Books, Set FF)

In the Desert (SUNSHINE™, Set E)

In the Rain Forest (TWiG® Books, Set FF)

My Home (The Story Box®, Set E)

My Secret Place (Wonder World™, Set I)

Over in the Meadow (The Song Box®, Set G)

Save a Tree for Me (The Song Box®, Set F)

Sleeping Out (The Story Box®, Set F)

Exploration

The Big Toe (The Story Box® Read-Togethers 3)

Caterpillar's Adventure (The Story Box® Read-Togethers 4)

What Is in the Closet? (The Story Box® Read-Togethers 4)

Where Is Skunk? (The Story Box®, Set G)

Perspective

Animals Hide and Seek (TWiG® Books, Set EE)

Biggles the Bug-Happy Bug (The Song Box®, Set H)

Camouflage (SUNSHINE™ Nonfiction, Set F)

Caterpillar's Adventure (The Story Box® Read-Togethers 4)

Fast, Faster, Fastest (TWiG® Books, Set F)

From the Air (Wonder World™, Set F)

Like My Daddy (Visions™, Set H)

The Mirror (The Story Box® Read-Togethers 4)

Shadows (Wonder World™, Set H)

Under a Microscope (SUNSHINE™ Nonfiction, Set J)

Relationships

Boo-Hoo (The Story Box® Read-Togethers 3)

Dog and Cat (The Story Basket®, Set A)

Hiking with Dad (Wonder World™, Set I)

"Jack Sprat" (*Heritage Readers™*, Book B)

My Buddy, My Friend (Visions™, Set G)

My Friend Jess (Wonder World™, Set H)

My Mom and Dad (The Story Box®, Set G)

One Cold, Wet Night (The Story Box® Read-Togethers 3)

Our Tree House (TWiG® Books Read-Togethers, Set 1)

"Stone Soup for Sharing" (*Heritage Readers™*, Book B)

There's a Hole in the Bucket (The Song Box®, Set G)

What Is in the Closet? (The Story Box® Read-Togethers 4)

Working for Dad (Visions™, Set F)

Relationships: Conflict

The Big Toe (The Story Box® Read-Togethers 3)

Bunny Hop (The Song Box®, Set H)

Don't You Laugh at Me! (SUNSHINE™, Set F)

Fire and Water (The Story Box®, Set H)
Gloves (The Story Box® Read-Togethers 4)
Lazy Mary (The Story Box® Read-Togethers 3)
The Meanies' Trick (The Story Box® Read-Togethers 4)
The Mirror (The Story Box® Read-Togethers 4)
Move Over! (The Story Basket®, Set C)
Mr. Bitter's Butter (The Story Basket®, Set C)
The Music Machine (SUNSHINE™ Read-Togethers, Set 2)
Once an Austrian Went Yodeling (The Song Box®, Set G)
The Scrubbing Machine (The Story Box® Read-Togethers 4)
Wishy-Washy Day (The Story Basket®, Set A)
Woosh! (The Story Box® Read-Togethers 3)

Relationships: Conflict/Cooperation

"Hugh Idle" (*Heritage Readers*™, Book B)
The Hungry Giant (The Story Box® Read-Togethers 3)
The Little Yellow Chicken (SUNSHINE™ Read-Togethers, Set 2)
Rum-Tum-Tum (The Story Box®, Set F)
"Stone Soup for Sharing" (*Heritage Readers*™, Book B)
The Wicked Pirates (SUNSHINE™ Read-Togethers, Set 2)

Relationships: Cooperation

Along Comes Jake (SUNSHINE™, Set F)
At the Car Wash (Visions™, Set H)
Busy Bees (The Song Box®, Set F)
"The Elves and the Shoemaker" (*Heritage Readers*™, Book A)
The Hungry Giant's Birthday Cake (The Story Basket®, Set C)
The Hungry Giant's Soup (The Story Basket®, Set A)

I Can Do It Myself (Visions™, Set H)
Our Tree House (TWiG® Books Read-Togethers, Set 1)
Sand Castles (Wonder World™, Set I)
Two Little Dogs (The Story Box®, Set G)

Relationships: Responsibility

The Big Roundup (Wonder World™, Set I)
Griffin, the School Cat (SUNSHINE™, Set G)
Tess and Paddy (SUNSHINE™, Set J)

Topics
Bees

The Bee (The Story Box®, Set E)
Busy Bees (The Song Box®, Set F)
Danger (The Story Box®, Set G)
The Hike at Day Camp (Visions™, Set F)
The Hungry Giant (The Story Box® Read-Togethers 3)
Over in the Meadow (The Song Box®, Set G)
Scared (TWiG® Books, Set E)

Buying and Selling

Annabel (The Story Basket®, Set A)
Boo-Hoo (The Story Box® Read-Togethers 3)
Little Car (SUNSHINE™, Set G)
The Marketplace (Visions™, Set G)
Miss Mary Mack (The Song Box®, Set G)
Mr. Bitter's Butter (The Story Basket®, Set C)
Mr. Whisper (SUNSHINE™, Set H)

Caterpillars and Butterflies

Cabbage Caterpillar (SUNSHINE™, Set J)
Caterpillar's Adventure (The Story Box® Read-Togethers 4)
Munch, Munch, Munch! (The Song Box®, Set E)
Where Is My Caterpillar? (Wonder World™, Set J)

Chores

Along Comes Jake (SUNSHINE™, Set F)
Dishy-Washy (The Story Basket®, Set C)
The Family (SUNSHINE™ Community Books, Set 2)
Hay Making (Wonder World™, Set H)
"Little Boy Blue" (*Heritage Readers*™, Book A)
Milking (Wonder World™, Set H)
The Scrubbing Machine (The Story Box® Read-Togethers 4)
There's a Hole in the Bucket (The Song Box®, Set G)
Wishy-Washy Day (The Story Basket®, Set A)
Working for Dad (Visions™, Set F)

City/Country

From the Air (Wonder World™, Set F)
Milwaukee Cows (The Story Box® Read-Togethers 4)

Clowns

The Clown in the Well (The Story Box®, Set H)
Face Painting (Wonder World™, Set H)
The Ha-Ha Party (SUNSHINE™, Set J)
Masks (Wonder World™, Set E)
Old Grizzly (SUNSHINE™, Set G)
Smarty Pants (The Story Box® Read-Togethers 3)

Dairy Animals

Goggly Gookers (The Story Basket®, Set A)
Milking (Wonder World™, Set H)
Milwaukee Cows (The Story Box® Read-Togethers 4)
"The Purple Cow" (*Heritage Readers*™, Book B)
Wake up, Mom! (SUNSHINE™, Set E)
What Comes from a Cow? (SUNSHINE™ Nonfiction, Set G)

Families

The Best Children in the World (The Story Box®, Set H)
The Family (SUNSHINE™ Community Books, Set 2)
Family Names (Visions™, Set E)
Grandma's Heart (Wonder World™, Set J)
Hiking with Dad (Wonder World™, Set I)
Lazy Mary (The Story Box® Read-Togethers 3)
Like My Daddy (Visions™, Set H)
"Little Red Riding Hood" (*Heritage Readers*™, Book A)
Mom's Birthday (SUNSHINE™, Set I)
My Mom and Dad (The Story Box®, Set G)

Fantasy Characters

Gravity (The Song Box®, Set E)
The Haunted House (The Story Box®, Set G)
The Hungry Giant's Soup (The Story Basket®, Set A)
"In the Cave of the One-Eyed Giant" (*Heritage Readers*™, Book B)
The Meanies Came to School (The Story Basket®, Set B)
The Meanies' Trick (The Story Box® Read-Togethers 4)
"Rumpelstiltskin" (*Heritage Readers*™, Book B)
Superkids (SUNSHINE™ Read-Togethers, Set 2)

Farm Animals

"Ask Mr. Bear" (*Heritage Readers*™, Book A)
Barn Dance (The Story Box®, Set F)
The Big Roundup (Wonder World™, Set I)
Boo-Hoo (The Story Box® Read-Togethers 3)
Donkey Work (Wonder World™, Set J)
Farms (SUNSHINE™ Nonfiction, Set H)
I Love Chickens (The Story Box®, Set F)
Mishi-na (SUNSHINE™, Set I)
Move Over! (The Story Basket®, Set C)

One Cold, Wet Night (The Story Box® Read-Togethers 3)
Wishy-Washy Day (The Story Basket®, Set A)

Farms

Barn Dance (The Story Box®, Set F)
Farms (SUNSHINE™ Nonfiction, Set H)
Hay Making (Wonder World™, Set H)
I Love Chickens (The Story Box®, Set F)
"Little Boy Blue" (*Heritage Readers*™, Book A)
Milking (Wonder World™, Set H)
The Mirror (The Story Box® Read-Togethers 4)
Move Over! (The Story Basket®, Set C)
Old Malolo Had a Farm (SUNSHINE™ Read-Togethers, Set 2)
There's a Hole in the Bucket (The Song Box®, Set G)
Wishy-Washy Day (The Story Basket®, Set A)

Feelings

The Big Toe (The Story Box® Read-Togethers 3)
Boo-Hoo (The Story Box® Read-Togethers 3)
Do Not Open This Book! (The Story Basket®, Set C)
"The Frog Prince" (*Heritage Readers*™, Book B)
It's Noisy at Night (Wonder World™, Set F)
Little Hearts (The Story Box®, Set E)
The Meanies' Trick (The Story Box® Read-Togethers 4)
Mr. Grump (SUNSHINE™, Set E)
Scared (TWiG® Books, Set E)
What Is in the Closet? (The Story Box® Read-Togethers 4)
Who Spilled the Beans? (The Story Basket®, Set A)
Why Cry? (SUNSHINE™ Nonfiction, Set J)

Feet

The Big Toe (The Story Box® Read-Togethers 3)
Bunny Hop (The Song Box®, Set H)
"The Elves and the Shoemaker" (*Heritage Readers*™, Book A)
"Feet" (*Heritage Readers*™, Book B)
My Feet Are Just Right (SUNSHINE™ Nonfiction, Set J)
The Poor Sore Paw (SUNSHINE™, Set H)
Whose Shoes? (TWiG® Books, Set F)

Fire

Chicken for Dinner (The Story Box®, Set E)
A Fire at the Zoo (SUNSHINE™, Set H)
I Smell Smoke! (SUNSHINE™, Set F)
Obadiah (The Story Box® Read-Togethers 3)
Touch (TWiG® Books, Set EE)

Food

Chicken for Dinner (The Story Box®, Set E)
How Many Hot Dogs? (The Story Box®, Set G)
The Hungry Giant (The Story Box® Read-Togethers 3)
The Hungry Giant's Birthday Cake (The Story Basket®, Set C)
"Jack Sprat" (*Heritage Readers*™, Book B)
Mom's Diet (SUNSHINE™, Set J)
The Pirate Feast (The Story Basket®, Set B)
The Predator (The Song Box®, Set F)
"Stone Soup for Sharing" (*Heritage Readers*™, Book B)
What Comes from a Cow? (SUNSHINE™ Nonfiction, Set G)

Gardens

The Bee (The Story Box®, Set E)
Caterpillar's Adventure (The Story Box® Read-Togethers 4)
The Earthworm (Wonder World™, Set I)
Goggly Gookers (The Story Basket®, Set A)
A Name Garden (SUNSHINE™ Nonfiction, Set H)
The Pumpkin (The Story Box®, Set G)
The Seed (SUNSHINE™, Set F)
"The Tale of Peter Rabbit" (*Heritage Readers*™, Book B)
What Do I See in the Garden? (Wonder World™, Set F)

Geography/Mapping

The Big Toe (The Story Box® Read-Togethers 3)
Dear Tom (Wonder World™, Set J)
The Map Book (SUNSHINE™ Nonfiction, Set J)
Party Time at the Milky Way (SUNSHINE™, Set I)
The Pirate Feast (The Story Basket®, Set B)

Giants

The Giant's Boy (SUNSHINE™, Set H)
The Giant's Stew (SUNSHINE™ Read-Togethers, Set 3)
The Hungry Giant (The Story Box® Read-Togethers 3)
The Hungry Giant's Birthday Cake (The Story Basket®, Set C)
The Hungry Giant's Lunch (The Story Box®, Set H)
The Hungry Giant's Soup (The Story Basket®, Set A)
"In the Cave of the One-Eyed Giant" (*Heritage Readers*™, Book B)
"Jack and the Bean Stalk" (*Heritage Readers*™, Book B)

Imagination

Behind the Rocks (Wonder World™, Set E)
"Block City" (*Heritage Readers*™, Book A)
Earthquake! (Wonder World™, Set F)
Fizz and Splutter (The Story Box®, Set F)
The Giant's Stew (SUNSHINE™ Read-Togethers, Set 3)
Mrs. Muddle Mud-Puddle (SUNSHINE™ Read-Togethers, Set 2)
The Night Train (The Story Box®, Set G)
What Is in the Closet? (The Story Box® Read-Togethers 4)
Why? (TWiG® Books, Set F)

Insects

Busy Bees (The Song Box®, Set F)
Cabbage Caterpillar (SUNSHINE™, Set J)
Caterpillar's Adventure (The Story Box® Read-Togethers 4)
Communities (Wonder World™, Set F)
"Feet" (*Heritage Readers*™, Book B)
In the Rain Forest (TWiG® Books, Set FF)
Munch, Munch, Munch! (The Song Box®, Set E)
One Cold, Wet Night (The Story Box® Read-Togethers 3)
Plop! (The Story Box®, Set E)
Spider Legs (TWiG® Books, Set FF)
Spider, Spider (SUNSHINE™, Set E)

Machines

Behind the Rocks (Wonder World™, Set E)
Engines (SUNSHINE™ Nonfiction, Set E)
The "Get-Up" Machine (SUNSHINE™, Set I)
Machines (TWiG® Books, Set E)
Move It (Wonder World™, Set E)
My Brother's Motorcycle (Visions™, Set G)
The Scrubbing Machine (The Story Box® Read-Togethers 4)

Mice

Gloves (The Story Box® Read-Togethers 4)
Mr. Beekman's Deli (The Story Basket®, Set B)
Pet Shop (The Story Box®, Set G)
"Three Blind Mice" (*Heritage Readers*™, Book A)

Mirrors

Like My Daddy (Visions™, Set H)
The Mirror (The Story Box® Read-Togethers 4)
Yippy-Day-Yippy-Doo! (SUNSHINE™, Set E)

Movement

Ballyhoo! (The Story Basket®, Set B)
Barn Dance (The Story Box®, Set F)
Bunny Hop (The Song Box®, Set H)
Buster (TWiG® Books, Set E)
Going to the Park with Granddaddy (Visions™, Set F)
Kitzikuba (The Story Basket®, Set B)
Move It (Wonder World™, Set E)
Obadiah (The Story Box® Read-Togethers 3)
The Roller Coaster (SUNSHINE™, Set G)
Shadows (Wonder World™, Set H)
Skating (The Story Box®, Set E)
Smarty Pants (The Story Box® Read-Togethers 3)

Music and Dance

Biggles the Bug-Happy Bug (The Song Box®, Set H)
Milwaukee Cows (The Story Box® Read-Togethers 4)
Rum-Tum-Tum (The Story Box®, Set F)

Parties

Biggles the Bug-Happy Bug (The Song Box®, Set H)
The Hungry Giant's Birthday Cake (The Story Basket®, Set C)
Mrs. Barnett's Birthday (SUNSHINE™, Set J)
Party Time at the Milky Way (SUNSHINE™, Set I)
The Pirate Feast (The Story Basket®, Set B)
Who's There? (The Story Box® Read-Togethers 4)

Pets

Annabel (The Story Basket®, Set A)
Baby Bumblebee (The Song Box®)
Bill Grogan's Goat (The Song Box®)
Buster (TWiG® Books, Set E)
Cats (Wonder World™, Set F)
Cats, Cats, Cats (The Story Basket®, Set B)
Donkey Work (Wonder World™, Set J)
Forty-Three Cats (SUNSHINE™ Read-Togethers, Set 3)
The Humongous Cat (SUNSHINE™ Read-Togethers, Set 1)
What Is in the Closet? (The Story Box® Read-Togethers 4)
Woosh! (The Story Box® Read-Togethers 3)

Problem-Solving

Boo-Hoo (The Story Box® Read-Togethers 3)
The Hungry Giant (The Story Box® Read-Togethers 3)
Miss Mary Mack (The Song Box®, Set G)
Move Over! (The Story Basket®, Set C)
Mr. Bitter's Butter (The Story Basket®, Set C)
Obadiah (The Story Box® Read-Togethers 3)
One Cold, Wet Night (The Story Box® Read-Togethers 3)
Sione Went Fishing (SUNSHINE™, Set I)
What Would You Do? (SUNSHINE™, Set J)

Quilts

Kitzikuba (The Story Basket®, Set B)
Lazy Mary (The Story Box® Read-Togethers 3)

Rain

City Storm (TWiG® Books Read-
Togethers, Set 1)

Kitzikuba (The Story Basket®, Set B)

One Cold, Wet Night (The Story Box®
Read-Togethers 3)

One Stormy Night (The Story Basket®,
Set A)

The Rain and the Sun (Wonder World™,
Set E)

Rain or Shine? (TWiG® Books, Set E)

"Rain, Rain, Go Away" (*Heritage
Readers*™, Book A)

Storm! (Wonder World™, Set J)

Umbrella (The Story Box®, Set E)

A Wet Day at School (SUNSHINE™, Set H)

Riddles

Birthdays (SUNSHINE™ Read-Togethers,
Set 1)

What's Black and White and Moos?
(TWiG® Books, Set F)

Where Are the Seeds? (Wonder World™,
Set E)

Who Uses These Tools? (TWiG® Books,
Set E)

Who's There? (The Story Box® Read-
Togethers 4)

Whose Shoes? (TWiG® Books, Set F)

Safety

Earthquake! (Wonder World™, Set F)

Gravity (The Song Box®, Set E)

I Smell Smoke! (SUNSHINE™, Set F)

My Brother's Motorcycle (Visions™,
Set G)

The Nine Days of Camping (TWiG®
Books Read-Togethers, Set 1)

Obadiah (The Story Box® Read-
Togethers 3)

Skating (The Story Box®, Set E)

Smarty Pants (The Story Box® Read-
Togethers 3)

What Would You Do? (SUNSHINE™,
Set J)

Sense of Sight

Behind the Rocks (Wonder World™, Set E)

City Senses (TWiG® Books, Set FF)

Dishy-Washy (The Story Basket®, Set C)

Do Not Open This Book! (The Story
Basket®, Set C)

Getting Glasses (Wonder World™, Set I)

I See You (TWiG® Books, Set E)

The Mirror (The Story Box® Read-
Togethers 4)

Under a Microscope (SUNSHINE™
Nonfiction, Set J)

Who Can See the Camel? (The Story
Box®, Set E)

Shelter

Baby Animals at Home (TWiG® Books,
Set FF)

"The Frog Prince" (*Heritage Readers*™,
Book B)

Gloves (The Story Box® Read-Togethers 4)

Hiking with Dad (Wonder World™, Set I)

A House for Me (TWiG® Books, Set FF)

My Secret Place (Wonder World™, Set I)

One Stormy Night (The Story Basket®,
Set A)

Trees Are Special (SUNSHINE™
Nonfiction, Set F)

Who Lives Here? (The Story Box®, Set E)

Who Loves Getting Wet? (SUNSHINE™
Read-Togethers, Set 3)

Time

Dig a Dinosaur (The Song Box®, Set E)

Forty-Three Cats (SUNSHINE™ Read-
Togethers, Set 3)

The "Get-Up" Machine (SUNSHINE™, Set I)

Grumbles, Growls, and Roars (TWiG®
Books Read-Togethers, Set 1)

Hiking with Dad (Wonder World™, Set I)

It's Noisy at Night (Wonder World™, Set F)

Lazy Mary (The Story Box® Read-
Togethers 3)

Munch, Munch, Munch! (The Song Box®,
Set E)

The Night Train (The Story Box®, Set G)

"Time to Rise" (*Heritage Readers*™, Book B)

Transportation

Boats (TWiG® Books, Set FF)

Engines (SUNSHINE™ Nonfiction, Set E)

Fast, Faster, Fastest (TWiG® Books, Set F)

Flying (The Story Box®, Set E)

My Brother's Motorcycle (Visions™, Set G)

The School Bus (SUNSHINE™ Community Books, Set 2)

Stop! (The Story Box®, Set E)

Who's There? (The Story Box® Read-Togethers 4)

Tricks

Carrots, Peas, and Beans (SUNSHINE™, Set G)

The Hungry Giant's Soup (The Story Basket®, Set A)

"In the Cave of the One-Eyed Giant" (*Heritage Readers*™, Book B)

The Meanies' Trick (The Story Box® Read-Togethers 4)

The Music Machine (SUNSHINE™ Read-Togethers, Set 2)

Washing

At the Car Wash (Visions™, Set H)

Dishy-Washy (The Story Basket®, Set C)

Do Not Open This Book! (The Story Basket®, Set C)

Horace (The Story Box®, Set G)

Mud Soup (The Song Box®, Set H)

Red Socks and Yellow Socks (SUNSHINE™, Set H)

The Scrubbing Machine (The Story Box® Read-Togethers 4)

Weather

The Giant's Boy (SUNSHINE™, Set H)

Kitzikuba (The Story Basket®, Set B)

One Cold, Wet Night (The Story Box® Read-Togethers 3)

One Stormy Night (The Story Basket®, Set A)

The Rain and the Sun (Wonder World™, Set E)

Rain or Shine? (TWiG® Books, Set E)

"Rain, Rain, Go Away" (*Heritage Readers*™, Book A)

Storm! (Wonder World™, Set J)

Umbrella (The Story Box®, Set E)

A Wet Day at School (SUNSHINE™, Set H)

Wind

The Pirate Feast (The Story Basket®, Set B)

A Wet Day at School (SUNSHINE™, Set H)

Woosh! (The Story Box® Read-Togethers 3)

Will It Rain on the Parade? (Wonder World™, Set J)

"The Wind and the Moon" (*Heritage Readers*™, Book B)

The Wind Blows Strong (SUNSHINE™, Set F)

Woodland Animals

Animals Hide and Seek (TWiG® Books, Set EE)

Bear Facts (The Song Box®, Set E)

The Giant's Stew (SUNSHINE™ Read-Togethers, Set 3)

Gloves (The Story Box® Read-Togethers 4)

The Hike at Day Camp (Visions™, Set F)

Hiking with Dad (Wonder World™, Set I)

Over in the Meadow (The Song Box®, Set G)

"Thumbelina" (*Heritage Readers*™, Book B)

Tracks (TWiG® Books, Set F)

Where Is Skunk? (The Story Box®, Set G)

Glossary

alliteration—the repetition of an initial sound in words in a sentence or phrase. This initial sound may be made by a single consonant, a vowel, a consonant blend, or a consonant digraph. Also a level of phonemic awareness in which children develop the ability to hear and generate words that begin with the same initial sound.

alphabetic principle—an understanding that each speech sound or phoneme is represented by its own graphic symbol

analogy—similarities between words that readers can use to decode unknown words. For example, if *cat* is known, students can use the known rime -*at* to help them decode the word *that*.

assessment—the process of data-gathering that occurs before evaluation takes place. Assessment can be formal (standardized, norm-referenced tests) or informal and ongoing (also called authentic assessment).

Assessment of Reading Behavior—a concise evaluation tool for scoring and analyzing students' reading behaviors, for determining the correct instructional reading level, and for determining the strategies and skills that need to be taught

authentic assessment—refers to qualitative assessment (that is, not standardized testing) that the teacher conducts on an ongoing basis in the classroom. Authentic assessment is usually anecdotal and based on a teacher's observations of student achievement over time. Authentic assessment captures the process of learning, as well as students' final products. It incorporates a variety of tools, including anecdotal observations, student journals, student work in progress, and skills checklists that the teacher can use routinely in the classroom. Also called *informal assessment*.

balanced reading program—a teaching philosophy that encompasses a blend of strategies and methods, including phonics and basic skills instruction, and immersion in meaningful literature and writing. Based on the assessed needs of students, this approach combines developmentally appropriate literature, language, and writing experiences with explicit instruction in skills. A balanced reading program includes reading aloud to students, shared reading, guided reading, paired reading, independent reading, model writing, process writing, content writing, guided writing, structure writing, journal writing, independent writing, and spelling

behaviors—how a child acts when encountering text; the demonstration of knowledge and use of strategies

benchmarks—predetermined indicators that measure a student's accomplishments. For example, by the end of the early or upper emergent level in reading, students should meet specific objectives in reading, writing, listening, and speaking.

blending—a level of phonemic awareness and a skill in phonics in which children develop the ability to combine isolated sounds, or phonemes, to make words; for example, blending the sounds /m/ /a/ /t/ to make the word *mat*

book boxes—containers of books organized by students' independent or instructional reading levels

book concepts—a concept of print that concerns the parts of a book, how to move through a book, how stories are structured, and how illustrations support and enhance the story's text. This includes learning about the front cover, back cover, title page, author, and illustrator.

brainstorming—the use of group discussion to generate ideas from students. Brainstorming is useful for broadening knowledge, solving problems, and developing a better understanding of concepts.

centers—places in the classroom that are set up for specific types of independent learning activities that offer opportunities for students to read and write and explore other content areas

chunks—groups of letters that form a part of a word; for example, *at* in *cat*, *be* in *between*.

cloze technique—an instructional strategy in which the teacher provides only part of a predictable sentence or idea and allows students to complete the sentence or thought. An example of a cloze sentence would be "The boy petted the big, brown _____." While reading this sentence aloud, the teacher would pause after *brown* and let the students say the next word.

cognitive web—a systematic way of organizing information to provide a framework for understanding and to help students make connections or build scaffolds between their own learning and what is to be learned. Cognitive webs include such things as discussions, activities, graphic organizers, or manipulatives.

concepts of literature—the variety of terms used to describe different aspects of literature, for example, character, setting, problem/solution, beginning/middle/end, mood, point of view, and genre

concepts of print—an understanding that print represents ideas and carries a message. Print concepts include book concepts, text concepts, word/letter concepts, and concepts of mechanics.

confirm—to verify a prediction in reading based on phonetic elements in a word, the meaning of the text, or the structure of the language

consonant blend—the combination of the sounds of two or more consonants with minimal change in those sounds; for example, /gr/ in *grow*

consonant digraph—two or more consonants that represent one speech sound; for example, /ch/ in *chin*

content-area centers—places in the classroom that are set up to help students develop integrated literacy connections to math, science, social studies, art, music, and so on

content writing—all writing done in the content areas (social studies, science, health, and so on). Content writing can be a personal response to an experience, an exploration of a concept, a list of directions, a reflection or summary of thoughts and feelings, a report or presentation of information on a topic, or a simple description of a process, event, or object. The most common medium at the emergent level for writing in the content areas is a journal.

context clues—information from the text that helps identify a word or a group of words and gain meaning from sentences.

conventional spelling—the stage of spelling at which words are spelled correctly

cooperative learning—small groups of children working together on a project. Cooperative learning helps students achieve independent goals and develop interpersonal relationships. It encourages them to solve problems and acquire knowledge as they are supported or challenged by their peers.

critical-level comprehension—the level of reading at which students can make judgments about the text, evaluate what was read, express personal opinions, or apply what they learned to a new situation

critical thinking—the ability to elaborate on ideas and create new ideas or alternative interpretations from one's learning

cross-checking—a reading behavior in which the reader uses one kind of cue or source of information as confirmation of comprehension or of decoding with another cue or source of information; for example, cross-checking the meaning of a word with the visual representation of a word

Daily News—the Daily News is a whole-class activity in which the teacher models fluent writing while prompting students for spelling, punctuation, and other skills. The Daily News usually begins with a student sharing something of interest orally with the class. The teacher then prompts the class while writing the date, the weather, and then a summary statement of the student's news item. At higher levels, the students take over the writing and editing.

decode—the ability to identify or analyze graphic symbols or written words in order to read a written message

developmentally appropriate—suitable for a specific level of learning

difficult reading level—the level at which text presents enough difficulties or challenges in word identification and comprehension that it is unsuitable for instruction. When a student reads a text with below 90 percent accuracy, the text is at the student's difficult reading level.

directionality—the ability to recognize that print moves from left to right and from top to bottom on a page. As children read from the beginning of a line to the end of a line and then return to the beginning of the next line, they are using return sweep.

early emergent readers—readers who are learning basic skills and concepts, for example that letters represent sounds, that clusters of letters form words, that books have a front and a back cover, and that the words and illustrations in a book tell a story. Children at this level are generally in kindergarten and the beginning of first grade.

encode—to represent what is heard or thought with symbols; for example, to encode oral language into writing

evaluation—the judging and appraising of students' growth and their products or knowledge of process

expanded KWL—refers to an expanded research process that adds to "what we know, what we want to know, what we learned" with other information; for example, "how we can find out," "how we can summarize our thoughts and feelings," "what new questions we have," or "what we want to learn next." Also called *KWHL*.

explicit instruction—a direct approach to teaching through the careful clarification of key concepts or specific skills. Explicit instruction may follow shared reading, guided reading, or model writing, and is done out of the context of the reading.

familiar books—books that students have been introduced to and that they have been able to satisfactorily read at either an independent or instructional level

flexible grouping—the arranging of students into small groups for a specific teaching purpose, such as reading at the same instructional reading level or working on a specific skill area. The groups are not static, but change to fit the needs and abilities of each student.

fluency—the clear expression of ideas in writing or speaking. In reading, it is the ability to decode words, to quickly and automatically read high-frequency words, and to maintain comprehension while reading either orally or silently.

four cueing system—the reading strategies readers use to decode and comprehend text. They are

schema (prior knowledge): "What do you know about…?"

graphophonic (letter-sound, phonics): "What would look right?"

semantic (meaning, context): "What would make sense?"

syntactic (structure, grammar): "What would sound right here?"

genre—a form of visual, musical, or written work composed in a particular style or with a particular content. Forms of literature such as poems, realistic fiction, fantasies, nonfiction, mysteries, biographies, and so on, are considered genres.

graduated text—books that show a gradual, developmentally appropriate increase in the difficulty of the text

grapheme—the visual representation or symbol of a sound or phoneme

graphic organizers—visual tools, such as outlines, charts, tables, diagrams, matrices, and webs, that can be used to identify key and related elements of ideas or topics. For example, students might create a chart on which they compare and contrast characters from two or more stories.

graphophonic cues—clues drawn from the relationship between the speech sound or phonology and the symbol/spelling or orthography of language. Graphophonic cues refer to the visual aspects of print, including the recognition and identification of letters and words. Often referred to as visual cues.

guided reading—guided reading involves small, flexible groups of children reading at the same instructional level. All students read together from their own copies of a book while the teacher guides individual students as needed. Guided reading sessions also include opportunities to teach reading strategies, design instruction that will accelerate students' growth in reading, conduct specific skill lessons, and evaluate students' progress.

guided writing—an instructional strategy in which the teacher works one-on-one with an individual student or with small groups. The teacher focuses on a single area of difficulty or a phonics skill in a brief lesson while reinforcing the child's current skill knowledge or writing strengths.

high-frequency words—words that appear with a high degree of frequency in spoken and written language. Many high-frequency words cannot be decoded and are difficult to attach meaning to, so they must be instantly recognizable; for example, *was, the, said.*

implant—to suggest or teach concepts before the actual teaching of the lesson that includes them. For example, a teacher will use and make students aware of difficult language patterns or vocabulary before reading a story.

implicit instruction—an approach to the teaching of skills or key concepts that is done within the context of meaningful reading and/or writing

in-context—used to describe instruction that is done through meaningful reading or writing experiences

independent reading—an activity that allows students to read on their own, to self-select their reading material, to practice skills, and to develop fluency

independent reading level—the level of reading material that a student can read with no word identification or comprehension challenges. A student can read and understand 95 percent to 100 percent of a text at his or her independent reading level.

independent writing— students writing on their own. Independent writing is the goal of all writing instruction. As students gain an understanding of writing conventions, they need a variety of opportunities to express themselves through their own writing.

inferential-level comprehension—the level of reading comprehension at which students make generalizations about a story, predict outcomes, or make inferences about the text

innovation—a new story that children write based on the sentence pattern and/or story structure of an existing story or book. The original structure of the story remains unchanged but the characters, setting, or events can be changed.

inquiry—a mode of research driven by the learner's desire to look deeply into a question or to pursue an idea of interest

instructional cycle—the model of instruction that begins with assessment, is planned based on that assessment, is modeled for students, provides for guided and independent practice, allows students to apply their knowledge, and ends with assessment

instructional reading level—the level of reading material that a student can read and understand with 90 percent to 94 percent accuracy. The purpose of instructional reading sessions is to "stretch" students' reading abilities with teacher guidance and feedback, and to help them handle new textual challenges. The most appropriate materials are those that are slightly more difficult than the student's independent reading level.

intervention—a means of providing explicit supplemental instruction for students functioning below grade level in reading

journal writing—a type of writing through which students learn to express themselves and develop writing and phonetic skills. In journal writing, students may respond to books they have read, make observations, or record feelings they have experienced.

known—letters, words, and/or concepts that are familiar to children. Working from the known supports students' learning of the unknown by linking what they know to something that is new.

KWL—a strategy for researching a topic. The letters KWL refer to what we **k**now, what we **w**ant to know, and what we **l**earned. See also *expanded KWL*.

language experience—a writing process in which a class discusses an experience such as a field trip, guest speaker, or special event while the teacher writes their ideas on chart paper. This writing can be used to teach skills, for reading practice, and as a model for student writing.

left-to-right progression—the concept that print moves from left to right on a page. Recognition of left-to-right progression is an important skill for early readers.

literacy centers—places created in the classroom to promote independent reading and writing and to encourage collaboration and cooperative learning. Literacy centers provide opportunities for students to engage in authentic and purposeful reading, writing, listening, and speaking activities as they practice and apply skills.

literal-level comprehension—an understanding of what is clearly stated in a text. At this level of reading students can find answers in the text to questions, such as who, what, when, and where questions.

literary elements—the parts that make up a story and that can be studied separately to help the reader understand it, such as character, setting, problem/solution, events, mood, author's intent, and point of view

literature circles—an instructional strategy in which small groups of students meet to talk about a book they have read

manipulating—a level of phonemic awareness and a skill in phonics in which phonemes in words are changed to form new words. One or more phonemes may be substituted for others, as in changing *bat* to *hat*; deleted, as in omitting the *c* in *cat* to make *at*; or added, as in changing *cap* to *clap* or *car* to *cart*.

manipulatives—objects that students can physically handle as they learn. Manipulatives help develop kinesthetic or tactile awareness. Examples are magnetic letters, felt letters, alphabet blocks, alphabet cards, counting rods, and geometric shapes.

miscue—an error made in reading text

mix and make (make and break)—an activity for putting the letters of a word together, mixing them up, and then reconstructing them

model writing—instruction in which the teacher models the process of writing and the decisions that one makes when writing

multiple intelligences—the individual capabilities proposed by Gardner (1983) that can be developed if presented in an appropriate learning environment. These learning modalities are linguistic-verbal, logical-mathematical, musical, visual-spatial, bodily-kinesthetic, interpersonal, intrapersonal, and naturalist.

one-to-one correspondence—the matching of speech to print. Children need to recognize that the words in print match the words spoken or read.

onomatopoeia—the use of words whose sounds imitate or suggest their meaning (for example, *buzz, purr, boom*)

onset/rime—the onset is the consonant(s) preceding the vowel(s) in a word or syllable. For example, *h* is the onset in the word *hat*. Rime refers to the vowel and any following consonants of a syllable or word. For example, *at* is the rime in the word *hat*.

open-ended question—a type of question that encourages students to explore their understanding of what was read and that does not have a "correct" answer. This type of questioning encourages divergent or creative thinking.

oral language—speaking and listening. Oral language development concerns the ability to listen and gain information from speech or to express oneself orally. The integration of listening and speaking enables students to create, analyze, evaluate, appreciate language, and communicate effectively.

orthography—the use of symbols in correct sequence or the use of correct spelling. Standardized spelling according to correct usage in a given language.

paired/partner reading—two students reading together. Students may be at the same reading level or at different reading levels. The process encourages students to share reading strategies and help each other problem solve their way through text.

phoneme—the smallest sound segment in a word. For example, *book* has three phonemes: /b/ /oo/ /k/. *Cat* has three: /k/ /a/ /t/. *Bench* has four: /b/ /e/ /n/ /ch/.

phonemic awareness—the ability to hear and distinguish individual sounds or phonemes in words. The ability to blend, segment, and manipulate these units of sound in speech.

phonetic spelling—the spelling of a word, represented by symbols, that reflects the sounds that children hear in a word. Also called *approximate spelling, inventive spelling*, or *developmental spelling*.

phonics—the system of teaching sound-symbol relationships used in reading and writing, based on the understanding that each letter of the English alphabet stands for one or more sounds. Phonics teaches the skills of blending these sounds to decode words and decoding words by using known parts or spelling patterns. It includes the use of recognizable spelling patterns and sound-symbol knowledge to encode, or write, words.

phonogram—a vowel and the ending consonant or consonants as in *-ed* in *red, bed*, and *fed*. See *word family*.

phonological awareness—an understanding of the sounds and the structure of spoken language. It includes an awareness of rhyme and alliteration and encompasses an understanding that oral speech can be divided into sentences, phrases, and words; and that words can be divided into syllables, onsets and rimes, and phonemes. Phonemes are the smallest sound segments that comprise words.

picture cues—the clues to comprehension or decoding that a reader gets from looking at the illustrations in a story

predict—to make an educationally sound decision about what text appears next or what may happen next in a story, based on what the reader knows about phonics, spelling patterns, word structure, and the text

predictable text—text that enables the student to make an assumption about what might come next or how a story might end

prior knowledge—knowledge that an individual brings to any learning situation based on his or her previous experiences. See *schema*.

process writing—an instructional writing model in which children learn to write by writing about their own experiences and for their own purposes. When children are developmentally ready they can begin taking their writing through the stages of planning, drafting, revising, editing, and publishing.

r-controlled vowel—a vowel followed by an *r* in which the *r* alters or modifies the vowel sound. For example, the vowels in *her, fur,* or *barn*.

read-alouds—stories that are read to children and enable them to enjoy literature that is above their instructional reading level. Read-alouds help develop skills such as oral language, comprehension, vocabulary, and sense of story.

recode—to change one form of information into another. Examples of recoding are transferring a written symbol, or grapheme, into its spoken form, and translating words read aloud into words heard inside one's head.

reproduction—the re-creation of a familiar story in a new format. For example, a teacher may write the text of a favorite story and have students illustrate it to make a Big Book reproduction. Reproductions could also include illustrated wall stories and transparencies, mobiles, character cut-outs, and so on.

resource centers—places in the classroom stocked with tools that help facilitate learning. Resource centers include the block center, the computer center, the simulation center, and so on.

retelling—a student's telling of a story that he or she has read or heard. Retellings are usually oral and can serve as a comprehension check, providing insight into the reader's ability to recall and sequence events, interpret and draw conclusions from a story, and summarize information. A retelling can also be a writing and illustrating project, such as making a retelling of a Big Book.

return sweep—the movement the eye makes to follow the print on a page from the end of one line of text to the beginning of the next line

scaffolding—a concept based on Vygotsky's (1987) emphasis on providing a solid instructional base and gradually releasing teacher support as students acquire and master skills. Scaffolding is often done through modeling, questioning, think-alouds, and so on, until the students become more independent in their learning.

schema—all of the prior knowledge and experiences that students bring to a learning situation

seen text—text that students have previously read. Taking an Assessment of Reading Behavior on seen text provides the teacher with information on how students are using reading strategies. It also serves as a means of planning instructional focus, monitoring progress at the current instructional level, and observing how students approach familiar text.

segmenting—a level of phonemic awareness and a skill in phonics in which words are broken down into their individual phonemes, as in breaking the word *dog* into the phonemes of /d/ /o/ /g/

self-correcting—the ability of readers to monitor themselves as they read, correcting their own mistakes by using different cues and cross-checking one cue against another

self-monitoring—the ability to be aware of one's own reading behaviors and strategies through rereading or reflection

semantic cues—clues taken from the general meaning of a story that readers use to figure out unknown words. Readers draw on their own experiences and knowledge to build their understanding of content and sense of story, giving them a context in which to identify new words. Also called *meaning cues*.

sentence puzzle—a sentence strip that has been cut apart into the words, letters, or spaces of a sentence to emphasize certain focus skills

sentence strips—long strips of paper, usually oaktag, on which students or teachers write a sentence or words. Sentence strips are used for sequencing, matching, word study, spelling, and other skill instruction.

shared reading—an instructional process in which the teacher involves children just learning to read in the reading and discussion of a Big Book. The teacher first reads the book aloud to the students, pointing carefully to each word and modeling how to read books. Repeated readings of the same Big Book deepen and reinforce students' understanding of phonological awareness, concepts of print, phonics, vocabulary, and sense of story.

sound-segment cards—small cards or strips of paper on which boxes are drawn to represent each sound, or phoneme, heard in a word

sound-symbol relationship—the relationship between the sounds, or phonology, and symbols/spelling of a language

spelling patterns—patterns of letters in words that represent a chunk of a word or a word family; for example, -at in *cat, sat, hat*

story structure—the organization of a story. Studying story structure can help readers understand and compare different stories, genres, or story elements (character, setting, problem, solution).

strategies—the thought processes or series of behaviors that readers go through in using the four cueing system. Strategies help students think and act like readers.

structure writing—a writing process in which children use a repeated sentence or phrase from a book, such as "The man got on," and substitute new words; for example, "The _____ got on." Used to develop phonics skills and knowledge of high-frequency words and language structures.

syllabication—the division of words into the minimal units of sequential speech sounds comprised of a vowel sound or a vowel-consonant combination (syllables)

syllable awareness—the ability to hear syllables and break words into syllables

syntactic cues—the understanding of the grammatical structure, word order, and language patterns, or syntax, of the English language that a reader draws on to help in the identification of and comprehension of unknown words. Also called *structure cues*.

theme—a major idea that covers the wide scope of a subject and that helps build connections between several topics. Examples of themes are relationships, exploration, community, and cycles.

think-aloud—a strategy in which the teacher verbalizes his or her thought process while modeling a skill or process

topic—a general category of ideas. Examples of topics are bears, pets, families, and the zoo.

unknown—letters, words, and/or concepts unfamiliar to students. Linking what students know to new or unfamiliar information supports their learning.

unseen text—text that students have not been introduced to. Taking an Assessment of Reading Behavior on unseen text shows the teacher the strategies that students are using independently at their instructional level. Using unseen text is beneficial in determining whether students are placed at their instructional level or as a diagnostic tool for placement at the next instructional level. It also allows the teacher to observe how students approach unfamiliar text.

upper emergent readers—readers who are beginning to use reading strategies, decoding skills, and the four cueing system to gain meaning from print. Children at this level are usually in first grade.

vowel digraph—a spelling pattern that has two adjacent vowels, the first of which is long and the second silent. For example, the *ai* in *rain*.

vowel diphthong—a spelling pattern with two adjacent vowels that are neither long nor short, but make a special sound of their own. For example, the *oy* in *toy*.

vowel pattern—the conventional placement of vowels and their surrounding consonants in a word. Most vowel patterns will fit into one of six categories: open vowel, closed vowel, vowel with silent *e, r*-controlled vowel, two vowels, and consonant plus *le*. Also called *spelling pattern*.

word family—a group of words that have the same ending sound, or rime, but a different beginning sound or onset; for example, *cat, fat, sat*. See *phonogram*.

word structure—how words are constructed, the use of prefixes, word endings, syllabication, contractions, possessives, and compound words

Bibliography

Adams, M. Jager. *Beginning to Read: Thinking and Learning About Print*. Cambridge, Mass.: MIT Press, 1990.

———. *Teacher's Tool Kit for Beginning Reading: Applying Reading Research to Classroom Practices*. Bothell, Wash.: Wright Group, 1998.

Adams, M. Jager, and M. Bruck. "Resolving the Great Debate." *American Educator* 19, no. 2 (1995): 7, 10–20.

Adams, M. Jager, R. Treiman, and M. Pressley. "Reading, Writing, and Literacy." In *Handbook of Child Psychology*. Vol. 4, *Child Psychology in Practice*, edited by I. Sigel and A. Renninger, 275–355. New York: Wiley, 1996.

Allington, R. L., and S. A. Walmsley, eds. *No Quick Fix: Rethinking Literacy Programs in America's Elementary Schools*. Newark, Del.: International Reading Association; New York: Teacher's College Press, 1995.

Anderson, R. et al. *Becoming a Nation of Readers: The Report of the Commission on Reading*. Washington, D.C.: The National Institute of Education, U.S. Department of Education, 1984.

Anderson, R., and P. D. Pearson. "A Schema-Theoretic View of Basic Processes in Reading Comprehension." In *Handbook of Reading Research*. Vol. 1, edited by P. D. Pearson, 255–291. White Plains, N.Y.: Longman Publishing Group, 1984.

Armbruster, B. B. "Content Reading in RT: The Last 2 Decades." *The Reading Teacher* 46, no. 2 (October 1992): 166–167.

Au, K. H., J. H. Carroll, and J. A. Scheu. *Balanced Literacy Instruction: A Teacher's Resource Book*. Norwood, Mass.: Christopher-Gordon Publishers, 1997.

Beck, I. et al. *Questioning the Author: An Approach for Enhancing Student Engagement with Text*. Newark, Del.: International Reading Association, 1997.

Beck, I., and C. Juel. "The Role of Decoding in Learning to Read." *American Educator* 19, no. 2 (1995): 8, 21–25, 39–42.

Booth, D. *Literacy Techniques for Building Successful Readers and Writers*. Markham, Ontario: Pembroke Publishers, 1996.

Brady, S., and L. Moats. "Informed Instruction for Reading Success: Foundations for Teacher Preparation." Position Paper, International Dyslexia Association, Baltimore, Md., 1997.

Braunger, J., and J. P. Lewis. "Building a Knowledge Base in Reading." Portland, Ore.: Northwest Regional Educational Laboratory's Curriculum and Instruction Services, National Council of Teachers of English, International Reading Association, 1997.

Campbell, B. "Multiple Intelligences in Action." *Childhood Education* 68, no. 4 (Summer 1992): 197–201.

Chall, J. Sternlicht. *The Reading Crisis: Why Poor Children Fall Behind*. Cambridge, Mass.: Harvard University Press, 1990.

———. *Stages of Reading Development*. New York: McGraw-Hill, 1996.

Cheyney, W. J., and E. J. Cohen. *Focus on Phonics*. Bothell, Wash.: Wright Group, forthcoming.

Christie, J. "Play and Story Comprehension: A Critique of Recent Training Research." *Journal of Research and Development in Education* 21 (1987): 36–43.

Christie, J., B. Enz, and C. Vukelich. *Teaching Language and Literacy: Preschool Through the Elementary Grades*. New York: Longman, 1997.

Clay, M. *Becoming Literate: The Construction of Inner Control.* Portsmouth, N.H.: Heinemann, 1991.

———. *The Early Detection of Reading Difficulties.* 3d ed. Exeter, N.H.: Heinemann, 1985.

———. *Reading: The Patterning of Complex Behaviour.* Auckland, New Zealand: Heinemann, 1979.

Combs, M. "Modeling the Reading Process with Enlarged Texts." *The Reading Teacher* 40, no. 4 (January 1987): 422–426.

Cunningham, A. E. "Explicit Versus Implicit Instruction in Phonemic Awareness." *Journal of Experimental Child Psychology* 50 (1990): 429–444.

Cunningham, A. E., and K. E. Stanovich. "Tracking the Unique Effects of Print Exposure in Children: Associations with Vocabulary, General Knowledge, and Spelling." *Journal of Educational Psychology* 83 (1991): 264–74.

Cunningham, P. M. *Phonics They Use: Words for Reading and Writing.* 2d ed. New York: Harper Collins College Publishers, 1995.

Daniels, H. *Literature Circles: Voice and Choice in the Student-Centered Classroom.* York, Maine: Stenhouse Publishers, 1994.

Dechant, E. *Whole-Language Reading.* Lancaster, Pa.: Technomic, 1993.

Dole, J. A. et al. "Effects of Two Types of Prereading Instruction on the Comprehension of Narrative and Expository Text." *Reading Research Quarterly* 26 (1991): 142–159.

Eldredge, J. L. *Teaching Decoding in Holistic Classrooms.* Engelwood Cliffs, N.J.: Merrill, 1995.

Eldredge, J. L., D. R. Reutzel, and P. M. Hollingsworth. "Comparing the Effectiveness of Two Oral Reading Practices: Round-Robin Reading and the Shared Book Experience." *Journal of Literacy Research* 28 (1996): 201–225

Elley, W. B. "Acquiring Literacy in a Second Language: The Effect of Book-Based Programs." *Language Learning* 41, no. 3 (1991): 375–411.

———. *Lessons Learned About Laric.* Christchurch, New Zealand: University of Canterbury, 1985.

———. "Vocabulary Acquisition from Listening to Stories." *Reading Research Quarterly* 24 (1989): 174–187.

Fitzgerald, J. "English-As-a-Second-Language Learners' Cognitive Reading Processes: A Review of Research in the United States." *Review of Educational Research* 65, no. 2 (Summer 1995): 145–90.

Foorman, B. R. "Research on 'The Great Debate': Code-Oriented Versus Whole Language Approaches to Reading Instruction." *School Psychology Review* 24 (1995): 376–392.

Fountas, I. C., and G. S. Pinnell. *Guided Reading: Good First Teaching For All Children.* Portsmouth, N.H.: Heinemann, 1996.

Fox, B. J. *Strategies for Word Identification: Phonics from a New Perspective.* Englewood Cliffs, N.J.: Merrill, 1996.

Freeman, J. *Books Kids Will Sit Still For: The Complete Read-Aloud Guide.* New York: Bowker, 1990.

———. *More Books Kids Will Sit Still For: A Complete Read-Aloud Guide.* New Providence, N.J.: R. R. Bowker, 1995.

Gardner, H. *Frames of Mind: The Theory of Multiple Intelligences.* New York: Basic Books, 1983.

Garner, R. "Metacognition and Self-Monitoring Strategies." In *What Research Has to Say About Reading Instruction*, edited by S. J. Samuels and A. Farstrup, 236–252. Newark, Del.: International Reading Association, 1992.

Genisio, M. H. "What Goes on at School? A Teachers' Focus Group Develops a Two-Step Plan to Communicate About Emergent Literacy Practices." *The Reading Teacher* 51 (1998): 514–19.

Genisio, M. H., and B. Bruneaw. "The Literacy Pyramid Organization of Reading/Writing Activities in a Whole Language Classroom." *The Reading Teacher* 51, no. 2 (October 1997): 158–160.

Goodman, Y. M. "Revaluing Readers While Readers Revalue Themselves: Retrospective Miscue Analysis." *The Reading Teacher* 49, no. 8 (May 1996): 600–609.

Graves, M. F., P. van den Broek, and B. M. Taylor, eds. *The First R: Every Child's Right to Read*. New York: Teacher's College Press; Newark, Del.: International Reading Association, 1996.

Guillaume, A. M. "Learning with Text in the Primary Grades." *The Reading Teacher* 51 (1998): 476–86.

Gunderson, L. *The Monday Morning Guide to Comprehension*. Markham, Ontario: Pippin Publishing, 1995.

Guthrie, J. T. "Educational Contexts for Engagement in Literacy." *The Reading Teacher* 49, no. 6 (March 1996): 432–445.

Guthrie, J. T. et al. "Relationships of Instruction to Amount of Reading: An Exploration of Social, Cognitive, and Instructional Connections." *Reading Research Quarterly* 30, no. 1 (January/February/March 1995): 8–25.

Hiebert, E. H., and B. M. Taylor, eds. *Getting Reading Right from the Start: Effective Early Literacy Interventions*. Boston: Allyn and Bacon, 1994.

Holdaway, D. *The Foundations of Literacy*. New York: Scholastic, 1979.

Honig, B. *Teaching Our Children to Read: The Role of Skills in a Comprehensive Reading Program*. Thousand Oaks, Calif.: Corwin Press, 1996.

International Reading Association (I. R. A.) and National Association for the Education of Young Children (N. A. E. Y. C.). "Learning to Read and Write: Developmentally Appropriate Practices for Young Children." *The Reading Teacher* 52, no. 2 (October 1998): 193–214.

Iversen, S., and G. Bancroft. *Foundations Early Emergent Teacher Guide*. Bothell, Wash.: Wright Group, 1997.

———. *Foundations Early Fluency Teacher Guide*. Bothell, Wash.: Wright Group, 1997.

———. *Foundations Upper Emergent Teacher Guide*. Bothell, Wash.: Wright Group, 1997.

Iversen, S., and T. Reeder. *Organizing for a Literacy Hour: Quality Learning and Teaching Time*. Bothell, Wash.: Wright Group, 1998.

Iversen, S., and W. E. Tunmer. "Phonological Processing Skills and the Reading Recovery Program." *Journal of Educational Psychology* 85 (1993): 112–20.

Johnson, A., and M. Graves. "Scaffolding: A Tool for Enhancing the Reading Experiences of All Students." *Journal of the Texas State Reading Association* 3, no. 2 (Fall/Winter 1996/97): 31–37.

Juel, C. "Effects of the Reading Group Assignment on Reading Development in First and Second Grade." *Journal of Reading Behavior* 22 (1990): 233–254.

———. *Learning to Read and Write in One Elementary School*. New York: Springer-Verlag, 1994.

———. "Phonemic Awareness: What Is It?" In *The Leadership Letters: Issues and Trends in Reading and Language Arts*, a series from Silver Burdett Ginn, 1996.

Juel, C., and D. Roper-Schneider. "The Influence of Basal Readers on First Grade Reading." *Reading Research Quarterly* 20 (1985): 134–152.

Krashen, S. D. *Second Language Acquisition and Second Language Learning.* Oxford: Pergamon Press, 1981.

Loughlin, C. E., and M. D. Martin. *Supporting Literacy: Developing Effective Learning Environments.* New York: Teachers College Press, 1987.

MacHado, J. M. *Early Childhood Experiences in Language Arts: Emerging Literacy.* New York: Delmar, 1995.

Marlow, L., and D. Reese. "Strategies for Using Literature With At-Risk Readers." *Reading Improvement* 29, no. 2 (Summer 1992): 130–132.

Martinez, M., and N. Roser. "Read It Again: The Value of Repeated Readings During Storytime." *Reading Teacher* 38, no. 8 (April 1985): 782–786.

Martinez, M., M. Cheyney, and W. Teale. "Classroom Literature Activities and Kindergarten Dramatic Story Re-enact-ment." In *Play and Early Literacy Development*, edited by J. F. Christi, 60–102. Albany, N.Y.: State University of New York Press, 1988.

Mason, J. "Reading Stories to Preliterate Children: A Proposed Connection to Reading." In *Reading Acquisition*, edited by P. B. Gough, L. C. Ehri, and R. Treiman, 123–140. Hillsdale, N.J.: Erlbaum, 1992.

McIntyre, E., and M. Pressley. *Balanced Instruction: Strategies and Skills in Whole Language.* Norwood, Mass.: Christopher-Gordon Publishers, 1996.

McNeil, J. *Reading Comprehension: New Directions for Classroom Practice.* New York: Harper Collins, 1992.

Moats, L. Cook. "Spelling: The Difference Instruction Makes." *The California Reader* 30, no. 4 (Summer 1997): 19–20.

Morrison, I. *Getting It Together: Linking Reading Theory to Practice.* Bothell, Wash.: Wright Group, 1994a.

———. *Keeping It Together: Linking Reading Theory to Practice.* Bothell, Wash.: Wright Group, 1994b.

Morrow, L. Mandel. "The Impact of a Literature Based Program on Literacy Achievement, Use of Literature, and Attitudes of Children from Minority Backgrounds." *Reading Research Quarterly* 27 (1992): 250–275.

———. *The Literacy Center: Contexts for Reading and Writing.* York, Maine: Stenhouse Publishers, 1997.

———. "Promoting Voluntary Reading." In *Handbook of Research on Teaching the English Language Arts*, edited by J. Jensen et al., 681–690. New York: Macmillan, 1991.

Morrow, L. Mandel, and J. Paratore. "Family Literacy: Perspective and Practices." *The Reading Teacher* 47, no. 3 (November 1993): 194–200.

Moustafa, M. *Beyond Traditional Phonics: Research Discoveries and Reading Instruction.* Portsmouth, N.H.: Heinemann, 1997.

———. "Children's Productive Phonological Recoding." *Reading Research Quarterly* 30 (1995): 464–476.

———. "Reconceptualizing Phonics Instruction." In *Reconsidering a Balanced Approach to Reading,"* edited by C. Weaver, 135–157. Urbana, Ill.: National Council of Teachers of English, 1998.

Nation, K., and C. Hulme. "Phonemic Segmentation, Not Onset-Rime Segmentation, Predicts Early Reading and Spelling Skills." *Reading Research Quarterly* 32 (1997): 154–167.

Nolan, T. E. "Self-Questioning and Prediction: Combining Metacognitive Strategies." *Journal of Reading* 35, no. 2 (October 1991): 132–138.

Ogle, D. "K-W-L: A Teaching Model That Develops Active Reading of Expository Text." *The Reading Teacher* 39 (1986): 564–70.

Olson, M. W., and T. C. Gee. "Content Reading Instruction in the Primary Grades: Perceptions and Strategies." *The Reading Teacher* 45, no. 4 (December 1991): 298–307.

Pearson, P. D. "Changing the Face of Reading Comprehension." *The Reading Teacher* 38, no. 8 (April 1985): 724–738.

Peterson, R., and M. Eeds. *Grand Conversations. Literature Groups in Action*. New York: Scholastic, 1990.

Phenix, Jo. "Putting Phonics in Its Place." *California Reader* 31, no. 3 (Spring 1998): 30–31.

Pikulski, J. J. *Preventing Reading Problems: Factors Common to Successful Early Intervention Programs*. Boston, Mass.: Houghton Mifflin, 1995.

Pressley, M., J. Rankin, and L. Yokoi. "A Survey of Instructional Practices of Primary Teachers Nominated as Effective in Promoting Literacy." *Elementary School Journal* 96, no. 4 (March 1996): 363–384.

Pressley, M. et al. "Beyond Direct Explanation: Transactional Instruction of Reading Comprehension Strategies." *Elementary School Journal* 92, no. 5 (May 1992): 513–555.

Rascon-Briones, M., and L. W. Searfoss. "Literature Study Groups in a Preservice Teacher Education Class." Paper presented at the meeting of the National Reading Conference, New Orleans, La., December 1995.

Richards, J. C., and J. P. Gipe. "Activating Background Knowledge: Strategies for Beginning and Poor Readers." *The Reading Teacher* 45, no. 6 (February 1992): 474–476.

Richardson, J. S., and R. F. Morgan. *Reading to Learn in the Content Areas*. 3d ed. Belmont, Calif.: Wadsworth, 1996.

Robb, L. *Whole Language, Whole Learners: Creating a Literature-Centered Classroom*. New York: Quill, William Morrow, 1994.

Routman, R. *Invitations: Changing As Teachers and Learners K–12*. Portsmouth, N.H.: Heinemann, 1991.

———. *Literacy at the Crossroads: Crucial Talk About Reading, Writing, and Other Teaching Dilemmas*. Portsmouth, N.H.: Heinemann, 1996.

Rumelhart, D. E. "Schemata: The Building Blocks of Cognition." In *Theoretical Issues in Reading Comprehension: Perspectives from Cognitive Psychology, Linguistics, Artificial Intelligence, and Education*, edited by R. J. Spiro, B. C. Bruce, and W. F. Brewer, 245–333. Hillsdale, N.J.: Erlbaum Associates, 1980.

Samuels, S. J. "Decoding and Automaticity: Helping Poor Readers Become Automatic at Word Recognition." *The Reading Teacher* 41, no. 8 (April 1988): 756–760.

Schwartz, R. M. "Self-Monitoring in Beginning Reading." *The Reading Teacher* 51, no. 1 (September 1997): 40–48.

Shanahan, T., and R. Barr. "Reading Recovery: An Independent Evaluation of the Effects of an Early Instructional Intervention for At-Risk Learners." *Reading Research Quarterly* 30 (1995): 958–96.

Share, D. L., and K. E. Stanovich. "Cognitive Processes in Early Reading Development: Accommodating Individual Differences into a Mode of Acquisition." *Issues in Education: Contributions from Educational Psychology* 1 (1995): 1–57.

Shefelbine, J. "Learning and Using Phonics in Beginning Reading." *Scholastic Literacy Research Paper*. Vol. 10. Scholastic, 1995.

Snider, V. "A Primer on Phonemic Awareness: What It Is, Why It's Important, and How to Teach It." *School Psychology Review* 24, no. 3 (1995): 443–455.

Snow, C., S. Burns, and P. Griffin, eds. *Preventing Reading Difficulties in Young Children*. Committee on the Prevention of Reading Difficulties in Young Children, Commission on Behavioral Social Sciences and Education, National Research Council. Washington, D.C.: National Academy Press, 1998.

Soundry, C. "Let the Story Begin! Open the Box and Set Out the Props." *Childhood Education* 69 (1993): 146–149.

Spear-Swerling, L., and R. Sternberg. *Off Track: When Poor Readers Become "Learning Disabled."* Boulder, Colo.: Westview Press, 1996.

Spiegel, D. "Blending Whole Language and Systematic Direct Instruction." *The Reading Teacher* 46, no. 1 (September 1992): 38–44.

———. "A Comparison of Traditional Remedial Programs and Reading Recovery: Guidelines for Success for All Programs." *The Reading Teacher* 49, no. 2 (October 1995): 86–97.

Stahl, S. A. "Saying the 'P' Word: Nine Guidelines for Exemplary Phonics Instruction." *The Reading Teacher* 45 (April 1992): 618–625.

Stanovich, K. E. "Matthew Effects in Reading: Some Consequences of Individual Differences in the Acquisition of Literacy." *Reading Research Quarterly* 21 (1986): 360–406.

Stanovich, K. E., and R. F. West. "Exposure to Print and Orthographic Processing." *Reading Research Quarterly* 24 (1989): 402–433.

Stotsky, S. "Research on Reading/Writing Relationships: A Synthesis and Suggested Directions." *Language Arts* 60 (1983): 627–642.

Strickland, D. S. "Emerging Literacy: How Young Children Learn to Read." In *Early Childhood Education*. 2d ed., edited by B. Persky and L. H. Golubchick, 337–344. Lanham, Md.: University Press of America, 1991.

———. *Teaching Phonics Today: A Primer for Educators*. Newark, Del.: International Reading Association, 1998a.

———. "Teaching Skills in a Literature-Based Classroom." New Orleans, La.: 34th Annual Convention of the International Reading Association, 1989.

———. "What's Basic in Beginning Reading? Finding Common Ground." *Educational Leadership* 55, no. 6 (March 1998b): 6–10.

Tancock, S. M. "A Literacy Lesson Framework for Children with Reading Problems." *The Reading Teacher* 48, no. 2 (October 1994): 130–140.

Taylor, B., B. Frye, and G. Maruyama. "Time Spent on Reading and Reading Growth." *American Educational Research Journal* 27 (1990): 351–362.

Taylor, B. et al. "Helping Struggling Readers: Linking Small-Group Intervention with Cross-Age Tutoring." *The Reading Teacher* 51, no. 3 (November 1997): 196–209.

Terrell, T. D. "A Natural Approach to Second Language Acquisition and Learning." *Modern Language Journal* 41 (1977): 325–37.

Tierney, R. J., and T. Shannahan. "Research on the Reading-Writing Relationship: Interactions, Transactions, and Outcomes." In *Handbook of Reading Research*, Vol. 2, edited by R. Barr, M. L. Kamil, and P. Mosenthal. New York: Longman, 1991.

Tompkins, G. E. *Literacy for the Twenty-First Century: A Balanced Approach*. Upper Saddle River, N.J.: Merrill, 1997.

Torgesen, J. "Intervention Research with Reading Disabled Children." *Their World* (1997/1998): 32–35.

Trelease, J. *The New Read-Aloud Handbook*. New York: Penguin, 1989.

Vygotsky, L. S. *Mind in Society: The Development of Higher Psychological Processes*. Edited by Michael Cole et al. Cambridge, Mass.: Harvard University Press, 1978.

———. "Thinking and Speech." In *The Collected Works of L. S. Vygotsky*. Vol. 1, *Problems of General Psychology*. Edited by R. W. Rieber and A. S. Carton, 39–243. New York: Plenum Press, 1987.

Weaver, C. *Reading Process and Practice: From Sociopsycholinquistics to Whole Language*. Portsmouth, N.H.: Heinemann Educational Books, 1994.

———, ed. "Reconsidering a Balanced Approach to Reading," Urbana, Ill.: National Council of Teachers of English, 1998.

———. *Teaching Grammar in Context*. Portsmouth, N.H.: Heinemann, 1996.

White, M. C., and S. M. Lawrence. "Integrating Reading and Writing Through Literature Study." *The Reading Teacher* 45, no. 9 (May 1992): 740–743.

Wilde, S. *You Kan Red This! Spelling and Punctuation for Whole Language Classrooms, K–6*. Portsmouth, N.H.: Heinemann, 1992.

Woloshyn, V., and M. Pressley. *Cognitive Strategy Instruction That Really Improves Children's Academic Performances*. 2d ed. Cambridge, Mass.: Brookline Books, 1995.

Yopp, H. K. "Developing Phonemic Awareness in Young Children." *The Reading Teacher* 45, no. 9 (May 1992): 696–703.

Index